Gregor Gossy

A Stakeholder Rationale for Risk Management

GABLER EDITION WISSENSCHAFT

Gregor Gossy

A Stakeholder Rationale for Risk Management

Implications for Corporate Finance Decisions

With a foreword by Univ.-Prof. Dr. Paul Wentges

GABLER EDITION WISSENSCHAFT

Bibliographic information published by the Deutsche Nationalbibliothek
The Deutsche Nationalbibliothek lists this publication in the Deutsche Nationalbibliografie; detailed bibliographic data are available in the Internet at http://dnb.d-nb.de.

Dissertation Wirtschaftsuniversität Wien, 2007

1st Edition 2008

Editorial Office: Frauke Schindler / Anita Wilke

Gabler Verlag is part of the specialist publishing group Springer Science+Business Media.
www.gabler.de

Cover design: Regine Zimmer, Dipl.-Designerin, Frankfurt/Main
Printed on acid-free paper
Printed in Germany

ISBN 978-3-8349-0985-5

To my parents

Foreword

Ordinarily, only the interests of shareholders, debtholders and corporate management are taken into account when analyzing corporate financial decisions, while the interests of the other non-financial stakeholders are neglected. In his study, Gregor Gossy investigates the interesting but under-researched implications of the firm's relationships with its non-financial stakeholders such as customers, employees and suppliers on corporate financial decisions. In particular, he develops a so-called stakeholder rationale for risk management and discusses whether this risk management approach contributes to a better understanding of the motives for and consequences of conservative corporate financial decisions in the areas of capital structure choice, corporate cash holdings and payout policy.

The underlying theory of the firm has a huge impact on corporate finance theory. In the first part of this book, therefore, Gregor Gossy discusses the relevant developments of the new institutional economics and combines them nicely with results of the resource-based view of the firm to get a well-founded stakeholder-oriented theory of the firm. On this basis, he develops his main hypothesis that the degree of conservativeness of a firm's financial policies is positively associated with the extent to which the firm is dependent on value enhancing specific investments of its stakeholders. In the second part of this study, he empirically tests his hypotheses for corporate cash holdings and capital structure decisions on a sample of 593 Austrian and German listed corporations.

Gregor Gossy presents a very ambitious work regarding the content as well as the methodology used. Both researchers and practitioners will profit from the author's ability to integrate two academic fields, strategic management and corporate finance, that have been developed quite separately over the years.

Paul Wentges

Preface

This dissertation was written during my employment as a research and teaching assistant at the Institute for Strategic Management and Management Control at the Vienna University of Economics and Business Administration. It could not have been written without the continued support of some people.

First, I would like to thank Univ.-Prof. Dr. Gerhard Speckbacher and Univ.-Prof. Dr. Paul Wentges for letting me become a member of the team of the Institute for Strategic Management and Management Control.

Grateful thanks go to my supervisor Univ.-Prof. Dr. Paul Wentges for giving me scientific guidance through my whole dissertation project.

Additionally, I would like to thank my co-supervisor ao.Univ.-Prof. Dr. Alois Geyer for his uncomplicated and unrestrained support regarding all empirical aspects of this work.

I am also grateful to all former and current colleagues at the Institute for Strategic Management and Management Control who supported me during all stages of the dissertation project.

Finally, I would like to thank my parents for their overwhelming love and support during all times.

Gregor Gossy

Table of Contents

List of Tables

List of Abbreviations

BDS	Bowen, R.M., DuCharme, L. and Shores, D.
BLUE	Best Linear Unbiased Estimators
CAPM	Capital Asset Pricing Model
COGS	Cost Of Goods Sold
c.p.	ceteris paribus
EBITDA	Earning Before Interest, Taxes, Depreciation and Amortization
etc.	et cetera
e.g.	exempli gratia
et al.	et alii
FD	First Differences
FE	Fixed Effects
GHM	Grossman, Hart and Moore
GLS	Generalized Least Squares
i.e.	id est
MM	Modigliani and Miller
NFS	Non-Financial Stakeholders
NOC	Net Organizational Capital
NPV	Net Present Value
OC	Organizational Capital
OL	Organizational Liabilities
OLS	Ordinary Least Squares
p.	page
pp.	pages
PCSE	Panel Corrected Standard Error
RBV	Resource-Based View
R&D	Research & Development
RE	Random Effects
ROA	Return On Assets
SFAS	Statement of Financial Accounting Standards
SLB	Sharpe, Lintner and Black
SME	Small and Medium sized Enterprises
SRI	Stanford Research Institute
SRRM	Stakeholder Rationale for Risk Management

TCE	Transaction Cost Economics
VRIN	Valuable, Rare, Imperfectly Imitable, Non-substitutable Resources
WLS	Weighted Least Squares

1 Introduction

1.1 Relevance of the topic

Titman's (1984) seminal contribution led to two streams of research by widening the boundaries of the firm and incorporating stakeholder liquidation costs into the firm's capital structure choice. The first stream of reseach investigates the relations between the capital structure choice and characteristics of the firm's products and the market where it operates, respectively (see, e.g., Maksimovic and Titman (1991), Franck and Huyghebaert (2006), Istaitieh and Rodríguez-Fernández (2006), Kale and Shahrur (2007) and Parsons and Titman (2007)).

The second stream initiated by Titman (1984) deals with the influences of non-financial stakeholder liquidation costs on corporate risk management and established the basis for a stakeholder rationale for risk management (SRRM) developed, among others, by Shapiro and Titman (1986), Cornell and Shapiro (1987), Wentges (2000) and Stulz (2003). This stakeholder rationale for risk management combines shareholder value-oriented reasoning for risk management with firm-specific influences on the firm's risk profile. It overcomes the purely financial perspective towards risk management that typically ignores factors influencing the firm's risk position. These factors are usually related to individual firm characteristics and the firm's environment. Recently, a growing body of literature from the field of strategic management has advanced the stakeholder rationale for risk management by revealing its interrelations to Barney's (1991) theory of the resource-based view of the firm (hereafter RBV) (see, e.g., Miller and Chen (2003), Wang et al. (2003) and Lim and Wang (2007)). The stakeholder rationale for risk management suggests conservative financial decisions in order to mitigate incentive problems and to induce valuable relation-specific investments on the part of non-financial stakeholders (NFS). Analyzing corporate risk management from a stakeholder perspective contributes to the ongoing discussion on why corporate financial decisions such as capital structure, dividend policy and cash holdings are conservative and if such decisions have detrimental performance implications (see, e.g., Minton and Wruck (2001), Mikkelson and Partch (2003), Cuijpers et al. (2005), and Bates et al. (2006)).

1.2 Objectives of the dissertation and research questions

The objectives of this research are twofold and can be separated into a conceptual and an empirical aspect.

The SRRM is mostly discussed from the perspective of financial literature without referring to theories from adjacent fields such as strategic management. From a conceptual perspective, this dissertation aims at uncovering the economic as well as financial and strategic theories underlying the stakeholder reasoning for risk management.

The second aspect of this research aims at contributing to the empirical literature investigating whether the firm-NFS relationship is a determinant of the firm's financial decisions. More precisely, the role of conservative financial decisions as an instrument of a stakeholder concept of risk management is investigated. It is analyzed whether firms that are more dependent on NFS-claims make more conservative financial decisions than firms that are less dependent on such claims. Primarily, the empirical part of the dissertation is intended to complement the findings of previous studies using elements from stakeholder and strategic management theories as determinants in empirical corporate finance research (see, e.g., Titman (1984), Banerjee et al. (2004), Franck and Huyghebaert (2006), Kale and Shahrur (2007), Barton and Gordon (1989), Holder et al. (1998), Vicente-Lorente (2001), and O'Brien (2003)). Thereby, this research complements the vast amount of empirical research on capital structure, liquidity and dividend policy using traditional financial explanatory theories, such as static trade-off and pecking order theories. To a lesser extent the empirical findings of this dissertation might also add to those papers with a focus on conservatism in finance (see, e.g., Minton and Wruck (2001) and Mikkelson and Partch (2003)).

From a methodological point of view, this study complements the scarce empirical literature operationalizing stakeholder theory by means of accounting data. Therefore, the dissertation also contributes to papers using stakeholder theory as a determinant in non-finance contexts such as accounting and strategic management (see, e.g., Bowen et al. (1995), Matsumoto (2002) and Miller and Chen (2003)).

1.3 Structure

The dissertation is structured into a theoretical part (chapters two to five) and an empirical part (chapters six and seven) and is organized as follows.

Chapter two discusses various definitions of the term "stakeholder" and provides a review of the most influential classifications of stakeholder theory with an emphasis on the instrumental perspective of stakeholder theory, as it is the predominant stream when used in the context of financial economics and strategic management.

The focus of chapter three lies primarily on neo-institutional theories of the firm. These theories are important for several reasons. First, elements of agency theory, transaction cost theory and property rights theory heavily influence a stakeholder conception of the modern firm because they give reason to the incomplete contractual relations between the firm and its environment. Second, the predominant corporate finance theories, which are discussed in chapter five, draw heavily on the lines of arguments built around these neo-institutional theories of the firm. Therefore, the theoretical development from a neoclassic to a neoinstititutional view of the firm is outlined. Additionally, the resource-based view (RBV) of the firm is introduced and is used to explain the performance-related aspects of the stakeholder-centered concept of the modern firm.

The essence of chapter four is to present the SRRM as a risk management concept that is appropriate for the modern stakeholder-centered firm. Implications for the scope of risk management, the relevance of corporate finance decisions as risk management instruments and effects on corporate performance are discussed. To emphasize the interdisciplinary character of the SRRM, it is contrasted with alternative risk management theories developed within the field of financial economics.

Chapter five extensively discusses traditional corporate finance theories. Starting from a neoclassic perspective, alternative theories such as the static trade-off and the pecking order theory, which are built around the neo-institutional theories of the firm, are used to explain capital structure, corporate payout and liquidity policy decisions.

Chapter six is devoted to the methodological aspects of this work. It addresses the advantages of panel data methodology over traditional multivariate regression models with either cross-section or time-series data. This chapter presents the underlying assumptions and pros and cons of alternative estimation methods for multivariate panel data regression models.

Chapter seven describes the empirical study that is carried out to investigate the determinants of capital structure and liquidity policy of Austrian and German firms. Accounting-based stakeholder literature and the traditional corporate finance theories presented in chapter five are used to develop linear regression models for each of the two areas of corporate financial decision making. These two models are tested on a sample of 593 Austrian and German firms to analyze whether the firm-stakeholder relations influence corporate finance decisions.

Chapter eight summarizes the main results of the dissertation and suggests paths for further research.

2 Stakeholder Theory

Stakeholder language has gained momentum across various academic fields in the last two decades. However, a coherent stakeholder theory is difficult to identify because various academic disciplines have produced several versions of stakeholder theory (Roberts and Mahoney, 2004: 399).

Stakeholder theory research addresses two central questions. These are first, to identify groups of stakeholders who deserve or require, for one or the other reason, management's attentions (Sundaram and Inkpen, 2004: 352) and second, to find out to what extent management's decisions are a function of stakeholder expectations and influences (Rowley, 1997: 889). In the following subsections, the historical roots of stakeholder theory are presented before turning to various stakeholder definitions offered by the literature. Finally, different classification schemes for stakeholder research are discussed.

2.1 Historical roots of stakeholder theory

Although scholars define Freeman's (1984) work linking the stakeholder concept with strategic management as the starting point for the intensive examination of stakeholder aspects in the field of organization studies (Sundaram and Inkpen, 2004: 352), the roots of the stakeholder concept go back to the Stanford Research Institute (SRI) in the 1960s (Carroll and Näsi, 1997: 46).[1] The term stakeholder, as defined by the SRI, refers to *"those groups without whose support the organization would cease to exist"* (Freeman and Reed, 1983: 89). Hence, it is no surprise that stakeholder analysis was an integral part of the SRI corporate planning process. The SRI argued that managers needed to understand the concerns of all stakeholders to assure the firm's long-term success (Freeman and Reed, 1983: 89). To some extent, the stakeholder notion was used as a counter movement to the then, and still, privileged place of stockholders in the business enterprise. Starting from the SRI's original definition, many other definitions of the term stakeholder have been proposed. In the following section, a brief review of the most relevant definitions in the context of this work is provided. For a comprehensive and chronological review on who is a stakeholder, the reader is referred to the extensive literature review by Mitchell et al. (1997: 855–863).

---

[1] Note that the SRI itself was heavily influenced by the concepts developed in the planning department of Lockheed (Freeman and McVea, 2001: 190; Freeman and Reed, 1983: 89).

2.2 Stakeholder definitions

Freeman and Reed (1983), for instance, suggest one broad and one narrow interpretation of the term stakeholder. The wider definition embraces *"any identifiable group or individual who can affect the achievement of an organization's objectives or who is affected by the achievement of an organization's objectives"* (Freeman and Reed, 1983: 91).[2] In a narrow sense, the authors define a stakeholder as *"any identifiable group or individual on which the organization is dependent for its continued survival"* (Freeman and Reed, 1983: 91). By relating the firm's survival to the dependence on its stakeholders, Freeman and Reed (1983) already emphasized the bilateral relationships between the firm and its stakeholders. Almost ten years later, Hill and Jones (1992) offer another definition by arguing that *"the term stakeholders refers to groups of constituents who have a legitimate claim on the firm"* (Hill and Jones, 1992: 133). They justify stakeholders' claims by their supplying of critical resources (Hill and Jones, 1992: 133), a view that is linking stakeholder theory to the resource-based view (RBV) of strategic management theory. In a 1995 paper, Clarkson distinguishes primary and secondary stakeholders, defining the former group as those *"without whose continuing participation the corporation cannot survive as going concern"* (Clarkson, 1995: 106). By primary stakeholders Clarkson explicitly understands shareholders, investors, employees, customers, suppliers, the governments and communities (Clarkson, 1995: 106). Secondary stakeholders, on the other hand, are defined as *"those who influence or affect, or are influenced or affected by, the corporation, but they are not engaged in transactions with the corporation and are not essential for its survival"* (Clarkson, 1995: 107). Clarkson names special interest groups or the media as examples for secondary stakeholders (Clarkson, 1995: 107). Berman et al. (1999) provide a similar definition to Clarkson's primary stakeholder concept when referring to key stakeholders (Berman et al., 1999: 489). Clarkson and Berman et al.'s separation into groups of stakeholders that diverge as to their contribution to the firm's success builds the basis for an instrumental understanding of stakeholder management as proposed by Donaldson and Preston (1995). Other authors group stakeholders in categories such as active vs. passive, economics vs. social, and core vs. strategic vs. environmental (Carroll and Näsi, 1997: 46).

---

[2] This definition is virtually identical to Freeman's classic (1984) definition: *"A stakeholder in an organization is (by definition) any group or individual who can affect or is affected by the achievement of the organization's objectives"* (Freeman, 1984: 46).

Building on financial economists' traditions of agency and contract theory, Cornell and Shapiro (1987) describe stakeholders as claimants who have contractual relations with the firm. Cornell and Shapiro (1987) were among the first authors, recognizing that there is risk involved with the position as a stakeholder. Clarkson (1994) also acknowledges stakeholders' position as risk-bearers. He distinguishes voluntary and involuntary stakeholders, dependent on the reason for their risk-bearing: *"Voluntary stakeholders bear some form of risk as a result of having invested some form of capital, human or financial, something of value, in a firm. Involuntary stakeholders are placed at risk as a result of a firm's activities. But without the element of risk there is no stake"* (Clarkson, 1994: 5; quoted in Mitchell et al., 1997: 857).

The essence of the above definitions is the insight that stakeholder theory stresses the importance of the firm's relations to internal and external groups that have a legitimate claim on the firm. The idea of stakeholder management, as formulated by Freeman (1984), is that managers must try to satisfy the needs of all groups who have a stake in the business. It is the management's task to balance the interests of shareholders, employees, customers, suppliers, communities and other groups in a way that ensures the survival and long-term success of the firm. Management should understand relationships to all stakeholders to achieve the organization's objectives. From an instrumental or managerial perspective of stakeholder theory this corporate goal is the maximization of shareholder value. However, it is acknowledged that all stakeholders have to be considered to generate that value (Freeman and McVea, 2001: 192 and 194).

2.3 Classifications of stakeholder theory

2.3.1 The classification by Donaldson and Preston (1995)

Donaldson and Preston (1995) assert that stakeholder theory and the stakeholder concept are used by many authors in very different ways. They argue that authors use various theories that are often contradictory in their arguments (Donaldson and Preston, 1995: 66). In their influential 1995 article Donaldson and Preston are able to classify past stakeholder research based on three cores which, in their opinion, underlie any piece of stakeholder literature. Their influential and often cited categorization of stakeholder theory distinguishes three reasonings: descriptive/empirical, instrumental and normative.

The descriptive arguments underlying stakeholder theory describe the nature of the firm and the way managers actually manage a corporation (Donaldson and Preston, 1995: 70).

The instrumental strand emphasizes the connections between stakeholder management and the achievement of traditional corporate objectives.[3] It states that managers must provide returns (economic or otherwise) to stakeholders in order to encourage them to engage in wealth-creating activities. Thereby, Donaldson and Preston (1995) assume a link between stakeholder management and organizational financial performance: *"corporations whose managers adopt stakeholder principles and practices will perform better financially than those that do not"* (Donaldson and Preston, 1995: 77). This idea that the concerns of stakeholders enter a firm's decision-making process only when they have strategic value to the firm is regarded as the essence of the strategic stakeholder approach to management (Shankman, 1999: 322; Berman et al., 1999: 491–492). As will be shown later, this instrumental stakeholder theory's prediction of financial outperformance goes hand in hand with the suggestions of the resource-based view of the firm.

The normative component of stakeholder theory discusses the moral obligations of the firm vis-a-vis its stakeholders (Donaldson and Preston, 1995: 71). This stream addresses the question of stakeholder identity from a moral standpoint. It tries to identify the normative foundations underlying stakeholder theory (Phillips, 2003: 25–26) and its effects on managers' behavior towards its shareholders and all other stakeholders. Furthermore, it assumes stakeholders to have an intrinsic value. Therefore, they need to be treated as "ends" rather than "means" to succeed in achieving corporate objectives (Jones and Wicks, 1999: 209). Many authors argue that the normative components of stakeholder theory are fundamental for its descriptive and instrumental understanding and build the basis of any stakeholder argument (see, e.g., Donaldson and Preston (1995), Mitchell et al. (1997) and Jones and Wicks (1999)).

---

[3] An instrumental understanding of stakeholder theory is therefore also used to integrate stakeholder theory and performance measurement (see, e.g., Atkinson et al. (1997)).

2.3.2 The classification by Roberts and Mahoney (2004)

Roberts and Mahoney (2004) provide a more recent categorization scheme for stakeholder literature by referring to the level of analysis from which one looks at an organization. Following their classification, a firm can be analyzed from three distinct levels, which the authors label as managerial agency, organizational and societal (Roberts and Mahoney, 2004: 402–404).

The managerial agency level stakeholder research

This stream of stakeholder literature is based on an instrumental understanding of stakeholder theory as proposed by Donaldson and Preston (1995). It argues from a "stakeholder as claimants" perspective inherent in the financial economics literature (see, e.g., Cornell and Shapiro, 1987). This neoclassical economic view is grounded on the idea of a single wealth-maximizing objective, which is to increase shareholder wealth through maximizing market returns. Hence, management regards NFS as instruments to achieve the ultimate goal of shareholder satisfaction. Although shareholder primacy is dominant, Jensen (2001) points at the important role of stakeholders even in this managerial agency view. He argues for an (enlightened) stakeholder conception of the firm that does not omit the firm's relationships with non-financial stakeholders, while increasing the long-term market value of the firm (Jensen, 2001: 16–17). The managerial-agency level stakeholder research emphasizes management's duty to act as agents of shareholders' property (Roberts and Mahoney, 2004: 402). Many studies, especially in the stakeholder-based accounting literature, follow this managerial-agency tradition. These studies build primarily on Cornell and Shapiro's (1987) interpretation of stakeholder management, which demands for strategically managing relations to external key-stakeholders in order to maximize the market value of the firm. Research in this tradition is, among others, provided by Cornell et al. (1989), Bowen et al. (1992 and 1995) and Burgstahler and Dichev (1997). These three papers use stakeholder language to assign the task of strategically managing stakeholder relationships through earnings management to the firm's management (Roberts and Mahoney, 2004: 407).[4]

---

[4] For a comprehensive overview of accounting studies within a stakeholder context see Roberts and Mahoney (2004).

Organizational level stakeholder research

The organizational level stakeholder research regards stakeholder analysis as a tool to develop strategies for achieving corporate objectives. As opposed to the managerial agency perspective, this stream's focus is on the organization's moral obligations vis-a-vis all of its stakeholders who have intrinsic rather than instrumental value. Studies following this normative tone argue for treating stakeholders as "ends" rather than "means". The discussion on what constitutes a legitimate claim and how to value them (see, e.g., Mitchell et al. (1997) and Trevino and Weaver (1999)) falls into this category of stakeholder research. Much of the corporate social responsibility literature can be assigned to these organizational level stakeholder studies (Roberts and Mahoney, 2004: 402–405).

Societal level stakeholder research

Societal level stakeholder analyses differ from the organizational and managerial approaches in their level of abstraction. The organizational level of stakeholder research analyzes the objective function an organization uses as decision criterion. Roberts and Mahoney (2004) refer to Jensen (2002) and Freeman (2000) as polar viewpoints regarding the selection of the corporate objective function. Jensen (2002), on the one hand, follows a neoclassic economics' view by arguing for maximizing long-term firm market value as the only objective function that is beneficial to societal welfare. Jensen's understanding supports a purely instrumental interpretation of stakeholder theory. Freeman, on the other hand, rejects the separation of the ethical aspects from the business aspects when making a business decision and proposes a model of "stakeholder capitalism" (Freeman, 2000: 172 and 174). This model implies that human beings are at the center of any process of value creation and trade, and underscores that decency and fairness are necessary in any business activity (Freeman, 2000: 177).

2.3.3 Concluding remarks

The managerial or instrumental perspective on stakeholder theory is an essential element for understanding the modern corporation (Cragg, 2002: 114). This view of the modern corporation receives support from elements of the neo-institutional economic theory of the firm (see, e.g., Hill and Jones (1992), Cragg (2002), Boatright (2002) and Jansson (2005)). Three, partially overlapping, streams out of this theoretical framework (i.e. positive agency theory, transaction cost theory, property rights theory) have contribute to explain economic value creation in the modern enterprise (Asher et al, 2005: 12). In the next chapter, competing and complementing theories of the firm are introduced in order to arrive at a definition of the modern firm that recognizes stakeholder theory as a central element.

3 The Theory of the Firm

According to Holmstrom and Tirole (1989), the theory of the firm tackles two central questions. First, why do firms exist, and second, what determines the firms' scale and scope. The theory of the firm offers a trade-off between the benefits and costs of integration to find an answer why not all economic transactions are organized within a single firm (Holmstrom and Tirole, 1989: 65–66). Departing from the irrelevance assumption of the firm in neoclassical perfect market theory, new institutional economic theory describes the boundaries of the firm within an environment of market frictions (Lockett and Thompson, 2001: 728).

In contrast to Holmstrom and Tirole (1989), Asher et al. (2005) emphasize different aspects of the theory of the firm. They point at the issues of economic value creation and the distribution of that economic value. These two points, they argue, have always been fundamental questions in the history of economic thought (Asher et al., 2005: 5).

In this chapter, the theories of the firm are outlined along three of those four elementary questions. Why do firms exist? What are the firm's boundaries? How is value created within the firm? The issue regarding the distributional aspect of the firm's value creation has not yet been given much research attention (Asher et al., 1995: 6) and will not be the focus of this work. Starting with neoclassic theory, the firm will later be analyzed within the framework of new institutional economics, before turning to the perspectives of Zingales (1998 and 2000) and Rajan and Zingales (1998) as well as those of the resource-based theory. The final subsection is devoted to integrating aspects from stakeholder theory, elements of new institutional theory and RBV-arguments into a stakeholder-centered conception of the modern firm.

3.1 The firm in neoclassical economic theory

Neoclassic theory treats the firm as a black box. Jensen and Meckling (1976) even denote it an empty box because the firm is simply regarded as a production function that seeks to maximize the present value of profits (Jensen and Meckling, 1976: 3). The firm is an entity into which resources go and out of which goods come. The transformational process within the firm is not subject to further analysis. The firms produce the products that are consumed by other economic entities (Demsetz, 1997: 426). Jensen and Meckling (1976) conclude that in neoclassic microeconomic theory the firm is simply an, however important, actor within a theory of markets (Jensen and

Meckling, 1976: 3). This view of the firm is maintained by holding the following very restrictive assumption: First, the markets function freely. Second, prices and technology are given and known by all parties. Third, owners are effective in controlling the use of their assets (Demsetz, 1997: 428). As a result of these assumptions, management does not play any role in the neoclassic firm (Stiglitz, 1985: 32–33; Demsetz, 1997: 428). Already Stiglitz asserts that the description of the firm in neoclassic economic theory provides an inadequate description of the modern industrial enterprise (Stiglitz, 1985: 32). This conclusion is even more relevant for a firm in the 21st century when the character of the firm shifts more and more from asset to service-based.

The new institutional theories of the firm achieve to overcome these unrealistic assumptions about the functioning of the firm and to develop theories addressing the question why a firm exists at all.

3.2 The firm within the framework of new institutional economic theory

The neo-institutional framework of the economic theory of the firm consists of several overlapping schools. These are agency theory, transaction cost theory and property rights theory, which are outlined in the following subsections.[5]

3.2.1 Positive agency theory

The development of positive agency theory is strongly connected to the seminal contributions by Ross (1973) and Jensen and Meckling (1976). The cornerstone of agency theory is the relationship between one actor or group (the agent) and another actor or group (the principal), where the agent has to fulfill certain obligations for the principal. The basis of this relationship of the two parties is an implicit or explicit contract. This perspective leads to a firm that is defined as a nexus-of-contracts between principals and agents (Shankman, 1999: 321). The main relationships analyzed in the financial economics literature are twofold. First, the manager-owner relationship and, second, the owner-bondholder conflict. In short, agency theory deals with two central issues. The first refers to the agency problem that arises when 1) there

[5] A detailed comparison of these theories is provided by Kim and Mahoney (2005), who contrast agency theory, property rights theory and transaction costs theory based on unit of analysis, focal dimension, focal cost concern, contractual focus, theoretical orientation, strategic intent and sources of market frictions (2005: 231).

are conflicting goals between the principal and the agent and 2) it is difficult or expensive for the principal to verify what the agent is doing and to determine if he has behaved according to the contract. The second issue addresses the different risk preferences of the principal and the agent that might induce different preferred actions (Eisenhardt, 1989: 58). The focus of agency theory is the selection of the most appropriate and efficient governance mechanism aligning the interests of the contracting parties. Efficient in this sense refers to the governance mechanism that reduces the spendings by either of the parties to limit opportunistic action of the other party to the contract. The sum of these costs (i.e. the principal's monitoring expenditures, the agent's bonding expenditures and any remaining residual loss) are referred to as agency costs (Eisenhardt, 1989: 58; Shankman, 1999: 321). The central concern of the governance mechanism is to safeguard the investments the contracting parties in the nexus make. The major contribution of agency theory is the insight that both, a firm's uncertain future and different parties' preferences to accept risk, influence the contracts between principal and agent (Eisenhardt, 1989: 65).

From an agency-theoretical viewpoint the firm can be seen as a nexus of interrelated contracts among the suppliers of factor inputs and the purchasers of outputs (Speckbacher, 2003: 271). This nexus-of-contracts perspective supports a stockholder-centered conception of the firm in which the duty of managers is to serve the interests of shareholders alone (Boatright, 2002: 1838). To serve the interests of shareholders (i.e. principals), managers (i.e. agents) are obliged to only allocate resources and carry out policies that increase the net present value (NPV) of the firm (Quinn and Jones, 1995: 24).[6] The standard line of reasoning to justify this view goes like this. Shareholders offer capital to contribute to a productive enterprise and thereby assume a large portion of risk of the enterprise. Hence, shareholders are residual risk bearers while all other stakeholders receive a fixed claim to safeguard their contributions. Due to this unique vulnerability to the firm's success, shareholders bargain for corporate control and the benefit of management's fiduciary duty as safeguards for their investments. Other non-financial stakeholders prefer different kinds of safeguards for their contributions, such as manufacturers' warranties or consumer and product safety laws, because they are assumed to be fully protected by complete contracts in an

[6] This duty on the part of the management underscores its particular role in this contractual understanding of the firm. Managers are in the center of the nexus of contracts and are the only group of stakeholders who enter into contractual relationships with all other stakeholders. Thereby, they have direct control over the decision-making apparatus of the firm (Hill and Jones, 1992: 134).

efficient markets setting (Boatright, 2002: 1841–1842; Speckbacher, 2003: 271; Hill and Jones, 1992: 132). Hence, under the complete-contract assumption of agency theory, the firm should be governed to maximize shareholders' value (Asher et al., 2005: 15), which is the discounted value of future expected cash flows. This highly rigorous and well-specified conceptualization of the firm with shareholders as the only residual claimants is still the prevailing perspective of the firm in corporate finance (Blair, 2005: 33; Asher et al., 2005: 13). Drawing on Zingales (2000) and Pitelis (2004), Asher et al. (2005: 13) indicate that this conception of the firm requires a very narrow view of contracts that is not consistent with real-world business experiences.

Seth and Thomas (1994) argue, with reference to Brealey and Myers (1988), that agency theory acknowledges firms having special advantages. Otherwise, positive NPV investment opportunities would not be available to the firm. The origins of such advantages are specialized resources the firm possesses. Although agency theory recognizes the value-creating capacity of specialized resources, financial economics and agency theory in particular do not deal with developing a theory on the sources of competitive advantage. This is the key question of strategic management's theory on the resource-based view of the firm. As will be shown later, both agency theory and the resource-based theory are compatible with each other (Seth and Thomas, 1994: 178–180).

3.2.2 Transaction cost theory

Building on the work of Coase (1937), transaction cost theory has mainly been put forward by Oliver E. Williamson and deals with two major issues. On the one hand, it emphasizes the administering, directing, negotiating and monitoring of the joint productive teamwork in a firm as opposed to a market solution. Additionally, it deals with the issue of assuring the quality of performance of contractual agreements (Alchian and Woodward, 1988: 66). Using a bipolar perspective, the market is the other alternative to govern transactions.[7] The notion of governance structures is to support an organization's high performance results. As opposed to property rights literature, transaction cost theory does not assume court ordering of contracts to be costless and efficacious (Williamson, 1998: 40). Rather, a costly private ordering is needed (Williamson, 1998: 28). This private ordering approach to governance

---

[7] Of course, Williamson asserts that there are also hybrid forms of governance lying between the market and the firm mode (1998: 37).

postulates that each generic mode of governance is defined by a distinctive contract law regime (Williamson, 2002: 177).

In the following section, the main insights tracing back to transaction cost theory, as far as relevant from the perspective of this work, are outlined. For a more detailed discussion see, e.g., Williamson (1985).

Transaction costs theory builds on a characterization of human beings that is strongly influenced by Herbert Simon's description of human behavior (see, e.g., Simon, 1985). It assumes human actors to be bounded rational, meaning that they act intendedly rational but their degree of rationality is, in fact, only limited.[8] Second, human agents are self-interested, a behavior that is referred to in transactions cost economics as opportunism (Willliamson, 1998: 30).[9] Given that all complex contracts are unavoidably incomplete, the problem with opportunism is that contracts are not self-enforcing when credible commitments are absent (Williamson, 1998: 31).

3.2.2.1 Characteristics of transactions

The natural unit of analysis in Williamson's theory is the transaction. Transactions in the sense of Williamson are not just spot exchanges or long-lasting series of spot exchanges. They are contractual, meaning that the parties become dependent on each other's promises to fulfill (Alchian and Woodward, 1988: 66). Building on the incompleteness of contracts and human's bounded rationality attribute, Williamson analyzes the attributes of transactions to which contractual hazards accrue and how to mitigate them (Williamson, 1998: 36). Transaction cost economics holds that three dimensions influence the study and costs of commercial transactions.[10] First, asset specificity, second, the frequency with which transactions recur, and, third, disturbances transactions are subject to (Williamson, 2005a: 47).

---

[8] Alchian and Woodward (1988) complement this definition by saying that bounded rationality always implies incomplete information about market opportunities, limited ability to predict the future and derive implications from predictions, and limited ability to prespecify responses to future events (Alchian and Woodward, 1988: 66).

[9] Williamson (1985) defines opportunism as *"a condition of self-interest seeking with guile"* (Williamson, 1985: 30).

[10] The costs inherent to Williamson's theory are ex-ante costs for establishing a contract and ex-post costs for administering, informing, monitoring and enforcing the contractually promised performance (Alchian and Woodward, 1988: 66–67).

Asset specificity is a cornerstone of transaction cost theory. It refers to investments in assets that, in contrast to general purpose investments, cannot be redeployed without a significant loss in value. Williamson (1985) attaches the following characteristics to asset specificity.[11] First, asset specificity refers to durable investments that are undertaken in support of a particular transaction. Opportunity costs of these investments are much lower for an alternative user or in an alternative setting. Second, in contrast to exchanges under a neoclassic setting, the identity of the transacting parties matters because a long-term relationship is positively valued by the business partners. Along with asset specificity, bilateral dependency develops, and, in combination with uncertainty (i.e. disturbances in the language of Williamson), incomplete contracts will be pushed out of alignment resulting in contractual complications (Williamson, 2005a: 47). The problem with these bilateral dependencies between the parties is that once the investment has been made, options that were available to the investor in the former stage are lost in the latter. Williamson labels this transition from precontract to postcontract the *Fundamental Transformation* (Alchian and Woodward, 1988: 67). Hence and third, safeguards to protect the investment arise that are unnecessary for non-specific transactions (Williamson, 1985: 55) (an assumption that is typically made in a neoclassic market setting).

The effect of frequency is relevant insofar, as the type of governance structures necessary to safeguard investments depends upon the number of transactions to be covered. Of course, it will be easier to recover for large transactions that recur more often than for smaller ones that occur only once (Williamson, 1985: 60).

Moreover, transactions are exposed to uncertainty, or disturbances to use Williamson's language. Williamson distinguishes non-behavioral and behavioral sources of uncertainty. While non-behavioral uncertainty goes back to communication problems and the mere fact that future contingencies are always unknown in advance, behavioral uncertainty is attributable to opportunistic actions (Williamson, 1985: 57–59). Opportunism covers the propensity for mutually reliant parties to mislead, distort, disguise, obfuscate, or confuse in order to expropriate wealth from the other party.

---

[11] Williamson dinstinguished the following types of transaction-specific assets: site specificity (specialization by proximity), physical asset specificity (e.g. a die for stamping), human asset specificity (usually arises from firm-specific training or learning by doing), dedicated assets (large discrete investments made in expectation of continuing business), temporal specificity and brand-name capital (Williamson, 1985: 55; 1998: 36; 2002: 176).

However, it also includes honest disagreements that might be costly to resolve (Alchian and Woodward, 1988: 66).

3.2.2.2 Holdup and moral hazard

As already specified, opportunistic actions intend to expropriate wealth from the other party of a contractual agreement. This attack against the higher-than-market value of the specific investment is referred to as *hold up*. What is attacked is the quasi-rent of the investor, which is simply the excess above the return necessary to maintain a resource's current service flow. A typical example in the literature of a holdup situation is a steel mill that is located near a public utility. Once the steel mill has made the investment, the power company could raise the power prices (Alchian and Woodward, 1988: 67; the authors heavily draw from Marshall (1936)).

Moral hazard occurs when there is informational asymmetry between the two parties involved in the contract and getting the information is costly. The problem with moral hazard is that one cannot count on what people promise they will do. These difficulties in evaluating performance ex-post will manifest themselves in the prices and contractual arrangements. Typical examples are the owner-manager, the inside owner-outside owner and the debtholder-equityholder relationships. The extent to which moral hazard might be a problem in a contractual arrangement depends on the plasticity of resources and on monitoring costs. When resources are plastic (i.e. they can be used in many different ways by the user), they are prone to moral hazardous exploitation. When, at the same time, monitoring of the user's performance is difficult, moral hazard problems will favor ownership of an asset by the user (Alchian and Woodward, 1988: 68–69).

3.2.2.3 The firm as a governance mechanism

Williamson uses the notion of transaction costs to discuss the issue of the firm's boundaries. Contrary to neoclassical economics, which describes the firm as a "black box"-like production function, transaction cost economics describes the firm as a governance structure, which is an organizational construction (Williamson, 1998: 32). Governance in the sense of Williamson is *"the means by which* ***order*** *is accomplished in a relation in which potential* ***conflict*** *threatens to undo or upset opportunities to realize* ***mutual*** *gains"* (Williamson, 1998: 37; original emphasis). As shown above, this conflict may occur when firm-specific resources are not all owned in common (Alchian and Woodward, 1988: 70–71).

According to transaction cost theory, the firm is just one alternative mode of governance. The firm is a means to integrate assets and thereby reduce the potential for opportunism of otherwise independent contractual parties. Williamson regards the essence of the firm as teamwork that requires long-term contractual agreements restraining the behavior of the participants (Alchian and Woodward, 1988: 70).

From this governance perspective, transaction cost economics has also been used extensively to explain the location of the appropriate boundaries of the firm. It has been applied to decisions on vertical integration, the make/buy-choice, or the use of franchising and joint-ventures (Lockett and Thompson, 2001: 728).

The essence of this governance perspective in the context of this work is twofold. First, it emphasizes the value-generating aspect related to continuing a relationship between contractual partners (Williamson, 2005b: 1). Second, it states that the likelihood of vertical integration increases with firm-specific investments because the market transaction costs associated with the threat of a hold-up go up (Klein, 1993: 213). In other words, vertical integration can mitigate the opportunism problem that is related to the quasi-rents in an incomplete contractual setting.

3.2.3 Property rights theory

3.2.3.1 Traditional property rights theory

Following Furubotn and Pejovich (1972), the traditional property rights approach analyzes the effect of different property rights assignments on penalty-reward structures and the choices these assignments leave to decision makers. Instead of treating the firm as the unit of analysis, this theory centers on the behavior of the individual within the firm and his adjustments to the economic environment (Furubotn and Pejovich, 1972: 1138). Hence, in the sense of this theory, property rights refer to the *"sanctioned behavioral relations among men that arise from the existence of things and pertain to their use"* (Furubotn and Pejovich, 1972: 1139). Since the assignment of property rights affects the utility function of the decision maker, it also affects the allocation of resources, the composition of output and the distribution of income. In order to be capable of predicting the effect of different sets of property rights, it is necessary to define more precisely what is actually meant by property rights. According to Furubotn and Pejovich (1972: 1139–1140), property rights refer to the right of ownership in an asset, which comprises the exclusive rights to 1) to use the asset, 2) change its form and substance, and 3) transfer rights in the asset completely through sale or partially through rental (Furubotn and Pejovich, 1972: 1139–1140; Richter and Furubotn, 1999: 82). A broader definition compassing not only the legal but also the social aspects of property rights (Kreps, 1990) gives Alchian (1965) who defines them as *"...the rights of individual to the use of resources ... supported by the force of etiquette, social custom, ostracism, and formal legally enacted laws supported by the states' power of violence of punishment"* (Alchian, 1965: 29; quoted in Kim and Mahoney, 2005: 226).

Developments in early, also referred to as traditional, property rights theory are closely related to the seminal work of Alchian and Demsetz (1972). Building on Coase (1937), these authors define the aspect of team production as the essence of the firm. Team production, in their definition, means a production process in which 1) several types of resources are used, 2) the product is not a sum of separable outputs of each cooperating resource, and 3) not all resources used in team production belong to a single person. In such a setting, it is difficult to define or determine the individual's contribution of each team member by only observing total output (Alchian and Demsetz, 1972: 779). Costly monitoring is necessary to avoid shirking on the part of the team members. The only economically meaningful arrangement is that the owners have the right to control the firm, the power to revise the contract terms with all team members and receive the residual rights to profit (Speckbacher, 2003: 271; Kim and Mahoney, 2005: 227). That is, the owners receive the property rights of the assets in use in order to achieve the most efficient outcome.

Alchian and Demsetz' (1972) analysis defines an organizational form that is known in the literature as the *classic capitalist firm* that is characterized by the following attributes (Alchian and Demsetz, 1972: 783 and 794):

- joint input production
- the existence of several input owners
- a central party that contracts with the joint input factors and has the right to renegotiate these contracts
- the central party holds the residual claims

- the exclusive right to sell the central contractual status is assigned to the central party
- the central party is called the firm's owner and the employer

In short, traditional property rights theory deals with the overall historical and institutional context that forms and changes property rights. On the other hand, modern property rights literature, which is introduced in turn, focuses on mathematical modeling of ownership and incentive structures to achieve the most efficient outcome (Kim and Mahoney, 2005: 224).

3.2.3.2 Property rights theory of Grossmann, Hart and Moore

The property rights theory of Grossman, Hart and Moore (Grossman and Hart (1986), Hart (1989), and Hart and Moore (1990)) (also referred to in the literature as the GHM model) has features in common with agency theory, transaction cost theory and the early property rights literature (Hart, 1989: 210). It stresses the incompleteness of contractual arrangements and is therefore often referred to as incomplete contract theory.[12]

The basic assumption is the following. In a neoclassical world, where it is costlessly possible to plan and write provisions for future events, parties to an exchange do not bear any contractual risk. In such a world, contracts costlessly specify all future contingencies, together with obligations and penalties for all possible states that are known in advance. Consequently, there is no need for a third party assuring that each business partner complies with the contract (Hart, 1991: 140). In reality, however, contracts are substantially imperfect. They are significantly incomplete, leaving out many contingencies. Additionally, contracts are often not enforced with rigor. Penalties for violation of contracts might be modest and, hence, breaching the ex-ante specified arrangement is not uncommon. Shavell (1998), for instance, identifies two reasons for why contracts are usually incomplete.

First, there are costs of writing complete contracts. The notion that there are transaction costs of writing contracts goes back to the works of Williamson (see, e.g., 1985) and Klein et al. (1978) and represents generally accepted knowledge in

---

[12] For a further discussion of incomplete contract theory see, e.g., Tirole (1999) and the literature cited there.

economics. Transaction cost literature argues that these contracting costs may be substantial. According to Hart (1995), such contractual costs derive from three different sources. First, the cost of thinking about all possible future states and planning how to deal with them. Second, the cost of negotiating with business partners about these plans. Third, the cost of writing down the plans in an enforceable way (Hart, 1995: 680).

The second reason Shavell (1998) identifies for contracts to be incomplete relates to the fact that expected consequences for violating contracts are often not very harmful because a tribunal might interpret an imperfect contract in a desirable way (Shavell, 1998: 438). Additionally, it might also be desirable to leave room to adjust the contract to new situations (Goldberg, 1976: 428). For these two reasons, events will occur where parties act differently from the way specified in the contract (Hart, 1991: 141). Such behavior, which is directed against the meaning of the contract, might be opportunistic and is more likely when there is a large surplus to be divided ex-post and whose division is unspecified ex-ante (Grossman and Hart, 1986: 692).

Grossmann and Hart (1986: 692) argue that in the case of incomplete contracts it might be optimal for one party to receive all the residual rights of control (i.e. all rights except those specifically mentioned in the contract). The property rights then fill the gap left in the incomplete contracts (Blair, 2005: 35). In the GHM model, these property rights are the residual control rights that are obtained when one has ownership over the firm.[13]

This definition of ownership has important implications for the nature of the firm. Hart and Moore (1990) assert that the owner of an asset has the exclusive right to decide who might and who might not use that asset.[14] Insofar, control over a physical asset translates directly into control over human assets (Hart and Moore, 1990: 1121). Consequently, the GHM model defines the firm as a bundle of physical assets (Hart and Moore, 1990: 1150).

---

[13] Note that in the definition of traditional property rights by Alchian and Demsetz (1972) ownership is equated with residual rights to income, as it holds the residual claim, while in the GHM model ownership is equated with residual rights to control (Kim and Mahoney, 2005: 227).

[14] Hart and Moore (1990) state that *"...the owner of a machine can decide who can and who cannot work on that machine, the owner of a building, the owner of an insurance company's client list can decide who has and who does not have access to the list"* (Hart and Moore, 1990: 1121).

3.2.4 The modern firm as a nexus of specific investments

Following the lines of new institutional economics, a theory of the firm has been developed that incorporates the importance of the valuable relationships between the firm and its environment. Proponents of this modern stakeholder view of the firm are Rajan and Zingales (1998) and Zingales (1998 and 2000), who define the modern firm as a nexus of specific investments that cannot be replicated by the market. Therefore, the value of this unique combination of complementary and co-specialized assets might be higher than the value of the sum of its parts (Asher et al., 2005: 16). This definition of the firm goes beyond the GHM model, which focuses on the physical investments of owners and therewith reduces the firm to a collection of physical assets. On the other hand, Rajan and Zingales define the firm in terms of unique assets, which are either physical or human, and in terms of people who have access to these assets (Rajan and Zingales, 1998: 390; Speckbacher, 2003: 274). This definition extends the boundaries of the firm and includes corporate stakeholders. Asher et al. (2005) criticize this instrumental approach to the view of the firm, as stakeholders are exclusively considered under the assumption that they have access to unique firm assets (Asher et al., 2005: endnote 3, p. 24).

Drawing on this view of the firm, where the value of the co-specialized investments is higher within the nexus than outside, two managerial tasks can be alleged. On the one hand, the management has the ex-post task to protect stakeholders' quasi-rents. On the other hand, given contractual incompleteness, it is responsible for creating conditions ex-ante that encourage investments by the firm's stakeholders. A business partner will not make any firm-specific investment when parts of the contract are implicit and he believes that his quasi-rents will be squeezed by the contractual partner once the investment is sunk. Zingales (2000) gives an example by discussing the specific role of employees in the modern firm. To maintain the incentive to specialize, he states, employees have to be granted a certain level of rents in the future. Moreover, he points out that employees might lose the incentive to specialize in the firm's assets in the case of a reduction in future growth prospects (e.g. as in the case of a temporary liquidity shock).

Such behavior on the part of the firm's stakeholders leads to underinvestment in firm-specific assets, which in turn reduces the value of the firm's organizational capital.[15] Zingales (2000) asserts that this permanent loss of organizational capital might be a new way of formalizing the costs of financial distress (Zingales, 2000: 1646). As will be shown in section 4.3, the stakeholder rationale for risk management extends Zingales' (2000) example that the firm suffers costs of financial distress due to an employee's disincentive to specifically invest in the firm to the entirety of the firm's NFS.

This modern view of the firm as a nexus of complementary and specific assets together with Willliamson's quasi-rent concept makes clear that other stakeholders besides shareholders are residual claimants (Asher et al., 2005: 18) and have something at stake. Hence, a firm's management should be aware of the role of its equityholders as well as non-financial stakeholders when it comes to creating and distributing economic value (Asher et al., 2005: 22).

3.3 The resource-based view of the firm

3.3.1 General

The resource-based view (RBV) of the firm goes back to ideas of Penrose (1959) about the growth of the firm. Penrose regards the firm as a bundle of productive resources (Seth and Thomas, 1994: 177). These resources are heterogeneously distributed among firms and create the unique character of each firm (Hoskisson et al., 1999: 438). In the 1980s, Penrose's ideas revived through articles by Wernerfelt (1984) and Barney (1986), which eventually led to Barney's (1991) influential article on *"Firm resources and sustained competitive advantage"* in the *Journal of Management* (Barney and Hesterly, 1996: 133). The central question the RBV addresses, as put forward by Barney, is to find out why firms are different and how firms achieve and sustain competitive advantage (Hoskisson et al., 1999: 437). Competitive advantage, in the sense of Barney, can be defined as an implemented value-creating strategy that is not simultaneously being implemented by any current or potential competitor. Sustainable in his sense means that other firms are unable to copy the benefits of this

[15] The link between organization capital as a fraction of firm value and the firm's stakeholders is presented in more detail in section 3.4.2.

strategy (Barney, 1991: 102).[16] To analyze these key points, Barney (1991) builds on Wernerfelt (1984), who suggests investigating the relationship between firm profitability and its resource position. Wernerfelt (1984) defines resources as any strength or weakness of a particular firm, independent of the resource's nature (be it tangible of intangible) (Wernerfelt, 1984: 172). In 1991, Barney classifies firm's resources into four types: 1) financial resources, 2) physical resources, 3) human resources, and 4) organizational resources[17] (Barney and Hesterly, 1996: 133).[18]

Barney's resource-based theory builds on two elementary assumptions. First, resources vary significantly across firms (i.e. assumption of firm heterogeneity), and second, productive resources cannot be costlessly transferred between firms (i.e. resource immobility) (Barney and Hesterly, 1996: 133; Priem and Butler, 2001: 24–25). Further, Barney (1991) argues that four characteristics define whether firm resources are capable of generating sustainable competitive advantage. They must be 1) valuable (meaning that such resources contribute to firm efficiency or effectiveness), 2) rare among its competitors, 3) costly to imitate for competitors (i.e. imperfect imitability), and 4) non-substitutable (meaning that there exists no strategically equivalent valuable resource that fulfills the same function) (Barney, 1991: 105–112; Barney and Hesterly, 1996: 134; Priem and Butler, 2001: 25). Building on Barney's (1991) VRIN (valuable, rare, imperfectly imitable, non-substitutable) framework, it is argued that the first two characteristics are each necessary but not sufficient conditions for competitive advantage, while the latter two are each necessary but not sufficient for sustainability of an existing competitive advantage (Priem and Butler, 2001: 25).

The non-transferability of resources is a central element of the resource-based view. Drawing on Dierickx and Cool (1989), Barney (2001) divides the reasons for why resources are imperfectly imitable into three categories. First, certain resources can

---

[16] Note that Barney (1991) does not assume that competitve advantage will last forever. The RBV simply asserts that this advantage will not be competed away through competing firms duplicating the original benefitial strategy (Barney, 1991: 103).

[17] From the perspective of this work it is worth noting that Barney (1991) regards stakeholder relations as a part of organizational resources: *"Organizational capital resources include ... as well as informal relations among groups within a firm and between a firm and those in its environment"* (Barney, 1991: 101).

[18] Some authors (e.g. Markides and Williamson (1996)) distinguish between resources and capabilities, with the latter being the human know-how and skills that are required to build assets and the former referring to all other assets (Combs and Ketchen, 1999: 868). Following Barney (1991), the term resources will be interpreted broadly in this work and encompass both resources and capabilities.

only be developed over time (so-called path dependency). This means that the development of resources depends upon a unique series of events in a firm's history. Second, often firms do not know by themselves what the reasons for their superior performances are (i.e. causal ambiguity). Hence, competitors are unable to imitate the resource responsible. Third, sometimes the resources the firm builds its superior performance on are socially complex (Barney and Hesterly, 1996: 134; Barney, 2001: 645). By socially complex, resource-based theorists mean that a firm's resources are built on complex social phenomena. In contrast to the causal ambiguity characteristic, it is known what drives the firm's outperformance. However, the ability to actively manage these resources is limited. Examples of such socially complex resources are a firm's reputation among various stakeholders, a firm's culture, or the teamwork among employees (Barney, 1991: 107–111; Barney and Hesterly, 1996: 134).

Originally developed to improve understanding about the strategy and (out) performance of the firm, recent pieces of literature show that the RBV is related to the financial policy of the firm. Particularly, resource-driven strategies shape the future financial decisions of the firm and can increase the cost of the firm's financial structure. Hence, resource-based strategies and financial policies need to be synchronized (Vicente-Lorente, 2001: 174).

3.3.2 Comparing the resource-based view to alternative theories of the firm

The RBV's main idea is to look inside firms and to explain performance differences among firms through resource heterogeneity. In the course of further developing the resource-based perspective, several strategy scholars analyze the RBV from a theory-of-the-firm perspective (Barney, 1996: 469). Connor (1991) and Conner and Prahalad (1996) develop a resource-based or knowledge-based theory of the firm. It is not the focus of this work to evaluate the RBV's ability to explain the nature and scope of the firm within a new theory of the firm.[19] However, the differences and similarities between the RBV and traditional theories of the firm other authors have identified are briefly outlined.

[19] For a critical discussion of Connor's (1991) argument of a resource-based perspective on firm existence see Mahoney (2001).

Neoclassical microeconomic theory

Unlike the RBV, neoclassic perfect competition theory assumes that firms are identical because perfect and complete information together with a specifiable production function makes sure that each firm has equal access to production technology. Resource mobility assures that each firm is able to obtain exactly the right fraction of required inputs. The core of the neoclassic firm is that the firm's input price equals the input's marginal productive value to the firm. Hence, the firm's profit-maximizing objective leads to a market equilibrium in which each firm yields zero economic returns (Connor, 1991: 123). Speaking with Lockett and Thompson (2001), the neoclassical theory of the firm turns out to be a misnomer for a theory of the short-run behavior of markets (Locket and Thompson, 2001: 727). The RBV sticks to the neoclassical view of the firm as a combiner of input factors. However, it does not rely on the neoclassic assumptions of a freely available and perfectly specifiable production function together with costless resource mobility and divisibility of input factors (Connors, 1991: 132).

Another important difference between microeconomic theory and the RBV is listed by Barney (2001). Neoclassic theory assumes that factors of production (what resource-based scholars define as resources and capabilities) are elastic in supply. This means that when the demand for a certain input factor increases, the prices for this factor will go up as well, which in turn drives up supply to achieve an equilibrium state. As argued above, the RBV identifies many reasons why the supply for resources is inelastic (path dependency, causal ambiguity, social complexity) and competitive advantage is sustainable (Barney, 2001: 644–645; Peteraf (1993)).

Transaction cost theory

Connor (1991) regards asset specificity as an important element of both the RBV as well as transaction cost economics (Connor, 1991: 133). Mahoney (2001) even extends this idea and claims that market frictions in general are critical concepts to both resource-based theory and transaction cost theory. Both, resource-based theory and transaction cost theory acknowledge incomplete markets and asymmetric information (Mahoney, 2001: 655).

Regarding differences between these two theories, the central point for Connor (1991) is the opportunism aspect. The main reason for a firm to exist in transaction cost theory is to reduce opportunism. The resource-based literature, however, tends to see the firm as a creator of unique productive value, not as an institution whose sole purpose lies in avoiding opportunistic action. Upon that argument, Connor (1991) builds a resource-based theory of the existence of firms that assumes away opportunism (Connor, 1991: 142). Mahoney (2001), in contrast, does not follow Connor's (1991) argument. He regards the RBV as a theory of firm rents, not as a theory of the existence of firms (compared to transaction cost theory). However, he considers both theories as complementary, with the former seeking to delineate the set of market frictions for achieving sustainable rents and the latter to explain the existence of the firm (Mahoney, 2001: 655).

3.4 A stakeholder-centered concept of the modern firm

3.4.1 Value creation in the modern firm

Building on the new institutional theory of the firm, an instrumental stakeholder perspective, and the RBV, a modern view of the firm has emerged. Starting point is Jensen and Meckling's (1976) perspective of the firm as a nexus of contracts (Coff, 1999: 121). This agency view represents a well-specified and precise definition of the firm in which shareholders are the firm's only residual risk bearers. Hence, the focus lies on maximizing the long-term economic value of the firm. However, in such as a Jensen and Meckling-world of complete contracts the inner workings of the firm are ignored.

Following stakeholder arguments, an organization can be viewed as a nexus of interdependent relationships among primary stakeholders (Clarkson, 1995: 107). Once the existence of implicit contracts and incomplete contracting is recognized, other stakeholders besides the equityholders are residual claimants. Their claims need to be protected to avoid underinvestment in relation-specific investments (Asher et al., 2005: 16–18). Although stakeholder theory is the opposite of the rigorous agency model, it is more realistic with respect to the day-to-day balancing act corporate managers are engaged in (Blair, 2005: 34).

The RBV of the firm argues that a firm's ability to outperform competitors depends on the unique interplay of human, organizational, and physical resources over time. As put forward by Barney (1991), firms using valuable, rare, imperfectly imitable, and non-substitutable resources, which are specific to the firm, may have a competitive advantage over their competitors. This leads to superior economic performance

(Barney (1991); Lockett and Thompson, 2001: 725) and higher firm value subsequently. Teece (1998: 75) and Hillman and Keim (2001: 127) argue that such socially complex and causally ambiguous resources might be reputation, knowledge-assets and long-term relationships with stakeholders. Wang et al. (2003: 51) argue similarly and regard all relation-specific investments made by the firm's NFS as potential sources of competitive advantage.[20] Harrison (2006) goes one step further, by interpreting the whole stakeholder network of the firm as a resource that fulfills the VRIN criteria.[21]

Recent pieces of literature address the relationship between the resource-based and stakeholder views and find that they are complementary rather than competing (see, e.g., Kim and Mahoney (2002), Blair (2005), Asher et al. (2005), Grandori (2005) and Harrison (2006)). Bringing together both the RBV and stakeholder arguments shows that the firm is composed of resources *and* relationships. The firm must manage both of them effectively in order to enhance the firm's ability to acquire and develop valuable resources (Harrison, 2006: 3). Consequently, this might lead to an increase in firm value.

3.4.2 Conceptualizing firm value through Net Organizational Capital

The central insight of a modern understanding of the firm is the fact that all stakeholders contribute to the creation of firm value because they are both valuable resources per se, as well as suppliers of valuable resources. As residual claimants, equityholders consequently benefit from value enhancing firm-specific investments made by NFS. The stockholders' proportion of the value created by these stakeholders depends on the payments required to induce stakeholders to make their resources available to the firm (Wang et al., 2003: 51). Cornell and Shapiro (1987) were the first authors analyzing these corporate financial implications of a modern contractual understanding of the firm and the contributions of non-financial stakeholders to firm value (Speckbacher, 1997: 633).

---

[20] Withouth referring to strategic management theory, Shapiro and Balbirer (2000) argue similarly to the RBV proponents, when stating that intangible assets such as brand names, reputation for quality and reliability, and specific human capital are important factors for building organizational capital, since they require specialized investments on the part of corporate stakeholders (Shapiro and Balbirer, 2000: 482).

[21] This is similar to Zingales' (1998) definitions of the firm as *"a nexus of specific investments"* and *"a network of specific investments that cannot be replicated by the market"* (Zingales, 1998: 498).

To show the financial impact of non-financial stakeholders' investments on firm value and shareholders' wealth position, Cornell and Shapiro (1987) introduce the concept of Net Organizational Capital (NOC). This concept builds on a contractual view of the firm in the sense of Jensen and Meckling (1976) but acknowledges an incomplete contract setting. However, their concept includes, in addition to explicit contracts, also implicit contractual relations (or claims in the language of Cornell and Shapiro) between the firm and its stakeholders. These implicit claims (or commitments) are defined as mutual understandings or promises between the business partners (Deephouse and Wiseman, 2000: 470) (e.g. a promise of continuing service to customers or a promise of job security to employees) and contain two essential characteristics. First, they are too nebulous and state contingent to be reduced to writing at reasonable cost. Second, implicit claims are closely connected to the firm's goods and services. These claims cannot be unbundled and traded independently from them. Rather, these non-formal contractual parts are inherent to any firm-stakeholder relationship and come together with the explicit contracts between the firm and its stakeholders (Cornell and Shapiro, 1987: 7).

The concept of Net Organizational Capital is an extended balance sheet that explains the close connection between implicit claims and firm value. On the one hand, there is Organizational Capital, OC, which Cornell and Shapiro define as the current market value of all implicit claims the firm expects to sell to its stakeholders in the future. Organizational Liabilities, OL, on the other hand, equal the firm's expected costs to honor both current and future implicit claims. The difference between OC and OL is Net Organizational Capital, NOC, which is positive when the implicit claims are sold to the firm's stakeholders at an average price that exceeds the average cost of honoring them (Cornell and Shapiro, 1987: 8). Wentges (2000) argues that the value stakeholders ascribe to their implicit claims with the firm depends on the perceived risk profile of the firm (Wentges, 2000: 204). Stakeholders' risk premia for this perceived risk profile are driven by their individual preferences, their potential to diversify risks, the weight of their implicit claims in their overall portfolio, but primarily the financial and non-financial rewards they expect to receive from the firm in the future (Wentges, 2002: 148). Hence, positive prospects regarding the firm's profitability and growth rate might improve stakeholders' perceived risk profile of the firm. Also, a sound financial condition of the firm might positively influence the perceived current and future risk profile of the firm. Since stakeholders' implicit claims are not contractually assured, stakeholders will additionally consider the firm's track record of honoring implicit commitments in the past when valuing them.

The usefulness of the NOC concept lies in linking the prices stakeholders are willing to pay for the firms' implicit contractual arrangements to firm value and ultimately to that fraction of firm value entitled to the equityholders. Therefore, all activities that increase NOC are consistent with the objective of shareholder value maximization. This clarifies the instrumental (Donaldson and Preston, 1995) or managerial agency (Roberts and Mahoney, 2004) character of the NOC concept.

To achieve the shareholder value objective the firm has to increase the current market value of its implicit claims (i.e. NOC). In a world of incomplete contracts, stakeholders' investments are not fully protected against opportunistic firm behavior. Hence, it is the management's task not only to understand the firm's entire set of stakeholder relationships from the perspective of value creation. Rather, it must also take steps to keep the sources of organizational and equityholders' wealth (i.e. the relation-specific investments) available to the firm.[22]

In the next chapter it is shown that implementing a risk management policy that reaches beyond the suggestions of traditional financial theory contributes to keeping stakeholders specifically investing in the firm and to increase the market value of the implicit claims the firm sells to these stakeholders. Although the distributional aspect of rent generation is only partly addressed in this work, the NOC concept together with resource-based arguments shows that both, equityholders and other NFS benefit from a continuing flow of complementary firm-specific investments.

---

[22] This task is compatible with Freeman's definition of stakeholder management which he describes as *"the idea that the tasks of managers in business are to manage the stakeholder relationships in a way that achieves the purpose of the business"* (Freeman and Gilbert, 1987: 397; quoted in Blair, 2005: 33).

4 The Theory of Corporate Risk Management

4.1 The foundations of modern finance

"One of the most important developments in finance theory in the last decades is the ability to talk about risk in a quantifiable fashion. If we know how to measure and price financial risk correctly, we can properly value risky assets. This in turn leads to better allocation of resources in the economy. Investors can do a better job of allocating their savings to various types of risky securities, and managers can better allocate the funds provided by shareholders and creditors among scarce capital resources." (Copeland et al., 2005: 101).

This quotation expresses the relevance of the development of a coherent theory to conceptualize and operationalize the risk inherent in a particular security. Such a coherent theory of risk represents a tremendous achievement in financial economics because it allows implementing the Net Present Value criterion. The foundation of such a theory was laid by the work of Markowitz (1952 and 1959) on portfolio selection under conditions of uncertainty. His theory represents a milestone for the development of modern capital market theory (Jensen, 1972: 358) and one of its most important elements, the Capital Asset Pricing Model (hereafter CAPM). Another pillar of modern finance goes back to the insights of Modigliani and Miller (hereafter MM) who assert the irrelevancy of corporate financial decisions for the value of the firm. The theory of risk management is closely connected to these two concepts. Therefore, a brief review of the key elements of the MM-framework and the CAPM, as far as relevant in the context of risk management, is presented before discussing the theories of corporate risk management.[23]

4.1.1 The Modigliani Miller-framework in the context of corporate risk management

Modigliani and Miller (1958) state that under the restrictive neoclassic assumptions[24] corporate financial decisions such as capital structure choice or dividend policy do not influence the value of the firm.[25] These decisions simply redistribute the income stream

---

[23] For a comprehensive review of the CAPM, the reader is referred to Sharpe (1991), Cochrane (1999), Fama and French (2004), and Perold (2004). The MM-framework and its implications for the field of corporate finance are discussed in greater detail in chapter 5.

[24] For a detailed discussion of these assumptions see, e.g., Fama (1978).

[25] Total firm value, i.e. the value of all assets, is defined as the sum of all expected cash flows discounted at the cost of capital. The firm value to the shareholders is equivalent to the difference between the value of the assets and the market value of debt (entity approach). Following the

among different investors. As long as investors can act in the capital markets at the same terms and conditions as the firm itself, the only way to impact firm value is by influencing the expected level of firm cash flows (Fenn et al., 2002: 15–16). Since corporate risk management is part of an overall financing policy, the MM-findings directly have important implications for the hedging policy of the firm.[26] In the MM-framework, any hedging policy is irrelevant because investors can alter their holdings of risky assets and undo any change in the firm's hedging policy by themselves. Under the MM-model, any investor's wealth position is unaffected by corporate risk management activities on the part of the firm (Smith and Stulz, 1985: 392). Additionally, shareholders have differing preferences regarding hedging that cannot be taken into consideration when hedging at the firm level (Bartram, 2000: 294). Following these arguments, a MM disciple would argue against doing any risk management at all since it is a purely financial transaction (Froot et al., 1994: 93). The immense importance of the MM-framework for corporate risk management, however, becomes apparent when it is used as a starting point for identifying conditions under which corporate risk management makes economic sense.[27] As will be shown in section 4.2.2, such a positive theory of corporate risk management can be derived by relaxing the neoclassic assumptions of the Modigliani-Miller framework.

4.1.2 Capital market theory in the context of corporate risk management

The concept of risk in financial theory is closely related to the insights of portfolio theory. The most important paradigm of risk is part of a set of results known in the financial economics literature as the SLB Model or the Capital Asset Pricing Model. The SLB Model was developed by Sharpe (1964), Lintner (1965) and refined by Black (1972). It represents an extension and simplification of the normative mean-variance portfolio model by Markowitz (1952 and 1959). Markowitz regards the issue of investor portfolio selection as a problem of utility maximization under conditions of uncertainty (Jensen, 1972: 358), an approach that defines a starting point for developing the SLB equilibrium model. The Markowitz model was the first theorizing a relationship between risk and return. In his model there are as many efficient

equity approach, shareholder value can be calculated as the sum of the free cash flows discounted at the return to equity (Bartram, 2000: 295).

[26] Following Miller and Chen (2003), hedging, in this work, is defined as *"investing in other activities or assets with expected payoffs that will offset the potential losses associated with current activities and assets"* (Miller and Chen, 2003: 357). In the risk management literature, the terms hedging and financial risk management are often used equivalently.

[27] Similar Smith and Stulz (1985: 392), Smith (1995: 24), or Bartram (2000: 294).

portfolios as there are investor risk preferences.[28] All efficient portfolios must lie on the mean-variance investment frontiers where investors can get a higher return only by accepting a higher level of risk (Chatterjee et al., 1999: 564). The SLB Model extends Markowitz's portfolio theory to a situation of equilibrium. The CAPM argues that all investors will hold the same efficient portfolio, the so-called market portfolio, regardless of their individual risk preferences. Thereby, the SLB Model is capable of determining the market price for risk and an appropriate risk measure for a single asset (Copeland et al., 2005: 147).

The CAPM is developed in a hypothetical world with the following neoclassic assumptions (see, e.g., Jensen, 1972: 385–359 and Copeland et al., 2005: 147–148):

- All investors are risk-averse and maximize the expected utility of their wealth
- Alternative portfolios are chosen on the basis of mean and variance of return
- Investors are price takers and have identical subjective expectations about means, variances, and covariances of return among all assets
- Assets returns have a joint normal distribution
- There is a risk-free rate of interest at which investors may borrow and lend unlimited amounts
- The quantities of all assets are fixed and all assets are perfectly divisibly and perfectly liquid
- Asset markets are frictionless, and information is costless and simultaneously available to all market participants
- There exist no market imperfections such as taxes, regulations, or restrictions on short selling

Under these assumptions, in short, the CAPM states that the equilibrium expected return of a risky asset, I, equals the risk free rate of return, R_f, plus a risk premium. The risk premium is the difference between the expected return on the market portfolio, M, and the risk-free rate of return times the quantity of risk. The quantity of risk is also called beta, β_i, and is quantified as the covariance of the returns to the security with those of the market portfolio over the variance of the market portfolio. Of course, the risk-free asset has a beta of zero as the covariance with the market portfolio is zero.

---

[28] Efficient in this context means that there is no other portfolio of assets that has the same or a higher exptected return at a lower risk and no other portfolio with the same or lower risk but a higher return (Schmidt and Terberger, 1997: 295).

The market portfolio has a beta of one, as the covariance of the market portfolio with itself is identical to the variance of the market portfolio (Jensen, 1972: 359; Schmidt and Terberger, 1999: 341–379). The beta measure not only quantifies a firm's risk premium but also the discount rate (i.e. the minimum return required by the firm's shareholders) that is used by fully diversified investors to compute a firm's NPV (Chatterjee et al., 1999: 556; Fatemi and Luft, 2002: 31). In short, the CAPM's central predictions are twofold: First, it implies that expected returns on securities are a positive linear function of their market betas. Second, market betas are sufficient to explain the cross-section of expected returns (Fama and French, 1992: 427). Mathematically the SLB Model's relationship between risk and return can be expressed as follows:

$$E(\tilde{R}_i) = R_f + \left[E(\tilde{R}_m) - R_f \right] \frac{\sigma_{im}}{\sigma_m^2}$$

$E(\tilde{R}_i)$........the expected value of the return of asset I

$E(\tilde{R}_m)$.......the expected value of the return of the market portfolio M

R_f...........the risk-free rate of return

σ_{im}..........covariance between the return of asset I and the return of the market portfolio M

σ^2_m..........the variance of the return of the market portfolio M

The CAPM divides the total risk of a firm into two parts. First, the systematic (market) risk that measures the dependence of an asset's return on fluctuations in the economy as a whole. The systematic risk, which is represented by the beta, is unavoidable and has to be born by the shareholder for investing in the equity market. Second, the unsystematic (unique) risk that is defined as the variance in a security's returns that cannot be explained by movements in the market portfolio. The CAPM assumes that all firm-specific activities are unsystematic (Chatterjee et al., 1999: 556 and 562–563). Hence, the terms unsystematic and firm-specific risks can be used synonymously in the terminology of the CAPM. Examples of such risks specific to a certain business are, for instance, the success of a new production process or a marketing campaign, a technological breakthrough jeopardizing an existing product, or a new competitor entering the market (Fenn et al., 2002: 15; Van Horne, 1995: 69). From these examples it becomes obvious that *"unsystematic risks obviously are associated with firm resources and competencies and with the relationship of the environment to the firm"*

(Bettis, 1983: 408). There, the close link of sources of unsystematic risk to issues and decisions of strategic management becomes apparent.[29]

The beta measure commonly used to account for the risk of an investment measures, by definition, only the systematic risk. However, the calculation of an individual stock's beta is dependent, among other things, on the standard deviation of that stock's returns. But a stock's standard deviation quantifies total risk, not just the systematic part. Peavy (1984) calls this observation a perplexing paradox. In a diversified portfolio context, beta is the only relevant risk measure because it captures all undiversifiable systematic risk. An individual stock's beta, however, is affected by the total risk of the stock's return (Peavy, 1984: 153). Bowman (1979: 628), for instance, analytically shows that beta is affected by financial characteristics of the company (e.g. leverage). Hence, to a certain extent, also nonsystematic risk affects beta (Peavy, 1984: 154).

Under the static equilibrium assumptions of the CAPM, investors hold a properly diversified stock portfolio and therefore are unconcerned about unsystematic risks. By definition, all firm-specific variations in the returns of individual securities cancel out in the long run when holding this well diversified portfolio.[30] Since unsystematic risk does not contribute to the variance of the rate of return of the entire portfolio of securities in the market, investors are not willing to price the unsystematic risk of an asset. Investors will only demand a premium for systematic risk. The higher the systematic risk of an asset, the higher the expected return investors will demand. A higher expected return, in turn, means higher costs of capital that reduce the NPV of the security, all else being equal. This relationship between expected return and unavoidable systematic risk and the valuation of securities is regarded as the essence of the CAPM (Naylor and Tapon, 1982: 1166–1167).

While under the Markowitz model corporate management can create shareholder value by reducing a firm's total risk, applying the equilibrium capital asset pricing model to

---

[29] Note, that there is some conceptual confusion about what constitutes the sources of unsystematic and systematic risk. Entry barriers, for instance, are regarded as determinants of systematic risks by industrial organization economists. Others argue that entry barriers are sensitive to unsystematic influences (Lubatkin and Chatterjee, 1994: 111–112). Therefore, Lubatkin and Chatterjee (1994) assert that systematic and unsystematic components of risk may not be fully independent as predicted by the SLB Model (Chatterjee, 1994: 114).

[30] More precisely, the CAPM implies 1) that all investors' portfolios comprise all the risky securities available in the market and 2) that investors hold the risky assets in the same proportions as these assets are available in the market, independent of the investors' preferences. Both requisites, however, are obviously not met in reality (Levy, 1978: 643).

corporate risk management has completely different implications (Chatterjee et al., 1999: 564). Since in a CAPM-world firm-specific risks are not incorporated in the beta measure and therefore not rewarded by the capital market, corporate managers might follow financial theory and ignore such risk factors. Hedging systematic risks, on the other hand, will not affect firm value as long as the risk, either borne by the firm or the capital market, is correctly priced. Under this condition, a hedging activity would only move the firm along the security market line and not change the value of the firm. Any management's hedging activity influencing the diversifiable risk is then undesirable from a shareholder perspective. Since these risks are not compensated by the CAPM, a change in the firm's exposure to these risks does not end up with a lower discount rate if, and only if, the owners hold well-diversified portfolios (Smith, 1995: 24; Peavy, 1984: 153). Therefore, under the assumptions of modern financial theory, the relevance of corporate risk management can only be analyzed by looking at its impact on the firm's cash flows rather than on the discount rate (Bartram, 2000: 296). Under MM, however, corporate risk management has no impact on the firm's cash flows, since risk management activities are purely financial transactions. Under these assumptions risk management is irrelevant (Stulz, 2003: 45).

4.1.2.1 A critical appraisal of the Capital Asset Pricing Model

4.1.2.1.1 Challenges from a financial economics' perspective

While early empirical tests of the CAPM supported the theory (see, e.g., Black et al. (1972), Fama and MacBeth (1973)), more and more disturbing results appear in the financial economics literature challenging the model. The discussion of the SLB Model focuses mainly on the predictive ability of beta for expected returns. The culmination of these critical contributions is the influential article by Fama and French (1992) published in the *The Journal of Finance.*[31] Similar to the results by Reinganum (1981), they are unable to find an empirical relationship between beta and expected returns for U.S. stock price data for the period 1963–1990. They conclude that the SLB Model does not describe the last 50 years of average stock returns (Fama and French, 1992: 428 and 464). Rather, they find that stock price risks are multi-dimensional (Fama and French, 1992: 428).[32] Fama and French (1993) develop a three-

---

[31] Building on their 1992 article, Fama and French further challenged the predictive validity of beta in later articles (Fama and French (1993), (1995), and (1996)).

[32] Unlike the relation between beta and average return, they report strong univariate relations between average return and size, leverage, earnings-price ratio, and book-to-market equity. Even in

factor asset-pricing model that includes a market factor and two risk factors related to size and book-to-market-equity that is able to capture much of the cross-section of average stock return (Fama and French, 1996: 55).

While Fama and French empirically challenge the beta-return prediction of the CAPM, Roll and Ross (1994) use an analytic approach to criticize the SLB Model. They detect additional weaknesses of the CAPM by showing that the discrepancies between the controversial empirical results and the theory of the CAPM are due to the specification of the market index proxy used to calculate beta. More precisely, they find *"that the SLB model may be of little use in explaining cross-sectional returns no matter how close the index is to the efficient frontier unless it is 'exactly' on the frontier"* (Roll and Ross, 1994: 111; original emphasis). Such exactitude, however, can never be verified empirically (Roll and Ross, 1994: 111). Finally, they conclude that *"if the SLB Model cannot tell us about average returns, then it is not of practical value for a variety of applications including the computation of the cost of capital and the construction of investment portfolios"* (Roll and Ross, 1994: 115).

4.1.2.1.2 Challenges from a strategic management's perspective

The numerous empirical anomalies discovered by finance researchers initiated a discussion of the usefulness of the CAPM for the field of strategic management starting with the contribution by Bettis (1983). He detects a conundrum regarding the role of risk in the strategic management context and states the main points of controversy between finance and strategy (Vicente-Lorente, 2001: 158). In particular, he seriously questions the implications of the CAPM for strategic management but especially corporate risk management. He identifies an implied recommendation in the CAPM to corporate management not to be concerned at all about firm-specific risks. This, he believes, is against the notion of strategic management.[33] Long before stakeholder and RBV arguments were introduced into strategic management theory, Bettis argued that business risks are associated with firm-specific resources and

---

multivariate tests, the relations between size and average return, as well as book-to-market equity and average return, remain strong (Fama and French, 1992: 428).

[33] This radical opinion towards CAPM was challenged by finance scholars. Peavy (1984), for instance, opposed Bettis' (1983) radical interpretation of modern financial theory. Peavy argues that *"such extreme negligence would place the firm at severe disadvantage to its actively managed competitors, causing investors to view the firm less favorably (more risky)"* (Peavy, 1983: 154). Rather, he states that modern financial theory only contends that firm-specific risks are diversified and, therefore, will not impact the wealth position of a properly diversified investor in the long run (Peavy, 1984: 154).

competencies and are strongly related to the firm-environment interface (Bettis, 1983: 408). This argument is related to the premises of strategic management theory. In order to gain competitive advantage, firms are assumed to make strategic, or hard-to-reverse, investments in products, resources, or people that create value for customers in ways that rivals will have difficulties imitating. Such actions intend to isolate a firm's earnings from competition. Thereby, the firm's future cash flows increase while the uncertainty related to these cash flow streams is reduced (Lubatkin and Schulze, 2003: 7). Therefore, firm-specific risks may not be omitted from a strategic management perspective. Put in Bettis (1983) words, *"management of unsystematic risk lies at the very heart of strategic management"* (Bettis, 1983: 408).[34]

Although controversially discussed between scholars from finance and strategy, Bettis' (1983) article lays the ground for further contributions from strategy researchers criticizing the CAPM's application in strategy research. Critical discussions on the usefulness of the CAPM in a strategy context provide, e.g., Amit and Wernerfelt (1990) and Chatterjee et al. (1999). Their main points of criticism are outlined below.

Amit and Wernerfelt (1990) offer three motives for why managers might indeed engage in reducing business risk. The first is the cash-flow motive stating that low business risk allows firms to operate efficiently and to acquire inputs more cheaply.[35] Their argument is based on the notion that in unstable environments, firms' operations might be less efficient (e.g. in production planning) and their earnings more volatile. In such a case, a risk-averse manager who is compensated on the basis of cash flows might be willing to work for less compensation when cash flow volatility is lower. Then, it is in the interest of shareholders to reduce business risk because lower business risk is associated with higher cash flows (Amit and Wernerfelt, 1990: 522). They empirically support their contention that reducing business risk has a positive effect on cash flows (1990: 529–530). Although Amit and Wernerfelt (1990) do not refer to the situation of corporate stakeholders in general, Miller and Chen (2003: 357) later identify a stakeholder argument for corporate risk management in Amit and Wernerfelt's original cash-flow motive.

---

[34] Note that 20 years after Bettis (1983), Lubatkin and Schulze (2003: 7) come to an identical conclusion.

[35] The other two arguments for reducing business risk, advanced by Amit and Wernerfelt (1990) are the agency motive and the rate-of-return motive (Wernerfelt, 1990: 521–523).

Building on the deficiencies of the CAPM, Chatterjee et al. (1999) address the dilemma of applying the SLB Model to issues of strategic management. Similar to Roll and Ross (1994), they question the practicability of the CAPM, especially for a usage in strategic management research.[36] Following Bettis' (1983) arguments, Chatterjee et al. (1999) question the CAPM's downplaying or even ignorance of the importance of firm-specific risks. They argue, that the *"CAPM is clearly at odds with strategic theory since it implies that managers should focus on that which they cannot influence[37], and should not be concerned with that which they can and, per strategic theory, should influence[38]"* (Chatterjee et al., 1999: 556). Rather, they strongly support strategic thinking within the context of risk management. They argue that investors care about firm-specific risks because most are not as fully diversified and markets are not as perfect as assumed under the CAPM. They support their assertion by drawing on three theories. First, on information economics, which identifies asymmetries in the market for information and heterogeneous beliefs among market participants. Second, the RBV of the firm stating that resources are distributed asymmetrically among firms and cannot be acquired costlessly. Finally, the industry structure view of strategy, which identifies asymmetries in the distribution of market power in input and output markets. In such a world, they assert, investors are exposed to three classes of firm-specific risks, which are tactical, strategic, and normative in nature (Chatterjee et al., 1999: 558). Due to strategic management's assumptions about the imperfect functioning of capital, factor, and product markets, they believe that their field is predestined to contribute to the issue of risk management (Chatterjee et al., 1999: 564).[39] This view, of course, is against standard financial theory's believe in neoclassic market behavior.

4.2 The financial theory of corporate risk management

The starting point of the literature on corporate risk management is Stulz' seminal 1984 article that introduces an economic reasoning why a firm's managers who are

---

[36] Robins comes to the same conclusion in his 1992 paper, when he claims that the CAPM is a suitable model when assets are tradeable but breaks down given the existence of firm-specific assets (Robins (1992); Kochar, 1997: 32). More generally, Roberts states *"that the CAPM can be an unreliable tool for managerial decision making"* (Robins, 1992: 531).

[37] Thereby, they mean reducing investors' exposure to macroeconomic uncertainties at a lower cost than what investors do on their own by adjusting their investment portfolio (Chatterjee et al., 1999: 556).

[38] (i.e. business risk)

[39] This interdisciplinary view on risk management is shared in *Long Range Planning's* special issue (2003; Vol. 36 (1)) on *"Risk: The Interface of Strategy and Finance"*.

assumed to act as agents of the firm owners, are concerned about expected profit and the distribution of firm returns around their expected value. His contribution explains why the firm's objective functions may be concave and thereby gives reasoning to risk avoidance (Allen and Santomero, 1998: 1475). Since then, a number of alternative positive theories and explanations for corporate risk management were identified in the financial literature.[40] Most of these theories relax singular neoclassic assumptions of modern financial theory to argue for a positive theory of risk management. Tufano (1996: 1106) distinguishes two streams of financial literature explaining why managers engage in risk management on the firm level. One stream of literature focuses on risk management as a means to maximize managers' private utility. A second strand of such a positive theory of risk management focuses on the extent to which corporate risk management contributes to enhancing the shareholder value of the firm. All explanations for risk management subsumed under these two literature streams are based on the standard financial paradigm with its neoclassic assumptions about perfect markets and a definition of the firm as a 'black box' maximizing shareholder value as the only corporate objective function.

However, recently, papers in the financial and strategic management literature have discussed stakeholder aspects of risk management by drawing on a modern stakeholder conception of the firm without omitting the shareholder value objective. The implications of this stakeholder approach to risk management differ substantially from the conclusions of the risk management explanations under the CAPM and MM assumptions. Building on neo-institutional insights the stakeholder rationale allows for a more realistic view of the scope of corporate risk management and acknowledges elements from both finance and strategic management theory.

In the following section, financial theory's explanations for risk management are reviewed. Following the literature, these financial theories are structured into a managerial utility and a shareholder value maximizing reasoning for corporate risk management. Then, the stakeholder rationale for risk management (SRRM) is introduced in section 4.3.

---

[40] At this point it is important to note that the various positive theories to explain corporate risk management rely on different corporate objectives (e.g. firm value, cash flows, pretax income) and value systems (market values, cash flows, book values). Therefore, these theories do not necessarily work in the same direction (Bartram, 2000: 297).

4.2.1 The managerial utility maximization hypothesis of corporate risk management

Two streams of literature arguing for a managerial explanation for risk management can be distinguished. Both go back to Stulz (1984), who states that corporate hedging is due to managers' poorly diversified personal wealth. For this reason, managers are assumed to be risk averse and prefer stable earning and/or income streams. By reducing the volatility of total firm value, managers improve their own utility at little or no expense to other stakeholders. Therefore, all else equal, managers with more wealth invested in a firm's equity will have greater incentives to manage the firm's risks (Haushalter, 2000: 111). Based on Stulz (1984), Smith and Stulz (1985) link managers' compensation plans to their hedging choice. While greater stock ownership leads to more risk management, greater option-like features are incentives to engage less in risk management.[41] However, the argument provided by Stulz (1984) and Smith and Stulz (1985) has two underlying weaknesses. First, it builds on the assumption that managers incur significant costs when managing risk for their own account. Otherwise, managers need not involve the firm in hedging the risk. Second, the argument by Stulz predicts that firms will hedge as much as possible until total variance is eliminated (Froot et al., 1993: 1632).

Another strand of managerial theories of hedging, which builds on informational asymmetry, goes back to papers by Breeden and Viswanathan (1996) and DeMarzo and Duffie (1995). These authors address managerial reputation as a reasoning for engaging in risk management activities. Assuming that investors cannot separate results attributable to either risk management or managerial talent, managers will use hedging to signal their skills and managerial ability to the capital and the labor markets (Santomero, 1995: 3; Tufano, 1996: 1111). This argument supports risk management activities that aim at reducing volatility or at least protecting firm value from large negative outliers in the distribution of returns (Allen and Santomero, 1998: 1475).

---

[41] This is due to the nonlinear payoff-characteristic of options that have a higher expected value when the underlying asset is more volatile (see, e.g., Tufano, 1996: 1109; Copeland et al., 2005: chapter 7, pp. 199–258). At this point it is worth noting that equity can also be interpreted as a call option on firm value. From this perspective, managers of a firm that is closer to financial distress (i.e. at-the-money in terms of option valuation) might prefer to manage less risk because the option-character of their stock holdings becomes more pronounced (Tufano, 1996: 1126).

4.2.2 The shareholder value maximization hypothesis of corporate risk management

4.2.2.1 Large undiversified shareholders

The CAPM states that shareholders holding well-diversified portfolios are unconcerned about firm-specific risks because these can be managed through costless diversification (see section 4.1.2). Mayers and Smith (1990) argue that the ownership structure of a firm influences its demand for corporate risk management. They assert that closely held firms are more likely to engage in risk management than firms with less concentrated ownership.[42] This argument is grounded in the risk aversion of undiversified shareholders, for whom the unsystematic risks do not cancel out. Rather, and in contrast to the CAPM, large undiversified investors are likely to incorporate the firm's total risk into their required rates of return (Stulz, 1996: 13). Usually, large shareholders cannot reduce these risks cheaply on an individual basis. Therefore, the firm has an incentive to engage in risk management (Mayers and Smith, 1990: 22–23; Smith, 1995: 24). Stulz (2003), however, emphasizes that the firm does not increase firm value when hedging, only for the reason that cheap homemade hedging is impossible to a large investor. Rather, hedging makes economic sense when the firm gains from having the large shareholders.[43] In this case, managing firm risks by corporate management represents an incentive for an undiversified shareholder to continue investments in the firm (Stulz, 2003: 66).

4.2.2.2 Taxes

One aspect of capital market imperfection refers to the existence of corporate taxes. The relevance for taxes as a rationale for risk management was introduced into the literature by Smith and Stulz (1985), who analyze the shape of the effective tax function. The progressivity of the marginal tax rate in the corporate tax system implies a convex nature of the effective tax function. According to Smith (1995: 26), this convexity in the U.S. tax system arises from three sources: statutory progressivity, limitations on the use of tax preference items (e.g. tax-loss carrybacks and carryforwards, or investment tax credits), and an alternative minimum tax. While the

---

[42] More precisely, Mayers and Smith (1990) refer their arguments to the demand for corporate insurance and not risk management. Similar to the theoretical explanations for risk management, however, they treat insurance purchases as a part of the firm's financing policy, which is assumed to be irrelevant under the strict MM-assumptions (Mayers and Smith, 1982: 282; (1990)).

[43] This gain can come, for instance, from monitoring on the part of the large undiversified shareholder. Usually, shareholder monitoring can increase firm value when either the investor has particular knowledge and skills in doing so and/or he is able to identify value destroying management action (Stulz, 2003: 66–67).

impact of statutory progressivity is generally small, tax preference items are of higher importance for the non-linearity of the tax function (Allen and Santomero, 1998: 1476). Due to this progressivity, risk management can enhance the value of the firm by reducing income volatility. Thereby, taxable income can be shifted from years of high returns to years of bad returns and the firm's expected tax liability falls, since earnings are smoothed (Smith and Stulz, 1985; Graham, 2005: 66). In the context of corporate taxes it is generally acknowledged that the effect of risk management increases with the degree of convexity of the tax function, the volatility of corporate income, and the part of the income that falls into the convex part of the tax schedule (Bartram, 2000: 311):

It is worth mentioning that the tax arguments build on reported income, not true economic profit. Hence, tax optimized reporting might be a result of this rationale for risk reduction (Santomero, 1995: 3).

Following Glaum (2002), the tax function argument may be less relevant for German firms. German financial accounting offers many opportunities for accounting and valuation. In general, management has great freedom to smooth firms' profits by accumulating and transferring hidden reserves. Thus, German accounting policies offer more efficient ways to manage taxable income than financial hedging (Glaum, 2002: 6 and 20). Due to high similarities between the Austrian and German accounting and tax laws, it can be reasonably assumed that the same is true in the Austrian context.

4.2.2.3 Underinvestment and asset substitution problems

The underinvestment and asset substitution problems are rooted in agency theoretical arguments tracing back to the seminal contribution by Jensen and Meckling (1976). Agency theory, in general, has had a strong impact on research in financial economics and has led to new explanations of classic economic problems. Central elements of an agency-oriented analysis are the interrelation between diverging interests, levels of information, and alternatives of action of different parties, resulting in the quest for optimal designs of relationships through incentive structures and contracts (Bartram, 2000: 298).

The agency problem in the context of risk management can be explained when the value of the firm is viewed as the sum of bondholders' and stockholders' claims on the company. Myers (1977) shows that once the firm issues claims of higher priority than equity (i.e. senior claim or debt), managers who act in the interest of shareholders have incentives not to realize all profitable investment projects when the firm's debt burden is sufficiently large. The reason for this problem – commonly referred to in the literature as the underinvestment or debt overhang problem – is that the benefits from the investment will primarily accrue to the debtholders in the event of bankruptcy (Nance et al., 1993: 270). These agency costs of underinvestment can better be controlled by risk management than by reducing leverage. By reducing the volatility of firm value and, hence, the probability of default, risk management eliminates the conflicts of interest and the loss of welfare from a suboptimal investment policy. The benefit from such a debt overhang problem is assumed to be more pronounced for firms with more growth options and a high debt ratio (Bartram, 2000: 298–299).[44]

Another problem related to the diverging interests of shareholders and debtholders refers to the possible opportunistic behavior once new debt has been issued. Shareholders might be induced to take on very risky projects, since the residual claims of shareholders can also be interpreted as a call option on the assets of the firm. This incentive is even stronger for firms with high amounts of debt. Rational bondholders will anticipate the incentive for an ex-post wealth transfer and will adversely adjust their price of debt or demand debt covenants (Mayers and Smith, 1982: 287; Mian, 1996: 422). By engaging in risk management the firm can ex-ante assure that risk-shifting will not take place. Corporate hedging lowers the riskiness of investment projects, meaning that both groups of suppliers of capital will be interested in realizing the (less risky) positive NPV project (Bartram, 2000: 299). Bessembinder (1991) states that it is essential for the firm to credibly commit itself ex-ante to maintaining the hedge over the life of the senior claim. This can either be done through debt covenants (Bessembinder, 1991: 531) or established reputation (Bartram, 2000: 300). Bartram (2000) defines bond ratings as a means to build up such reputation. A drawback to building up reputation through bond rating is that it is limited to corporations that use the credit market for funding. More generally, it can be assumed that conservative financial policies deliver the same results. By increasing the future probability of fulfillment of fixed financial commitments and reducing the future probability of a

---

[44] For empirical evidence on that hypothesis see, e.g., Gay and Nam (1998) and Géczy et al. (1997).

cash shortfall, the bondholders' risk that the firm will offset the hedge during senior claims' life time is minimized.

4.2.2.4 Investment policy and capital market imperfections

Building on the strand of previous work on hedging based on arguments of capital market imperfections, Froot et al. ((1989), (1993), and (1994)) extend Myers' (1977) debt overhang argument. Froot et al. (1993) argue that risk management enables firms to pursue optimal investment policies by coordinating corporate investment and financing policies more efficiently. Their model builds on three key assumptions. First, firm value is created through investment in positive NPV projects. Second, accessing external capital markets is more costly than internally generated funds due to market imperfections.[45] These may include transactions costs to obtain external funds, asymmetric information regarding the riskiness of the investment projects of the firm, or the costs of potential future bankruptcy or financial distress. Third, the firm knows its set of investment opportunities that can be ranked in terms of an NPV criterion (Allen and Santomero, 1998: 1477; Gay and Nam, 1998: 54). Generally, a firm's cash flows show some sort of fluctuation, creating variability as to the amount of funds that has to be raised externally, or the amount of investment. Variability in investment, however, is undesirable because of decreasing marginal returns to investment (Froot et al., 1993: 1630).[46] Since the marginal cost of external funds increases with the amount raised due to imperfect capital markets, variability in the firm's cash flows is expensive when there is a lack of internal liquidity. Therefore, risk management can enhance the value of the firm by aligning the demand for funds with the internal supply. Risk management allows firms to transfer excess supply to periods of a liquidity shortage (Froot et al., 1993: 1630; Tufano, 1998: 68). Thereby, risk management guarantees realizing an optimal investment policy and avoids higher costs of capital. This benefit of hedging is assumed to be largest for firms with substantial informational

---

[45] This view is consistent with the pecking order theory of financing by Myers (1984) and Myers and Majluf (1984). See also section 5.1.1.2.2.

[46] Minton and Schrand (1999) empirically find that cash flow volatility is strongly negatively related to the level of investment in capital expenditure, R&D expenditure, and advertising expense. Although investment volatility is undesirable according to Froot et al. (1993), the authors find that firms rather forego investment opportunities instead of completely smoothing cash flow volatility to maintain investment levels and avoid external capital markets (Minton and Schrand, 1999: 455). Hyun-Han and Stulz (2000) and Allayannis et al. (2005) complement the evidence provided by Minton and Schrand (1999). Both papers show that cash flow volatility is significantly and negatively associated with firm value and hence costly for shareholders (Hyun-Han and Stulz, 2000: 20–21; Allayannis et al., 2005: 26).

asymmetries between managers and shareholders (e.g. firms with high growth options) (Mian, 1996: 423; Smith, 2005: 12).

4.2.2.5 Direct costs of bankruptcy and financial distress

The bankruptcy-cost argument for hedging goes back to Smith and Stulz (1985), who assert that the transaction costs related to bankruptcy induce firms to engage in hedging activities. Hedging reduces the variability of the future value of the firm and therefore reduces the probability of incurring bankruptcy costs. The decrease in the expected present value of bankruptcy costs accrues to the shareholders. According to the argument by Smith and Stulz (1985), shareholders primarily benefit from hedging because bankruptcy involves real costs such as costs of administration and reorganization, the loss of debt tax shields, and the loss of valuable growth options (Smith and Stulz, 1985: 397–398; Nance et al., 1993: 269; Haushalter, 2000: 110).[47] While the core argument of Smith and Stulz (1985) focuses on direct bankruptcy costs, further analysis by Stulz (1996) shows that there are also indirect costs of bankruptcy that have to be taken into account when referring to states of financial distress. These indirect costs are not only related to states of bankruptcy but mainly to states of illiquidity that can even be reached before the firm is forced into bankruptcy procedures. This state is generally referred to as financial distress. These indirect costs are closely connected to the firm's explicit and implicit contracts with its stakeholders. This argument in favor of hedging is one of the key elements of the stakeholder rationale for risk management and is presented in turn.

Overall, the argument of financial distress costs as reasonings for risk management is supported by several studies. Most of these studies find an empirical relationship between corporate risk management and the probability of bankruptcy, which is, for instance, measured by the firm's financial structure (debt ratio or leverage) or its credit rating. Moreover, empirical evidence shows that the risk of financial distress is positively related to the volatility of cash flows, the dependence on business cycles, and the degree of operating leverage (Bartram, 2000: 305).

---

[47] For a formal analysis of these arguments see Smith and Stulz (1985: 395–398).

4.3 A stakeholder rationale for risk management

Hitherto risk management was explained from a pure investor perspective using the neoclassic MM-assumptions as starting point of the analysis. The stakeholder rationale for risk management (SRRM), however, is grounded on a stakeholder-centered concept of the modern firm as presented in section 3.4.

The concept of a stakeholder rationale for risk management primarily goes back to arguments developed in pieces of finance literature by Mayers and Smith (1982), Titman (1984), Smith and Stulz (1985), Shapiro and Titman (1986), Cornell and Shapiro (1987), Wentges (2000), and Stulz (2003). In the last few years, the stakeholder approach to risk management has been advanced by scholars from the field of strategic management, who point, among other things, at connections to the resource-based theory. Among the first were Amit and Wernerfelt (1990) and Aaker and Jacobson (1990). More recent contributions are provided by Miller (1998), Miller and Chen (2003), Wang et al. (2003), and Lim and Wang (2007). Although the stakeholder reasoning for risk management has recently received more attention in the fields of finance and strategic management, Lim and Wang (2007: 645) assert that it is still relatively underdeveloped. Previous work has been primarily conceptual with empirical evidence being rare in this field.[48]

4.3.1 Non-financial stakeholders as risk bearers

4.3.1.1 Contractual incompleteness and opportunistic firm behavior

The stakeholder argument for risk management acknowledges that the firm consists of a vast network of contracts with multiple stakeholders (i.e. financial as well as non-financial) jointly working for the purpose of creating wealth through developing mutually specialized assets.[49] The value of the firm can be conceptualized through Cornell and Shapiro's (1987) NOC concept. Hence, the stakeholder rationale for risk management is based on a modern conceptualization of the firm integrating elements from new institutional economics, stakeholder theory, and the RBV (see section 3.4).

---

[48] The only empirical evidence explicitly building on a stakeholder rationale for risk management, the author of this dissertation is aware of, is provided by Miller and Chen (2003), Banerjee et al. (2004), and Aabo (2004). Barton et al. (1989) and Holder et al. (1998) implicitly build their arguments on a stakeholder motive for risk management.

[49] This definition is similar to Zingales (1998), who defines the firm as *"a nexus of specific investments: a combination of mutually specialized assets and people"* (Zingales, 1998: 498). Thereby, he focuses on the economic essence of a firm which he describes as *"a network of specific investments that cannot be replicated by the market"* (Zingales, 1998: 498).

The reason why non-financial stakeholders are also risk bearers of the firm (see, e.g., Post et al. (2002)[50] or Rajan and Zingales (2000: 222)) is rooted in the incompleteness of contracts (Grossman and Hart (1986), Hart (1989), Hart and Moore (1990); see also section 3.2.3.2).

These insights of new inistitutional economic theory show that the contractual benefits of NFS are partially implicit and incomplete with the quasi-rents of the stakeholders being subject to post-contractual opportunism by the firm.[51] Such opportunistic action on the part of the firm's management might for instance include stopping servicing products, reducing product quality, or providing a less safe work environment. Hence, not only shareholders, but also stakeholders can, at some time, be risk bearing residual claimants (i.e. they have something at stake). The threat of opportunistic action taken by the firm in which stakeholders specifically invest is the essential risk factor for NFS.[52] Therefore, a firm whose value significantly depends on relation-specific assets by its NFS needs to provide some sort of guarantee to assure them a fair ex-post treatment of their implicit claims. As will be shown in the subsequent sections, the corporate financial policy recommendations of the stakeholder rationale for risk management might be such a guarantee.[53]

---

[50] Post et al. (2002) state that *"the stakeholders in a firm are individuals and constituencies that contribute either voluntarily or involuntarily, to its wealth-creating capacity and activities, and who are therefore its potential beneficiaries and/or risk bearers"* (Post et al., 2002: 8).

[51] Such a post-contractual attack against the quasi-rents of the party, once it is locked into the relationship, is referred to as hold-up in the literature (see, e.g., Picot and Schuller (2001) and section 3.2.2).

[52] Note that Wang and Barney (2006) specify a different risk factor also leading to underinvestment in firm-specific assets that is independent on opportunistic firm behavior. They argue that underinvestment may be caused by a loss in value of the underlying asset controlled by the firm to which an employee makes his investments specific to. They show that risky core firm assets can reduce employee incentives to make relation-specific investments without any threat of opportunistic behavior (Wang and Barney, 2006: 467). It can be assumed that their arguments are not limited to employees but can be applied to the role of non-financial stakeholders in general.

[53] Note, that a governance system that governs the ex-post distribution of the firm's surplus might also be such a form of guarantee. Such a governance system can be defined as a *"complex set of constraints that shape the ex-post bargaining over the quasi-rents generated in the course of the relationship"* (Zingales, 1998: 497). To be efficient, a corporate governance system must aim at achieving the following objectives: 1) to maximize the incentives for value-enhancing investments, 2) to minimize inefficient ex-post bargaining, and 3) to allocate the residual risk to the least risk-averse parties (Zingales, 1998: 500).

4.3.1.2 Costs of financial distress and the firm's financial standing

One can imagine two reasons for why firms might behave opportunistically against their NFS. First, there might be a self-interested owner-management breaching implicit commitments to further increase current profits of shareholders. Such behavior, to be economically reasonable, of course, presumes that managers do not believe in negative terms of trade effects that indirectly hurt firm value. Another reason for why firms do not fulfill implicit commitments is grounded in the firm's financial standing. While a financially healthy firm, which is aware of the risk-bearing role of non-financial stakeholders, has no reasonable incentive to cut expenses to NFS, a financially distressed firm does. In a situation of financial distress, the generation of substantial amounts of cash has absolute priority to keep the firm in business (Shapiro and Titman, 1986: 217). Therefore, the probability of post-contractual opportunistic behavior against stakeholders' implicit claims is strongly linked to the firm's financial standing (Asher et al., 2005:17).

This financial distress-argument brings the transaction costs of such a situation into play. In the stakeholder literature for risk management particularly the indirect costs of financial distress are emphasized.[54] The sources of these indirect costs of financial distress are mainly the negative terms of trade effects that are imposed on the firm by NFS. Another important aspect refers to the probability of getting into a situation of illiquidity (Rawls and Smithson, 1990: 11). In the following two subsections the sources of indirect costs of financial distress, as well as the drivers of encountering a situation of financial distress, are discussed.

4.3.1.2.1 Sources of indirect costs of financial distress

Indirect costs of financial distress are grounded in the explicit and implicit contractual relations with the firm's stakeholders. Non-financial stakeholders have sunk investments in firm-specific tangible and intangible assets that relate a high proportion of their wealth to the future financial situation of the firm. Hence, NFS do not hold the well diversified portfolio of investments assumed in the CAPM due to asset specificity reasons (Miller, 1998: 500). Usually these stakeholders are risk-averse and find it difficult to diversify the risks related to their firm-specific investments with available capital market instruments (Stulz, 1996: 13). Cornell and Shapiro (1987: 7), for

[54] The existence of direct costs of financial distress as an argument for risk management is stressed in section 4.2.2.5.

instance, give the example of an employee who receives an implicit promise from the firm that he will not be laid off except under extraordinary conditions. However, this employee can neither market that claim nor buy an oppositional claim on the market to offset his risk position to be protected if the company defaults. Thus, the employee will require some form of security or adjust his wage demand.[55] The situation for other non-financial stakeholders is equivalent. Workers and managers will worry about promises regarding job security and internal training and qualification. Customers, for instance, will care about the future fulfillment of warranty obligations or the availability of service and spare parts and might, as a result, be reluctant to buy a product (Smith and Stulz, 1985: 399; Shapiro and Titman, 1987: 218; Smith, 1995: 25). Similarly, suppliers make their investment decisions dependent upon their view of the long-term viability of the firm (Shapiro and Titman, 1987: 219; Banerjee et al. (2004); Kale and Shahrur (2007)). These types of firm-specific investments by the firm's stakeholders require some sort of contractual arrangement protecting them against opportunistic renegotiation of the ex-ante defined terms of trade through corporate management (Milgrom and Roberts, 1992: 31). Absent any contractual protection against opportunistic firm action, NFS are expected to seek other ways of compensation for their risk bearing. Knowing that the implicit payoffs from the firm-specific investments are not fully guaranteed before making the investment, it is very likely that rational non-financial stakeholders will either incorporate a risk premium into their terms of trade with the firm, or avoid making the investments all together (see, e.g., Mayers and Smith, 1982: 283; Smith, 1995: 25; Stulz, 1996: 13).[56] Since underinvestment in relation-specific capital lowers overall firm productivity, firms are advised to compensate NFS for their risk bearing (Jaggia and Thakor, 1994: 284). Such compensation by the firm can take several forms, like a discount to buyers, favorable compensation packages for managers, workers, and employees, or premium prices to suppliers (Miller, 1998: 500).

All these forms of compensation represent costs that are related to the probability of opportunistic behavior especially in situations of financial distress. These costs impact the value of the firm given the NOC concept (see also section 3.4.2). Other sources of indirect costs of financial distress, apart from the adverse and costly terms of trade-

---

55 See also Berk et al. (2007) for a similar argument.

56 Except for demanding compensation, NFS can also adapt their attitude towards the firm. Smith (1995) argues that employees, workers, or managers can, for instance, also reduce their loyalty or even their work effort (Smith, 1995: 25). It can be reasonably assumed that other NFS might behave similarly.

effects might, for instance, arise because of the management's lack of attention for value-enhancing activities. In situations of cash shortages management might be unable to devote adequate time to running the business in the interest of its shareholders.

4.3.1.2.2 Probability of default

Given that financial distress occurs when a firm's cash flows are insufficient to cover its fixed claims, the probability of encountering financial distress is determined by two drivers. First, the amount of fixed claims the firm has to fulfill and second, the volatility of its cash flows (see, e.g., Rawls and Smithson, 1990: 11; Pritsch and Hommel, 1997: 683). This volatility argument is essential for the stakeholder reasoning for risk management. It goes that indirect costs of financial distress are a positive function of cash flow volatility. As described by the NOC concept, these costs of transferring risk to NFS are indirectly but ultimately borne by the firm's shareholders (Miller and Chen, 2003: 359). Therefore, Stulz (1996) argues for eliminating the probability of lower-tail outcomes of the firm's cash flow distribution as these are the source of financial distress or underinvestment in relation-specific assets (Stulz, 1996: 23–24).

4.3.2 Implications of a stakeholder reasoning for risk management

Following the stakeholder rationale for risk management and ignoring the suggestions of the CAPM has several implications for the nature of corporate risk management. These consequences refer to the scope of the risks to be considered by corporate managers and to the particular role of corporate financial decisions as risk management instruments. Additionally, implications for corporate performance can be expected.

4.3.2.1 Widening the scope of corporate risk management

Several arguments support the notion of integrating NFS into the firm's risk management policy. When drawing on a modern view of the firm, it is evident that a risk management policy must include not only explicit but more importantly also all implicit contractual relations between the firm and its stakeholders.[57]

---

[57] Similarly argues Spremann (1996: 485), who regards implicit stakeholder commitments as an essential part of a firm's risk management policy.

From the financial theory of risk management it is known that the probability of financial distress is a positive function of cash flow volatility (see, e.g., Stulz, 1996: 12). Therefore, reducing cash flow volatility diminishes the risk premiums demanded by NFS and enhances shareholder value through increasing NOC (Shapiro and Titman, 1986: 216; Cornell and Shapiro, 1987: 7).

The scope of the firm's risk management activities to achieve this volatility reduction is subject to discussion. As argued in this work, the CAPM's perspective is insufficient to integrate the position of not-fully diversified non-financial stakeholders into corporate risk management. From the incomplete contract theory of the firm it is known that other stakeholders, besides shareholders, are residual claimants whose claims need to be protected (Asher et al., 2005: 18). The willingness of these stakeholders to make firm-specific investments is clearly a function of the sum of the firm's systematic and unsystematic (i.e. total) risk. The fundamental decisions to do business with the firm and about the prices non-financial stakeholders are willing to pay for implicit claims depend upon their perception of expected future payouts from the business relationship, which are jeopardized by a situation of financial distress. It can be assumed that stakeholders' assessment of their future payouts depends on two factors. First, the perception of the firms' current and future financial situation. Obviously, the financial situation of the firm is determined by the overall risk profile (Franck and Huyghebaert, 2006: 8), which includes all sources of risks. Second, stakeholders' assessment is, even partly, determined by the firm's track record of ex-post fulfillment of implied stakeholder commitments (Wentges, 2000: 204). In this context, trust has been identified as a crucial element in stakeholders' decisions to specifically invest in a firm (see, e.g., Williamson, 1993: 98; Das and Teng, 1996: 832; Wicks and Berman, 2004).[58] Therefore, a strong reputation for fulfilling implicit claims, even in situations of financial difficulties, additionally supports stakeholder-centered risk management activities of the firm. Consequently, corporate management has to credibly signal ex-ante that implicit stakeholder commitments will be honored ex-post, independent from the firm's future financial situation. Thereby, the management can build up an ex-post reputation of non-opportunistic firm behavior. This reputation allows NFS to ex-ante differentiate between firms that promise to

[58] Following Noteboom et al. (1997), trust can be defined as a subjective probability that a partner will not abuse one's dependence. Then, anything that contributes to such subjective probability and restrains the partner from opportunistic conduct would belong to trust (Noteboom et al. (1997: 312).

maximize stakeholders' payout ex-ante but honor claims only to an extent that maximizes the short-term ex-post value of NOC (Cornell and Shapiro, 1987: 9).

4.3.2.2 The role of corporate financial policy

The role of financial policy as alternative or complementary means of risk management has recently been identified in financial literature. Several examples illustrate this new vein in risk management literature. Mikkelson and Partch (2003), for instance, recognize the interdependence of the fields of financial decisions and risk management and encourage future research to *"explore cash holdings, financial leverage, and risk management in combination to more fully understand the motives for and consequences of conservative financial policies"* (Mikkelson and Partch, 2003: 293). A more recent call comes from Acharya et al. (2005), who regard the cash-debt interplay as an *"interesting new dimension researchers can explore in studying corporate hedging"* (Acharya et al., 2005: 5).

Two arguments are proposed to support corporate financial policy's role as a cornerstone of a stakeholder rationale for risk management.

4.3.2.2.1 Signaling through financial policy

Cornell and Shapiro (1987) assert that: *"...firms that expect to provide high payoffs on implicit claims will attempt to distinguish themselves ex-ante. Under some circumstances, this can be done by choosing the appropriate dividend payout rate or financial structure"* (Cornell and Shapiro, 1987: 9–10). Shapiro (1990) again underlines the role of financial stability for all non-financial stakeholders when he says that: *"A key element of corporate competitiveness is the firm's ability to inspire sufficient trust and confidence such that customers, employees, and other stakeholders are willing to develop relationships with the firm. One prerequisite for such confidence is that the firm be seen as financially sound and viable over the long run"* (Shapiro, 1990: 509). Excessive risk taking could adversely affect non-financial stakeholders' wealth position and jeopardize the firm-specific organizational assets (Shapiro, 1990: 509). Several other authors argue similarly and emphasize the importance of conservative financial decisions for the NFS of the firm. Miller (1998), for instance, says that: *"...the generation of slack resources may be wholly consistent with the long-term interests of diverse stakeholders, despite conflicts over claims to current cash flows"* (Miller, 1998: 500). Wang et al. (2003) identify, among others, the capital structure decision as one alternative risk management mechanism in a stakeholder concept of risk management. They argue that a higher debt burden implies a higher probability of financial distress. Hence, by changing a firm's capital structure, corporate managers can change the firm's risk profile and influence stakeholders' incentives to make firm-specific investments (Wang et al., 2003: 53).[59] Identical arguments are provided by Kale and Shahrur (2007), when they state that the firm's capital structure affects the incentives of suppliers and customers to make relation-specific investments as long as the firm's liquidation decision is causally linked to its bankruptcy status (Kale and Shahrur, 2007: 324).

As shown, extant literature discusses the role of conservative financial decisions as a means of signaling financial stability to non-financial stakeholders. This implicitly assumes both, corporate management and NFS to be aware of the relationship between the firm's financial policy and the probability of fulfillment of its implicit stakeholder commitments.

More precisely, stakeholders can be classified based on their awareness of the positive relationship between the probability of fulfillment of their implicit claims and the degree of conservativeness of the firm's financial decisions. Furthermore, one has to distinguish between stakeholders that are informed about the firm's financial decisions to which they make their investments specific to and such that are uninformed. When assuming that stakeholders are either uninformed about the firm's financial policy and/or unaware of the relationship between financial policy and fulfillment of their implicit claims, signaling through conservative corporate financial policies, however, becomes an inadequate instrument to induce firm-specific investments.

4.3.2.2.2 Increasing management's flexibility

However, there is a second reasoning for why corporate management might favor conservative financial decisions that is independent from a signaling argument. A firm's management can deliberately make conservative financial decisions in order to increase its financial ability to make value-enhancing investment decisions at its own discretion in the future. This argument for building financial slack in the firm's balance sheet is also implicitly found in Myers' (1984) and Myers and Majluf's (1984) pecking

[59] Stulz (1996) argues similarly when he states that *"risk management can be viewed as a direct substitute for equity capital"* (Stulz, 1996: 16).

order theory of capital structure (see also section 5.1.1.2.2). Their theory asserts that firms tend to retain earnings and to finance new investment according to the following order. First, internally, then with low-risk debt, and finally with risky equity only as a last resort (Myers and Majluf, 1984: 219; Harris and Raviv, 1991: 306). The pecking order style of financing is explained by asymmetric information problems that are more severe for firms with comparatively high intangible assets relative to firm value (Harris and Raviv, 1991: 308). Since these intangible assets are often firm-specific in nature and developed jointly between the firm and its non-financial stakeholders, pecking order and stakeholder arguments go hand in hand. However, Myers and Majluf (1984) do not give a normative recommendation of possible investment targets. Following stakeholder theory, available funds can be devoted to make investments in the fulfillment of implicit stakeholder claims. Arguing from a resource-based perspective, such management actions might strengthen the ties between the firm and its stakeholders and positively influence the firm's rent generating ability.

Berk et al. (2007) argue likewise, but only related to the firm's capital structure decision, when they assert that financial flexibility is an important factor as it enables managers to share human capital risk more effectively with employees than firms with low financial flexibility (Berk et al., 2007: 24).

However, increasing management's discretionary power over the firm's funds does not come for free. Building up financial slack might lead to a situation equivalent to the well known free-cash flow problem identified by Jensen (1986).

To summarize, conservative financial policies, on the one hand, increase management's flexibility to make investments in implicit stakeholder claims, which is desirable from the RBV. On the other hand, these policies circumvent monitoring by external capital markets and therefore might create substantial agency costs (similar Jensen, 1986: 323).

Drawing on the signaling and the flexibility arguments the following hypothesis can be formulated:

> H 1: The degree of conservativeness of the firm's financial policies is positively associated with the extent to which the firm is dependent on implicit claims with its non-financial stakeholders, cp.

Hypothesis 1 can be divided into the following three hypotheses:

H1.1: The firm's debt level is negatively associated with the extent to which the firm is dependent on implicit claims with its non-financial stakeholders, cp.

H 1.2: The firm's level of cash holdings is positively associated with the extent to which the firm is dependent on implicit claims with its non-financial stakeholders, cp.

H 1.3: The firm's dividend payout-ratio is negatively associated with the extent to which the firm is dependent on implicit claims with its non-financial stakeholders, cp.

4.3.2.3 The performance effect

Implementing the suggestions of the stakeholder rationale for risk management supports achieving the corporate objectives of a managerial agency or instrumental version of stakeolder theory, which are especially relevant when the firm is dependent on building competitive advantage and valuable intangible assets through relation-specific investments on the part of its NFS. Shapiro and Titman (1986) identify certain industry-specific and firm-specific characteristics of firms for which the financial distress-based stakeholder argument for risk management is especially relevant. They argue that firms whose products and services contain certain industry-specific product characteristics should consider NFS in their risk management activities. These product characteristics are the following (Shapiro and Titman, 1986: 221-222; Shapiro and Balbirer, 2000: 482–483): 1) products that require repairs, 2) goods or services whose quality is an important attribute but difficult to evaluate in advance (e.g. air transportation services), 3) products with high switching costs (e.g. IT products), and 4) products whose value to customers depends on services and complimentary products supplied by independent firms.

Additionally, they identify the following firm-specific factors calling for a SRRM and conservative financial policies (Shapiro and Titman, 1986: 222; Shapiro and Balbirer, 2000: 483–484): 1) high growth opportunities, 2) large excess tax deductions, and 3) the degree to which firms depend on intangible assets. Firms showing these characteristics will benefit disproportionately from adapting their risk management to the needs of their non-financial stakeholders because states of financial distress are more likely and substantially costly.

Similar to the arguments initially developed by Shapiro and Titman (1986), Wang et al. (2003) emphasize the role of firm strategy when deciding about the scope of the risk management activities. They assert that firms implementing a differentiated strategy with more unique products are more dependent on firm-specific investments from stakeholders and hence have stronger incentives to engage in risk management activities (Wang et al., 2003: 57). This reasoning is similar to Titman's (1984) argument that firms that impose high costs on their customers when going out of business will use capital structure decisions to mitigate customers' disincentive to buy products.

Drawing on an instrumental or managerial justification of stakeholder theory, a positive performance effect of conservative financial arrangements for firms that are heavily dependent on stakeholders' implicit claims can be predicted. The performance aspect of the stakeholder reasoning for risk management is also supported by literature analyzing conservative financial decisions (see, e.g., Minton and Wruck, 2001). A recently published study by Mikkelson and Partch (2003) does not find any empirical support for the often stated assertion that conservative financial policies such as high cash holdings or high leverage harm stockholders. This is especially true for firms investing heavily in R&D.

Consequently, it can be hypothesized that the firm's performance is associated with its dependence on implicit claims and its corporate finance decisions:

> H 2: Among firms that are heavily dependent on implicit claims of their non-financial stakeholders, those firms that choose conservative financial decisions will outperform firms that choose non-conservative financial decisions, cp.

In the subsequent section empirical evidence is outlined to further support the hypothesized consequences of the stakeholder rationale for risk management.

4.3.3 Empirical evidence

Rarely, pieces of empirical evidence use stakeholder language in corporate finance. Hitherto, some empirical studies have focused on integrating isolated stakeholder arguments into classic corporate finance research on the financial determinants of a firm's capital structure, payout policy, or liquidity policy (see, e.g., Opler and Titman (1994), Balakrishnan and Fox (1993), Graham and Harvey (2001)). One reason why the amount of empirical evidence is scarce is the difficulty to operationalize the theoretical constructs by means of accounting data (Franck and Huyghebaert, 2006: 2).

Especially product uniqueness, defined as a ratio of R&D expenses to sales, is usually employed as a proxy for stakeholders' costs in the event of liquidation in a number of studies[60] (see, e.g., Titman and Wessels (1988), Barton et al. (1989), Opler and Titman (1994), Balakrishnan and Fox (1993), Vicente-Lorente (2001), and O'Brien (2003)).

While a growing body of empirical literature uses stakeholder arguments for analyzing the capital-structure decision, empirical work analyzing stakeholder arguments as determinants of a firm's cash level but especially dividend policy is only scarce (notable exceptions are the contributions by Holder et al. (1998) and Minton and Wruck (2001)). The empirical results of these studies, however, are supportive and encouraging for the notion that conservative financial policies are important and effective instruments of a stakeholder rationale for risk management.

However, empirical evidence explicitly or implicitly building on a stakeholder theoretical argument for risk management is rare. Only recently Aabo (2004), Miller and Chen (2003), and Banerjee et al. (2004) use the stakeholder rationale for risk management as a theoretical starting point for their empirical analyses. Hitherto, the corporate performance effect of stakeholder-oriented financial decisions has been almost neglected in empirical research. In the following subsections, the main empirical results that are relevant from the theoretical perspective of the stakeholder rationale for risk management are reviewed.[61]

---

[60] The usage of product uniqueness as a variable for stakeholder theory goes back to Titman (1984) and is usually measured by relative R&D expense.

[61] Note that these articles relating stakeholder theory to corporate finance issues are discussed in greater detail in chapter 5.

4.3.3.1 Evidence from financial economics literature

4.3.3.1.1 Evidence on capital structure choice

Barton et al. (1989) analyze the effect of stakeholder theory on capital structure using a sample of 179 large U.S. firms for the 1970–1974 periods. They use the concept of Net Organizational Capital to account for stakeholder theory.[62] Using regression analysis they showed that related firms have lower levels of debt than unrelated firms. Moreover, they find a significantly negative relationship of profit with debt levels. Since higher profits ultimately result in lower debt levels, they interpret this finding to be consistent with stakeholder theory predictions for capital structure differences in large firms (Barton et al., 1989: 40–43). However, they report difficulties in directly measuring NOC and encourage developing further proxies to measure NOC.

Graham and Harvey (2001), provide contradictory results on the capital structure decision. Surveying 392 CFOs, they find high-tech firms to be less likely to limit debt in order not to concern non-financial stakeholders. This is clearly contrary to the stakeholder theory's predictions. On the other hand, they find many growth firms to claim that customers might not purchase their products if they are worried about the debt level which might cause the firm to go out of business. Assuming that growth firms produce unique products, this piece of evidence, however, is consistent with the stakeholder rationale for risk management (Graham and Harvey, 2001: 227).

Myers (2001) reports that industry debt ratios are found to be low or negative when profitability, business risk, or the level of intangible assets are high. For example, marketing- and advertising-intensive companies have traditionally operated at low debt ratios, as their profits derive mainly from intangible assets (Myers, 2001: 83).

---

[62] Following Cornell and Shapiro (1987), Barton et al. (1989) argue that NOC is built through implicit contracts between the firm and its stakeholders (Barton et al., 1989: 43). Since a direct measure of NOC is impossible, Barton et al. (1989) use Rumelt's (1974) categories of diversification strategies as a proxy to indirectly distinguish firms by level of NOC. In order to classify firms, they use information on the relationship of products and businesses from annual reports. They separate between two major strategy categories. First, firms whose business activities are related to similar skills and/or resources. Second, firms whose business activities are not related to a common set of skills or resources (Barton et al., 1989: 37). The underlying idea behind this proxy is that firms producing related products are more likely to have common stakeholders for generating the products and higher levels of NOC (Barton et al., 1989: 43). Hence, a failure in one product line might have negative spillover effects on related business lines that limit the firm's ability to sell implicit claims to these stakeholders (p. 38).

For a sample of Spanish manufacturing firms for the periods 1993–1999, Istaitieh and Rodríguez (n.d.) provide empirical evidence showing that factors from stakeholder theory affect management's capital structure choice. More specifically, their results show that firms with high reputation or high client concentration and employees' bargaining power are associated with low leverage (Istaitieh and Rodríguez, n.d.: 25).

Banerjee et al. (2004) investigate how a firm's financing choices are determined in a bilateral supplier-customer relationship. Analyzing a sample of U.S. manufacturing firms for the periods from 1979 to 1997 and segment customer data from the Compustat database, they show that firms in industries producing specialized goods will maintain lower debt ratios if their procurements from dependent suppliers constitute a higher proportion of their costs. Their results also support their hypothesis that suppliers in specialized industries will maintain lower debt ratios if they depend on relatively few customers for a large proportion of their sales (Banerjee et al., 2004: 26–27). Regarding the low leverage of dependent suppliers they find that suppliers' voluntarily choose low leverage to avoid direct and indirect costs of financial distress rather than being forced to such a financial policy by its principal customers (Banerjee et al., 2004: 26).

Following the stream of arguments established by Titman (1984) and Maksimovic and Titman (1991), Franck and Huyghebaert (2006) investigate the influence of non-financial stakeholder relationship costs as determinants of the capital structure choice of first-time business start ups. Relevant from a stakeholder-based argument for risk management are their findings that the size of NFS liquidation costs significantly affects capital structure choice in the direction of lower debt levels. Further, they report that supplier bargaining power has an impact on the relation between NFS liquidation costs and capital structure. However, they do not find equivalent results for the bargaining power of customers and employees (Franck and Huyghebaert, 2006: 5–6).

The paper by Kale and Shahrur (2007) goes into the same direction as the study by Franck and Huyghebaert (2006). They also investigate the link between a firm's leverage and the characteristics of its suppliers and customers. Building on the literature of Titman (1984) and Maksimovic and Titman (1991), they examine whether firms use leverage as a mechanism to induce suppliers and customers to undertake relations-specific investments. Additionally, they consider the relation between a firm's debt level choice and its bargaining position relative to its customers/suppliers (Kale and Shahrur, 2007: 322). They find significant support for the negative relation between the firm debt levels and to the intensity of R&D investments by its suppliers and customers. Moreover, they find that leverage is lower when the firm enters into strategic alliances and joint ventures with its suppliers and customers. They find evidence to suggest that the firm's leverage and the R&D investments of its suppliers and customers are simultaneously determined (Kale and Shahrur, 2007: 358–359). Their empirical results are highly consistent with the stakeholder arguments for risk management's preference for conservative financial policies.

4.3.3.1.2 Evidence on dividend policy

Holder et al. (1998) examine the influence of non-financial stakeholders on a firm's dividend payout ratio by extending the Barton et al. (1989) study on debt policy in high or low-NOC firms to the dividend policy puzzle. Using a sample of 477 U.S. firms from the periods of 1983–1990, they show that more focused firms (i.e. firms with high NOC) have significantly lower payout ratios. They conclude that managers consider the claims of non-financial stakeholders when choosing a target dividend-payout ratio (Holder et al., 1998: 80).

4.3.3.1.3 Evidence on cash holdings

Mikkelson and Partch (2003) investigate the relationship between conservative levels of cash holdings and operating performance. Based on data from the *Compustat* database for the periods of 1986–1999 they analyze a sample of 89 publicly traded U.S. non-financial firms to identify the characteristics of corporate cash holdings and to test the consequences of persistent, substantial holdings of cash on corporate performance. Mikkelson and Partch (2003: 276) find that high cash firms in their sample differ from a comparison group in two ways. First, firms in their group of high cash are smaller, less leveraged, have higher market-to-book ratios, and grow faster than firms in the comparison group. Additionally, the firms in the high cash group are characterized by a higher percentage of single-segment firms. Mikkelson and Partch explain the latter characteristic by the inability of single-sourced firms to transfer funds internally among business units (Mikkelson and Partch, 2003: 276 and 282). Regarding the use of excess cash by high cash firms, Mikkelson and Partch (2003: 291– 292) find that these firms have extraordinarily high investment expenditures, mainly for R&D, and do not make unusually high total payouts to security holders. An alternative interpretation for these high R&D expenses is offered by the stakeholder rationale for risk management. Firms with single-source cash flows have a higher risk to fail on implicit claims because such firms are expected to maintain high cash levels to always be able to fulfill explicit and implicit commitments to stakeholders. A regression analysis of operating performance on characteristics of high cash firms does not uncover evidence of underperformance by firms that retain high cash reserves. In general, the findings by Mikkelson and Partch (2003) are consistent with prior empirical evidence on the determinants of cash holdings (see, e.g., Kim et al. (1998); Opler et al. (1999); Ozkan and Ozkan (2004)) and with the stakeholder theory's predictions.

4.3.3.1.4 Evidence on corporate hedging

Drawing on a corporate governance background, Aabo (2004) investigates the linkage between risk management in non-financial companies and the attitude towards stakeholder/shareholder satisfaction. His key question is to analyze the extent to which an aim of stakeholder satisfaction at the corporate level leads to a risk management strategy that differs from one pursued by companies with an aim of shareholder satisfaction (Aabo, 2004: 1). Using a questionnaire design, he finds for a sample of 42 Danish non-financial companies listed on the Copenhagen Stock Exchange as of the end of 2001 that those firms with an aim of stakeholder satisfaction hedge more extensively than companies with an aim of shareholder satisfaction (Aabo, 2004: 19).

4.3.3.2 Evidence from strategic management literature

Miller and Chen (2003: 360) analyze the relations between measures of firm's risk relevant to a broad category of stakeholders, and firm's costs. They build their argument on Amit and Wernerfelt's (1990) cash-flow motive for risk management, which states that performance volatility reduces firms' cash flows (Amit and Wernerfelt, 1990: 522; Miller and Chen, 2003: 357). However, they split Amit and Wernerfelt's original single argument into two distinct aspects: First, the harmful effect of risk on a firm's operating efficiency and, second, stakeholders' demand for compensation for their risk bearing (Miller and Chen, 2003: 357). Using regression analysis based on a panel data set of industrial publicly-traded U.S. companies for the period from 1978 to 2001, Miller and Chen (2003) empirically analyze these two effects of risk on a firm's costs. They use two ratios to measure costs. First, cost of goods sold over sales and, second, sales, general and administrative cost over sales.

They argue that these ratios cover the costs associated with many stakeholder relationships (Miller and Chen, 2003: 362).[63] As risk variables, they use several measures: 1) standard deviation of ROA, 2) an ROA root lower partial moment measure to account for downside risk, 3) a measure covering the variation of sales, and 4) a second-order root lower partial moment of sales to average sales to reflect employees' and suppliers' possible aversion to downward shifts in production. To examine the moderating effect of bankruptcy risk on firms' costs, Miller and Chen include Altman's Z score as a further measure. Their results are consistent with the proposition that risk increases firms' costs. This relation holds even when controlling for industry average cost, as well as firm and time effects. Moreover, both contemporaneous and lagged risk are positively associated with firms' cost levels (Miller and Chen, 2003: 371–372).

4.3.3.3 Evidence from accounting literature

Previous studies on accounting decisions lend support to the role of conservative financial policies as a risk management instrument. These works empirically show that stakeholders use accounting numbers to evaluate a firm's ability of and reputation for fulfilling implicit commitments (Bowen et al. (1995), Matsumoto (2002), Cuijpers et al. (2005)).

Following arguments from Cornell and Shapiro (1987) and Maksimovic and Titman (1991) that a firm's financial image is relevant to stakeholders' assessment of the firm's reputation for fulfilling implicit commitments, Bowen et al. (1995) empirically find that the firm's management has higher incentives to choose income-increasing accounting methods when it is more dependent on implicit claims of different NFS. They base their findings on measuring reported accounting numbers (Bowen et al., 1995: 260) and the idea that management believes at least some stakeholders use accounting data in their assessment of the firm's reputation for fulfilling implicit claims. This notion also underlies the stakeholder rationale for risk management. While Bowen et al. (1995: 291) assume that stakeholders are unlikely to completely adjust (positively biased) reported accounting data for income-increasing accounting methods stakeholder theory, as outlined in chapter 2, can be interpreted in the opposite

[63] Miller and Chen (2003) state that cost of goods sold refers to compensation of suppliers and employees while sales, general and administrative cost reflects the relationships to managers, support staff, sales force, and customers (Miller and Chen, 2003: 362).

direction. In contrast to the BDS-argument, the stakeholder-based argument for risk management contends that NFS will recognize the detrimental effect of non-conservative financial decisions on the probability of fulfillment of their implicit commitments through a reduction in financial stability.

More recently, Cuijpers et al. (2005) investigate whether the firm's orientation in terms of shareholder versus stakeholder orientation affects the properties of their financial reporting. Analyzing 173 Dutch non-financial firms for the period from 1991 to 2000 they argue that for firms adopting a stakeholder-oriented reporting system, financial reporting plays a substantially different role than in shareholder-oriented firms. According to their results, a stakeholder-oriented financial reporting aims at maintaining a strong financial position and avoiding excessive payouts to any of the firm's stakeholders. Among other things, they find that such firms practice more earnings smoothing and report more conservatively. Therefore, they conclude that stakeholder-oriented reporting incentives mitigate the effect of shareholder-oriented accounting regulation accounting practices (Cuijpers et al., 2005: 26–27).

The accounting-oriented approach to measure a firm's stakeholder dependency used by Bowen et al. (1995) and reapplied by Matsumoto (2002), seems to be capable of verifying the stakeholder rationale for risk management's proposition of a positive association between the extent to which a firm depends on its non-financial stakeholders and the degree of conservativeness of its corporate finance decisions. This is because the stakeholder rationale's implications for a conservative set of financial policy are usually reflected in the firm's accounting data.

4.3.4 Concluding remarks

The stakeholder argument for risk management reflects elements of the theory of the firm, strategic management research on the stakeholder view and the RBV. The essence of this economic rationale for limiting risk is that total risk is costly when a contractual view of the firm with multiple stakeholders is assumed. These costs reduce the cash flows of the firm and thereby adversely impact firm value (shown through the concept of NOC). This cash flow effect, in general, is independent from proximity to bankruptcy because firms may default on implicit contracts long before they default on explicit contracts. NFS bear the risk of losing their quasi-rents because of opportunistic firm behavior. Nevertheless, it is possible that proximity to bankruptcy intensifies the negative effects. Hence, non-financial stakeholders are especially averse to performance volatility and downside results (Miller and Chen, 2003: 358; Deephouse and Wiseman, 2000: 470).

Moreover, the stakeholder theory of risk management is consistent with the standard financial objective of maximizing shareholder value. At the same time it explicitly considers the role of stakeholders' value-enhancing investments through widening the boundaries of the firm. By accepting this view of the modern firm, risk management can contribute substantially to value generation and superior firm performance by encouraging necessary relation-specific investments by non-financial resource providers. Conservative financial policies together with a high reputation for the ex-post fulfillment of implicit claims are elements of a risk management concept that integrates non-financial stakeholders. Implementing the stakeholder rationale for risk management supports achieving several corporate objectives. It contributes to avoiding underinvestment in value-enhancing firm-specific assets. Rather, it even encourages relation-specific investments on the part of NFS. A positive performance effect is assumed by reducing the firm's contracting costs with key stakeholders.

From a managerial point of view, implementing a stakeholder-based approach to risk management may of course bear an individual risk factor. Since managers are subject to periodic shareholder vote, the firm's management relies on shareholders' consent with the notion of a stakeholder-driven process of value creation of the firm that deviates from the stockholder-centered agency perspective. Otherwise, the firm's management might be replaced (Asher et al., 2005: 17).

5 Theories of Corporate Finance Decisions

In the preceding chapter, the stakeholder rationale for risk management was, among other things, introduced as one explanation for conservative corporate financial decisions. The following section is dedicated to alternative theories explaining capital structure, dividend policy, and liquidity policy decisions.

The aim of this section is twofold. First, to provide a brief outline of existing and accepted theories explaining corporate finance decisions and, second, to provide the basis for developing testable regression models of corporate finance decisions that integrate elements from a stakeholder-oriented risk management framework, as well as elements from traditional financial theories as additional control variables. In the following subsections, an overview of the theoretical arguments and empirical evidence of the classic and most influential contributions in this field is presented. The literature presented has been selected, either because of its influence on the field of corporate finance or because it is to some extent related to a stakeholder-based reasoning for corporate financial decisions.

5.1 Capital structure

This section presents capital structure theories built on neoclassic economics and neo-institutional economic theory as well as strategic considerations influencing the capital structure choice. For further theoretical and empirical evidence on capital structure see, e.g., the literature reviews of Harris and Raviv (1991) and Graham and Harvey (2001).

5.1.1 Theoretical evidence

5.1.1.1 Neoclassical theories of capital structure

Before the classic article of Modigliani and Miller (1958), the conventional view of capital structure posed that there is an optimal capital structure that minimizes the average capital costs and thus maximizes the total market value of the firm (i.e. the sum of the market value of debt and equity). The main assumptions of this traditional theorem are that the costs of capital decrease (i.e. the value of the firm increases) by substituting expensive equity capital for cheap debt capital. However, there is a point where the cost of equity increases due to the higher financial risk of the cash flows generated by the firm. Furthermore, an increase in the debt level increases the cost of debt because debtholders will charge a higher risk premium. This traditional view of capital structure has important implications for a firm's investment policy. Since the cost of capital is dependent on the capital structure of the firm, the firm's investment policy is dependent on the way investment projects are financed. From the above it can be seen that the traditional perspective of capital structure is grounded on subjective behavioral assumptions of financial claimants regarding an adequate compensation for a given degree of risk (Modigliani and Miller, 1958: 276–279; Schmidt and Terberger, 1999: 245–252; Brealey and Myers, 2000: 486–491).

The modern theory of capital structure was introduced by Modigliani and Miller (1958), who use a completely different approach to tackle the capital structure puzzle. Instead of relying on behavioral assumptions of the firm's financial stakeholders, they use an arbitrage argument. Given that a certain commodity (i.e. the total value of a firm's stream of cash flows) cannot sell at more than one price in the market, they posit that there is no such thing as an optimal capital structure (Modigliani and Miller, 1958: 279). Based on *"drastic simplifications"* (Modigliani and Miller, 1958: 296) Modigliani and Miller develop an equilibrium model with three well known propositions.[64] MM argue that the market value of any firm is independent of its capital structure and is given by discounting its expected return at a rate appropriate to its risk class (Proposition I) (Modigliani and Miller, 1958: 268; Miller, 1977: 262). As a consequence financial leverage is irrelevant. This result even generalizes to any mix of securities issued by the firm. It doesn't matter whether the debt is short- or long-term, straight, or convertible or some mixture of all of these or other types (Myers, 2001: 84). Secondly, they state that the expected yield of a share (i.e. the required rate of return of equity capital) is equal to the appropriate discount rate for a pure equity stream in the risk class, plus a premium related to the financial risk of the firm. The financial risk is determined by the debt-to-equity ratio times the spread between the discount rate and the risk-free rate (Proposition II) (Modigliani and Miller, 1958: 271). Proposition III asserts that the cut-off point for investment (i.e. the cost of capital) will be completely unaffected by the type of security used to finance the investment (Modigliani and Miller, 1958: 288). Hence, it is legitimate to separate investment and financing decisions of the firm.

---

[64] For a discussion of the neoclassic assumptions underlying the MM-theorem see, e.g., Copeland et al. (2005: 559).

Following the MM-arguments, there will be no systematic variation in capital structure across firms. The proof of Proposition I dramatically influenced the development of financial research (Stulz, 2000: 120). The proof is based on the idea of arbitrage between the value of a levered and an unlevered firm, rational investors will take advantage of. If a levered firm sells for more than an unlevered firm, any investor can make a risk-free profit by selling short the levered firm and buying the unlevered firm (Stulz, 2000: 122). Different to prior capital structure arguments, this arbitrage opportunity is independent from the investor's attitude towards risk (Modigliani and Miller, 1958: 269).

Among others, MM assume a world without taxes and costless bankruptcy procedures. Further neoclassical developments of MM's theory of capital structure focus on these two critical types of market imperfections, which obviously occur in reality. By relaxing the no-tax-assumption it can be shown that the value of the firm increases with the debt-ratio because the interest charges related to the use of debt capital are tax deductible. Therefore, financial leverage decreases the firm's corporate income tax liability and increases its after-tax operating earning stream (Kraus and Litzenberger, 1973: 911). The different taxation of equity and debt in the real world implies an optimal capital structure, as alleged by the traditional perspective, which is determined exclusively by debt capital.[65] Thereby the value of the firm is maximized. To take advantage of these gains from leverage, however, stockholders must incur increasing risks of financial distress and the direct and indirect costs related to that state (Miller, 1977: 262). Kraus and Litzenberger (1973), for example, explain the problem of optimal debt-equity mix by a model which trades off this tax advantage of debt against the costly disadvantage of bankruptcy (Kraus and Litzenberger, 1973: 912; Ross, 1977: 23–24).

5.1.1.2 Neo-institutional theories of capital structure

The logic of Modigliani and Miller (1958) is now widely accepted. However, other theories were developed to explain why financing can matter (Myers, 2001: 81). Starting from the modern MM capital structure perspective, the theoretical focus shifted from the valuation of an income stream to looking at *"the effect of the structure*

---

[65] Despite the tax advantage of debt there are arguments against a capital structure consisting of debt capital (e.g. personal income tax, restrictions by lenders, the need for reserve borrowing). For a further discussion of this point see, e.g., Modigliani and Miller (1963: 442)

of claims on the incentives of the individuals whose decisions would determine the income stream" (Brennan, 1995: 9). Those neo-institutional models of capital structure introduced the breakdown of the neoclassical paradigm and were initiated by the work of Jensen and Meckling (1976) (Brennan, 1995: 12). In their review of financial theories of capital structure, Harris and Raviv (1991: 299) classify the neo-institutional theories under four categories of determinants of capital structure. These are based on 1) an agency approach, 2) an asymmetric information approach, 3) the influence of the nature of the products or competition in the product/input market, and 4) corporate control considerations.[66]

5.1.1.2.1 Agency cost models of capital structure

The initial model based on agency costs is the paper by Jensen and Meckling (1976), who provide the first arguments that capital structure is more than simply a way of allocating a given income stream. Rather, they posit that capital structure could affect the nature of the income to be distributed. This view represents a serious attack on the fundamental ceteris paribus assumptions of the MM paradigm (Brennan, 1995: 12). To differentiate themselves from the neoclassical approaches, Jensen and Meckling (1976) use the term 'ownership structure' instead of 'capital structure'. Therewith, they emphasize that it is not just about the relative amounts of debt and equity but also about the distribution of equity between corporate insiders (i.e. managers) and outsiders (Jensen and Meckling, 1976: 53). Additionally, they use a nexus of contract conception of the firm as introduced by Alchian and Demsetz (1972).

Jensen and Meckling (1976) identify two different types of conflicts. The first conflict refers to the shareholder and manager relationship. Since managers do not hold 100 percent of the equity of the residual claim, they can transfer parts of the cost of value-destroying activities, which only favor the manager himself (e.g. by consuming perquisites such as plush offices, building empires, etc.), to outside shareholders. Since shareholders anticipate that interests are not fully aligned, they will incorporate the monitoring costs into the price they are willing to pay for an equity issue. Jensen and Meckling argue that these agency costs of outside equity can be reduced by increasing leverage. If the manager's absolute investment in the firm is held constant, his fraction

[66] In short, the theory linking capital structure to corporate control considerations argues that takeover targets will increase leverage to avoid a possible takeover. For a review of the most influential papers relying on corporate control considerations, see Harris and Raviv (1991: 319–325) and the literature cited there.

of equity would increase, thereby reducing the effect of diverging interests between the two parties (Jensen and Meckling, 1976: 11–12; Harris and Raviv, 1991: 300). Furthermore, an increase in the debt level commits the management to use free cash flow for interest expense instead of spending it at its own discretion (Jensen, 1986: 324). Hence, an increased likelihood of bankruptcy, which comes along with higher leverage, aligns the incentives of risk-averse managers and stockholders.

Further work dealing with the conflict between equityholders and managers is provided by Harris and Raviv (1990) and Stulz (1990). In the former paper, managers and investors disagree over the optimal time for a liquidation decision. In the latter paper by Stulz (1990) both parties disagree over the investment decision of the firm. In both models the problem is mitigated through debt. For a detailed discussion of the conflicts described and the implications for the extent of the debt level see the respective papers. A short review can be found in Harris and Raviv (1991: 302–303).

The second conflict raised by Jensen and Meckling (1976) deals with diverging interests of debtholders and equityholders. Jensen and Meckling (1976: 41–45) show that high debt levels have a negative incentive effect, inducing managers to engage in risky investment activities, which promise very high payoffs, even if they have a very low probability to turn out successfully. Because of limited liability of equity claims, equityholders benefit from such risky projects while debtholders bear the full negative consequences. As debtholders anticipate this expropriation of wealth, they will pay less for a new debt issue. This effect, which is called the 'asset substitution effect', represents the agency costs of debt financing (Harris and Raviv, 1991: 301; Jensen and Meckling, 1976: 52; Brennan, 1995: 14). Thus, from the owner-manager's standpoint, the optimal proportion of outside funds (i.e. equity vs. debt) for a given level of internal equity is determined by the minimum of total agency costs (i.e. monitoring and bonding expenditures, and residual loss) (Jensen and Meckling, 1976: 54). A similar effect has been observed by Myers (1977), who shows that there are situations when equityholders are not willing to provide new capital for positive-NPV projects. The reason is that when a firm is likely to go bankrupt, equityholders bear the total cost of the investment. The returns of this investment, however, are mainly captured by the debtholders. This problem is known as the underinvestment problem or debt overhang problem in the finance literature (Balakrishnan and Fox, 1993: 5; Schmidt and Terberger, 1999: 419; Bartram, 2000: 298; Graham and Harvey, 2001: 223). Important implications can be drawn from these agency insights. Leverage is expected to be positively associated with free cash flow and negatively related to a firm's growth opportunities (Harris and Raviv, 1991: 305; Rajan and Zingales, 1995: 1451).

5.1.1.2.2 Asymmetric information models of capital structure

Many markets are characterized by informational differences between buyers and sellers (e.g. the labor market (Akerlof, 1970: 488)). In financial markets, however, such information asymmetries are especially pronounced. Usually, borrowers know their collateral and future behavior better than lenders who provide external finance. Similarly, entrepreneurs have inside information regarding their own project they wish to fund (Leland and Pyle, 1977: 371). As shown by Akerlof (1970), without transfer of information, markets often perform poorly and market value of products necessarily represents average quality (Akerlof, 1970: 490 and 500; Leland and Pyle, 1977: 383). Based on these insights, a stream of literature deals with informational problems, financing and capital structure decisions are subject to. In the following paragraphs a short outline of the most prominent contributions in this field of capital structure research is given.

Myers (1984) and Myers and Majluf (1984) move away from the static trade-off framework that implies an optimal target debt-to-equity ratio with moderate borrowing (Myers, 1984: 588) at which the benefit of the last dollar of debt just offsets the costs (Fama and French, 2002: 1). Based on the notion of asymmetric information between the management and external investors, they develop a pecking order theory of capital structure that does not end in an optimal target level (Myers, 1984: 582–590). Rather, they argue that capital structure is driven by a firm's desire to finance new investment according to the following order. First, internally, then with low-risk debt, and finally with risky equity only as a last resort (Myers and Majluf, 1984: 219; Harris and Raviv, 1991: 306). Their pecking order theory is based on a commonality of interests between current (i.e. old) shareholders and corporate insiders (i.e. managers). However, asymmetric information leads to heterogeneous expectations between insiders and potential new outside debt or equity investors (Watson and Wilson, 2002: 561). The basic idea is that the owner-manager's objective is to maximize the 'true' value of the firm's existing shares. Thus, if the firm has good investment projects, the owner-manager will not want to issue new shares because some of the benefits of the new positive-NPV projects will have to be shared with new shareholders. On the other hand, if prospects are poor, the owner-manager may want to issue new shares to shift some of the costs to new shareholders (Watson and Wilson, 2002: 561). Since new equity investors will assume that managers are not on their side, they will adjust the price they are willing to pay (Myers, 1984: 583). If underpricing by new investors is severe, the new positive-NPV project will be rejected. Hence, instead of passing up a positive-NPV investment, firms will use other types of securities (e.g. internal funds or riskless debt) for which information asymmetry and thus undervaluation are less a problem. Therefore, information asymmetry can lead to a pecking order style of financing (Myers, 1984: 584) with several important implications. First, financial slack is valuable to the firm since it avoids the costs of asymmetric information. Second, financial markets regard equity issues as a negative signal (Myers and Majluf, 1984: 220). Therefore, share prices empirically tend to decline when new share issues are announced. Third, debt issues can be interpreted as a sign that outside investors undervalue the firm's 'intrinsic' value. Fourth, observed debt ratios will reflect the cumulative requirement for external financing. Fifth, and opposed to Jensen (1986), a negative relationship between leverage and free cash flow is predicted. Finally, the problem of asymmetric information is predicted to be more severe for firms with comparatively high intangible assets relative to firm value. Such firms are expected to accumulate more debt over time (Myers, 1984: 585–590; Watson and Wilson, 2002: 561; Harris and Raviv, 1991: 308 and 326).[67]

Another strand of literature belonging to the asymmetric information category goes back to Ross' (1977) seminal contribution. Starting from both, the MM irrelevancy proposition and Spence's (1974) insight that good firms have an incentive to signal their quality by undertaking some action that would be too costly for poor firms to imitate (Balakrishnan and Fox, 1993: 8), Ross develops a model where capital structure serves as a signal of private information of corporate insiders (Harris and Raviv, 1991: 311). He attacks the MM-assumption that the market knows the (random) return stream of the firm and values this stream to determine the value of the firm. However, Ross points out, what is really valued is the perceived stream of returns. Thus, changes in the financial structure can alter the market's perception of that stream, even though it is in fact unchanged. This is the basis of the relationship between signaling and capital structure (Ross, 1977: 25). In Ross' model the capital market interprets debt issues of managers with insider information as a valid signal of higher quality leading to an increase in the value of the firm (Ross, 1977: 37). Since

[67] For a recent literature review and empirical evidence on trade-off and pecking order theories of debt see, e.g., Frank and Goyal (2005).

lower quality firms have higher marginal expected bankruptcy costs for any debt level, managers of such firms have no incentive to imitate higher quality firms by being more levered (Williamson, 1988: 577; Harris and Raviv, 1991: 311).

Leland and Pyle (1977) provide a model similar to that of Ross (1977). They consider the fraction of ownership retained by managers as a signal of firm quality. Although a larger proportion of equity reduces managerial welfare because of management's risk aversion, the decrease is smaller for managers of higher quality projects. Hence, managers of higher quality firms can signal this fact by having higher leverage in equilibrium (Blazenko, 1987: 841; Harris and Raviv, 1991: 313).[68]

Instead of the formalistic idea of signaling equilibria as in the models by Ross (1977) and Leland and Pyle (1977), the term signaling can, however, also be interpreted in a broader sense. Balakrishnan and Fox (1993) argue that it can be used to describe situations where a firm wants to commit itself to taking a particular course of actions in order to gain credibility with the other players in the game (Balakrishnan and Fox, 1993: 8). This game-theoretic interpretation can be extended to the role of corporate stakeholders who are, in fact, the 'players' surrounding the firm. This interpretation is similar to Brav et al. (2004: 14), who use the term 'convey' instead of the term 'signal' to differentiate between a purely academic and a more real-world meaning of the term. This broader understanding of signaling is consistent with its meaning in the context of a stakeholder motive for risk management. This is especially true when considering that investments in reputational assets, even though they are firm-specific and intangible, can form a safeguard for stakeholders. When stakeholders interpret investments in brand name, R&D etc. as reputational in nature these investments may require continued expenditure. Hence, they can be regarded as commitments by the firm to fulfill implicit claims in the future, which then in turn increase NOC (see also Balakrishnan and Fox (1993: 8 and 11) for a similar analytical argument from the perspective of a firm's creditors and further empirical evidence).

5.1.1.2.3 Capital structure models based on product/input market interactions

The literature linking capital (or financial) structure and factor-product market characteristics draws on elements of a stakeholder theory of capital structure, market

[68] However, in a survey of 392 CFOs, Graham and Harvey (2001: 222) find only little empirical evidence that a firm's debt policy is affected by factors consistent with signaling.

structure, and firms' strategic behavior to determine an optimal debt-to-equity-mix (Istaitieh and Rodríguez-Fernandez, 2006: 50).[69]

Most of the models belonging to this stream use capital structure as a commitment or strategic device. Here, rival firms can observe the capital structure choice of its competitors and anticipate its effect on subsequent investment and production decisions (Istaitieh and Rodríguez, n.d.: 6). One classic paper in this area of research is that of Brander and Lewis (1986). They investigate the effect of the capital structure choice on output markets. Drawing on the ideas of Jensen and Meckling (1976), they argue that increased levels of debt create incentives for equityholders to pursue riskier strategies in the output market. They refer to this as the 'limited liability effect of debt financing', since shareholders usually ignore low returns in bankruptcy (Brander and Lewis, 1986: 956). In their model, financial structure (i.e. debt) is used as a commitment variable to pursue a more aggressive strategy in the output market (i.e. increase of output) (Brander and Lewis, 1986: 969). Hence, following the arguments of Brander and Lewis (1986), leverage is expected to be positively associated with such a strategy. However, Grinblatt and Titman (1998) stress that increased debt can also make a firm act less aggressivley due to financing problems (Grinblatt and Titman, 1998: 589). Other authors in this field, such as Bolton and Scharfstein (1990), argue that conservatively financed competitors take steps to drive their financially constrained competitors out of a profitable market by reducing their rival's cash flow (Bolton and Scharfstein, 1990: 93). This financial underperformance adversely affects the agency relationship between the rival's investors and managers and might lead to a stop of funding. As a consequence, the highly levered firm exits the market (Bolton and Scharfstein, 1990: 104).

Another linkage between capital structure and behavior on the output market is related to financial distress. Highly levered firms will tend to make output decisions that drive their rivals out of the market in order to improve their own financial situation (Brander and Lewis, 1986: 956).

Another approach in this field, which is more interesting from the perspective of this work, refers to interrelations between the debt-equity-choice and characteristics of the

---

[69] For a recent literature review discussing the relationship between capital structure and factor-product markets see, e.g, Istaitieh and Rodríguez-Fernandez (2006) and Parsons and Titman (2007).

products of the firm and the market in which the firm operates (Harris and Raviv, 1991: 318). Here, the initiating paper is Titman's (1984) analysis of capital structure's impact on a firm's liquidation decision. Drawing on a contractual perspective of the firm, as suggested by Jensen and Meckling (1976) and Alchian and Demsetz (1972), Titman analyzes the effect of indirect bankruptcy costs imposed on non-financial stakeholders of the firm on stockholders' and bondholders' incentives to liquidate the firm. Titman argues that in the case customers and other stakeholders of a firm rationally assess its probability of liquidation, the firm will indirectly bear those liquidation costs via the current price a consumer is willing to pay for the firm's products and services. Since stockholders will suffer from such indirect costs through a decrease in firm value, a value-maximizing firm has an ex-ante incentive to adopt a policy of liquidating only when the liquidation value exceeds the value of going concern plus the costs imposed on a firm's stakeholders (Titman, 1984: 138). Unfortunately, the firm also has an ex-post incentive to omit the costs imposed on its stakeholders when deciding about liquidation. In order to assure the ex-ante behavior and to avoid the detrimental ex-post effect on the firm's current market value[70], a firm must bond itself ex-ante to an optimal liquidation policy. Titman (1984: 139 and 143) proposes the choice of capital structure as a means to achieve a specific liquidation policy in a world where contracts are incomplete and costly to write. He states that an increase in the firm's debt level in turn increases its probability of bankruptcy and thus worsens the terms of trade. These less favorable terms of trade are a cost of debt financing that need to be integrated in the capital structure decision of the firm (Titman, 1984: 140). Since stockholders have the lowest priority claim to the liquidation proceeds and bondholders the highest, both parties have differing objectives about deciding when to liquidate the firm (Titman, 1984: 144). Titman shows that capital structure can be arranged so that stockholders never wish to liquidate, bondholders always wish to liquidate when the firms is in bankruptcy, and the firm will default only when the net gain to liquidation is higher than the costs to customers (Titman, 1984: 149; Harris and Raviv, 1991: 318). Several important implications can be drawn from Titman's work. First, it can be assumed that firms for which the effect of customer's power is more important will have less debt, ceteris paribus, than firms for which this effect is less pronounced (Istaitieh and Rodríguez,

---

[70] Shapiro and Titman (1986) and Cornell and Shapiro (1987) extended Titman's (1984) notion of the impact of firm risk on its current market value via the terms of trade with *"customers and other associates of a firm"* (Titman, 1984: 138). Cornell and Shapiro (1987) introduced the concept of Net Organizational Capital to measure the impact of the terms of trade on the firm's market value of equity (see also section 3.4.2).

n.d.: 17). Second, firms that impose high costs on their stakeholders when going out of business will have lower debt-to-equity ratios, other things being equal. Then, Titman explicitly names the computer and automotive industry as examples where stakeholders bear high costs in the event of default. Moreover, he expects firms in the hotel industry and in retailing to impose only little costs on their customers in a bankruptcy (Titman, 1984: 150).

A line of arguments similar to that of Titman (1984) is used by Maksimovic and Titman (1991) who analyze the relationship between a firm's financial policy and the quality of its products. In contrast to Titman, who states that stakeholders may be reluctant to do business with a highly levered firm, which imposes high costs on its stakeholders when going out of business (Titman, 1984: 150), Maksimovic and Titman provide a model where stakeholders may be reluctant to do business with a firm even if stakeholders suffer no such costs at all (Maksimovic and Titman, 1991: 176).[71] Contrary to an all-equity firm, a levered firm may have an incentive to reduce the quality of its products in order to increase current cash flows and avoid immediate bankruptcy or a debt issue. Thus, reducing quality can be interpreted as obtaining an involuntary loan from customers. As consumers recognize this incentive, they will incorporate it into the price they are willing to pay for the firm's products (Maksimovic and Titman, 1991: 177 and 194). Hence, the firm's current and future cash flows will be negatively affected. Debt financing and the alternative use of a firm's assets (i.e. its degree of specificity) may determine managements' incentives whether to reduce the quality of its products or to maintain a high-quality reputation. Maksimovic and Titman formally show that capital structure as well as dividend policy play an important role in transactions between a firm and its stakeholders when the terms of trade underlying these transactions are determined partly by reputational aspects (Maksimovic and Titman, 1991: 194).

In their 1991 literature review, Harris and Raviv emphasize the potential of this capital structure theory related to product and factor market characteristics. They expect further interesting results from this stream of literature and encourage further research using strategic variables other than price and quantity to analyze their impact on capital structure (Harris and Raviv, 1991: 319 and 351).

---

[71] Maksimovic and Titman (1991: 194) explicitly name industries that produce nondurable goods and offer services, such as hospitals, pharmaceutical companies, and the airline industry.

5.1.1.2.4 Transaction cost arguments for capital structure

Williamsons (1988) makes an important contribution to the theory of capital structure by using a transaction cost reasoning to analyze the different roles of debt and equity, which he regards not simply as forms of financial instruments but rather as examples of different governance structures. He parallels the financing decision with the classic decision about the boundaries of a firm (i.e. vertical integration) asserting that from a transaction cost economics (TCE) approach, debt is the natural financial instrument. It represents a form of market mode while equity is the financial instrument of last resort and thus similar to an internal supply solution (Williamson, 1988: 576 and 581). The explanation for that is grounded in the redeployability characteristics of assets. When asset specificity deepens, the terms of debt financing will be adjusted adversely, because debtholders' pre-emptive claims against the asset in question will decrease in value in the event of default (Williamson, 1988: 580–581). As it is usually assumed that tangible assets are easier to collateralize, lenders are expected to be more willing to supply debt financing for such assets. Ceteris paribus, leverage should be higher (Rajan and Zingales, 1995: 1451 and 1455). The consequences of Williamson's analysis are similar to those of the pecking order theory of financing. Both, the pecking order theory and Williamson's TCE approach regard equity finance as the financing instrument of last resort. However, the underlying reasoning is different. While admitting that, similar to previous works, intangible investments in R&D and advertising have poor redeployability properties, Willliamson underlines that this is also true for many tangible assets (Williamson, 1988: 588).

Combining the arguments of Williamson (1988) with those of Jensen and Meckling (1976), Vilasuso and Minkler (2001) present a model of a firm's capital structure that integrates both transaction cost and agency cost reasonsing into a single framework (Vilasuso and Minkler, 2001: 56). Their model demonstrates that only both theoretical lenses together accurately describe the optimal capital structure of the firm. They show that for highly specific assets, equity is capable of reducing transaction costs by limiting opportunistic ex-post behavior. Over time, they argue, equity is also favorable to debtholders since they will be protected from excessive risk taking, thereby reducing agency costs of debt (Vilasuso and Minkler, 2001: 65).

5.1.1.3 Stakeholder theory of capital structure

Grinblatt and Titman (1998), with reference to the contributions of Titman (1984), Shapiro and Titman (1986), Cornell and Shapiro (1987), and Maksimovic and Titman (1991), argue for a stakeholder theory of capital structure: *"The stakeholder theory of capital structure suggests that the way in which a firm and its nonfinancial stakeholders interact is an important determinant of the firm's optimal capital structure. We argue that these nonfinancial stakeholders may be less willing to do business with a firm that is financially distressed."* (Grinblatt and Titman, 1998: 578). They explicitly consider the environment in which the firm operates as an important determinant of its overall corporate strategy including its debt-to-equity ratio (Grinblatt and Titman, 1998: 579). Assuming a new institutional economics' perspective of the firm in a world with incomplete contracts, they explicitly consider the following NFS: customers, employees, competitors, suppliers, and the community. As indicated in the quotation above, the relationships between the firm and these non-financial stakeholders are particularly determined by the (indirect) bankruptcy costs they have to bear in the event of financial distress of the firm (Grinblatt and Titman, 1998: 580; Titman, 1984). As outlined in section 4.3 even without any danger of liquidation, only the management's incentive to increase the firm's current cash flow at the expense of the future cash flows heavily concerns a firm's stakeholders (Shapiro and Titman (1986), Cornell and Shapiro (1987), Maksimovic and Titman (1991)).

In their 1998 contribution, Grinblatt and Titman discuss the relevance of the relationships between the firm and its NFS for corporate financial decisions with a special emphasis on the capital structure choice. However, they do not address the link to the rent-generating aspect of these relationships that underlies the SRRM as outlined in chapter 4.3.

5.1.1.4 Capital structure and corporate strategy

Apart from mainstream finance, authors from the field of strategy suggest joining strategy literature and financial literature to address the capital structure question (see, e.g., Bettis (1983), Barton and Gordon, 1987: 67, Vicente-Lorente, 2001: 158).

Barton and Gordon (1987: 68) were among the first strategy researchers who called to overcome the oversimplifications of the financial paradigm. In their 1987 article, they argue for a strategic managerial theory of capital structure at the firm level that is compatible with a finance-based theory of capital structure (Barton and Gordon, 1987: 74). Following previous work in strategic management, they argue that the capital structure decision and financial decisions are usually ones that are made at the top management level and are determined by many contextual variables as well as managerial values. This argument implies that the debt-to-equity choice is dependent on the corporate strategy of the firm. Therefore, the capital structure decision is better analyzed from a top management perspective and not from a purely functional finance perspective (Barton and Gordon, 1987: 70 and 1988: 623). Similar behavioral (rather than financial) reasonings are provided by Lowe et al. (1994: 247) who posit that the significance of the debt/equity ratio is influenced by 1) the apparent norm of the specific industry, 2) traditions within the firm, 3) credit limits placed by lenders, and 4) management's judgment of the firm's debt capacity. Combining financial theory with behavioral contributions to strategy, Barton and Gordon present five propositions that describe the capital structure decision from a top management's view (Barton and Gordon, 1987: 71). Their first three propositions are related to management values and aspirations, the fourth and fifth are associated with external threats/opportunities and internal strengths/weaknesses of the firm (Barton and Gordon, 1988: 623).[72] Some of their propositions are noticeable from a broader stakeholder perspective of risk management. Propositions one and four are related to the management's attitude towards risk and its approach to risk management. It is posited that the terms at which creditors are willing to lend are determined by the firm's financial context. In their 1988 article, Barton and Gordon (1988: 624) connect proposition four to the firm's risk of default.[73] This is consistent with the stakeholder perspective of risk management that alleges that the terms of trade between the firm and all its stakeholders are determined by the firm's risk of default on explicit and implicit claims. Their third proposition is identical with Myers' (1984) pecking order theory. However, Barton and Gordon argue differently. Barton and Gordon's preference for internal funds over external financing is not grounded in informational asymmetries but in top management's desire for maximum control and flexibility, which would be limited by restrictions of debt covenants (Barton and Gordon, 1987: 72 and 1988: 624). It can be concluded that, although not explicitly mentioned by Barton and Gordon (1987), many arguments of the SRRM implicitly play an important role in their calling for a research program that enables strategic explanations of the firm's capital structure decision.

---

72 For an enumeration of the five propositions see Barton and Gordon (1987: 71–72).

73 See also the more recent work by Jordan et al. (1998: 2) for a similar conclusion.

Barton and Gordon (1987: 73) suggest using Rumelt's (1974: 29–32) corporate strategy typology in order to introduce strategy variables into capital structure research. Rumelt's typology (1974: 80) is based on the corporate diversification strategy of the firm and thus related to top management's perception of and reaction to risk (Barton and Gordon, 1987: 73).[74] Barton and Gordon's sympathy for this typology is due to the fact that in the Rumelt study, capital structure is, among other things, found to vary significantly among different strategy groups, although not controlling for other possible causes of capital structure (Barton and Gordon, 1987: 73).

5.1.2 Empirical evidence

The theory of capital structure is characterized by a vast body of empirical research with heterogeneous methodologies (Vicente-Lorente, 2001: 164). In the following subsections, first the empirical determinants agreed upon in capital structure research are presented. Subsequently, the most important empirical research streams from the perspective of this work are discussed. These are empirical studies in the tradition of Titman (1984)/Maksimovic and Titman (1991), as well as the empirical literature discussing strategic aspects of the capital structure choice.

5.1.2.1 General

From an empirical standpoint the characteristics of firms and industries are important determinants of leverage ratios. Harris and Raviv (1991) report that several empirical studies generally agree that leverage increases with fixed assets, non-debt tax shields, growth opportunities, and firm size. On the other hand, the debt level decreases with volatility, advertising expenditure, R&D expenditures, uniqueness of product, probability of default and profitability (Harris and Raviv, 1991: 334).

The underlying reasons for most of the above empirical determinants of capital structure mentioned by Harris and Raviv (1991) were explained in the previous section. However, the effects of firm size, non-debt tax shields, and profitability on the capital structure choice seem to have received little attention up to this point.

---

[74] Rumelt's arguments are grounded on applying the portfolio theory of finance to the selection of businesses. Therefore each alternative choice of strategy represents a different approach towards risk (Rumelt, 1974: 80; Barton and Gordon, 1987: 73).

Leverage ratios can be related to firm size in several ways. First, the effect of size can be interpreted as a proxy for informational asymmetries between corporate insiders and outsiders and are expected to decrease with firm size. Following this argument, it is easier for large firms to issue informationally sensitive securities like equity which, in turn, are less levered (Rajan and Zingales, 1995: 1457). Second, and contrary, size can also be regarded as an inverse proxy for bankruptcy because larger firms tend to be more diversified. Hence, large firms should be more highly levered (Rajan and Zingales, 1995: 1451; Titman and Wessels, 1988: 6). The latter interpretation is also consistent with the stakeholder theory of risk management (see, e.g., Wang et al. (2003)). Moreover, direct bankruptcy costs appear to be a larger portion of a firm's value as that value decreases (Titman and Wessels, 1988: 6).

Additionally, it can also be argued that larger firms have easier access to capital markets and borrow at more favourable interest rates, which would also imply a positive relationship between leverage and size (Ozkan, 2001: 179–180).

The role of profitability is equivalent to the role of cash flow as discussed by Myers and Majluf (1984) and Jensen (1986). The former predict a negative relationship based on the pecking order theory while the Jensen paper predicts a positive association if the market for corporate control is effective (Titman and Wessels, 1988: 6; Rajan and Zingales, 1995: 1451).

The issue of non-debt tax shields is introduced into the corporate finance literature by DeAngelo and Masulis (1980), who argue that tax deductions for depreciations and investment tax credits are substitutes for the tax benefits of debt finance. This is particularly true when part or all of these tax shields go unused, for example when the firm faces financial distress (Balakrishnan and Fox, 1993: 3). Hence, firms with large non-debt tax shields relative to their expected cash flow are expected to rely more on equity finance (Titman and Wessels, 1988: 3).[75]

Industrywise it is noticeable that several empirical studies find negative levels of net debt for pharmaceutical firms (Myers, 2001: 82–83), which is consistent with Titman (1984) and the SRRM. However, it is worth mentioning that the debt level in the

---

[75] Note that Harris and Raviv report that leverage generally increases with non-debt tax shields according to several studies (1991: 334 and 336). This finding is contradicting the relationship hypothesized by Titman and Wessels (1988).

airline industry is found to be relatively high by a pair of studies (Harris and Raviv, 1991: 335), which is inconsistent with theoretical predictions (see, e.g., Maksimovic and Titman, 1991: 194; Grinblatt and Titman, 1998: 583). Myers (2001) reports that in general industry debt ratios are low or even negative when profitability and business risk are high. Also intangible assets are associated with low debt ratios. He stresses that marketing-intensive and advertising-intensive companies whose profits flow mainly from intangible assets have traditionally operated at low debt ratios (Myers, 2001: 83; see also Barclay and Smith, 1999: 13).

5.1.2.2 Studies considering strategic aspects of the capital structure choice

The Barton and Gordon (1987) paper initiated substantial empirical research relating the capital structure decision to corporate strategy. This development had been additionally fostered by Harris and Raviv (1991: 351), asserting that models relating capital structure to strategic variables promise interesting results. The papers most related to this piece of research are presented below.

5.1.2.2.1 Barton and Gordon (1988)

In their 1988 paper, Barton and Gordon analyze 279 U.S. firms of the Fortune 500 list of industrial companies for the 1970–1974 period. They reduce Rumelt's nine sub-categories to four types of firm strategy named single, dominant, related, and unrelated. Following Rumelt (1974) and Barton and Gordon (1987), the authors hypothesize that firms with single and related strategies will have a low, dominant strategy firms a positive, and unrelated firms the highest positive relationship to debt levels (Barton and Gordon, 1988: 625). Controlling for relevant financial variables (i.e. profitability, size, sales growth, capital intensity, and earnings variability), they find that the relationship between contextual financial variables and capital structure is contingent on the strategy category. Hence, they conclude that depending on a firm's diversification strategy, management reacts differently to financial context when choosing a certain debt level. If true, they argue, this result is inconsistent with a purely financial view of capital structure (Barton and Gordon, 1988: 629).

5.1.2.2.2 Barton et al. (1989)

The stakeholder theory of capital structure formulated by Shapiro and Titman (1986) and Cornell and Shapiro (1987) is tested empirically in a study conducted by Barton et al. (1989). Controlling for other variables, Barton et al. (1989) analyze the effect of stakeholder theory on capital structure using a sample of 179 U.S. firms for the 1970–1974 period.

They use Cornell and Shapiro's (1987) concept of Net Organizational Capital (NOC) to account for stakeholder theory. Given Myer's (1984) pecking order theory, firms that are on the bottom of the hierarchy (i.e. retained earnings) will probably have to move up the hierarchy. This upgrade will increase future financing costs. Hence, Cornell and Shapiro (1986: 12) expect firms with many implicit claims attached to their products (i.e. high NOC) to bond themselves for future periods by being financed predominantly with equity instead of debt. Barton et al. (1989: 37) use Rumelt's (1974) categories of diversification strategies as a proxy to indirectly distinguish firms by level of NOC. In order to classify firms, they use information on the relationship of products and businesses from annual reports. They separate between two major strategy categories. First, firms whose business activities are related to similar skills and/or resources and, second, firms whose business activities are not related to a common set of skills or resources. Drawing from stakeholder theory, they assume that related firms have higher levels of NOC than unrelated firms (Barton et al., 1989: 40). To control for alternative financial capital structure theories they employ profit, size, growth, earning volatility, uniqueness of product, tax shields, and asset structure as additional independent variables. Those control variables are in line with the consensus determinants of capital structure identified in Harris and Raviv (1991: 334). Barton et al. (1989) hypothesize and show that related firms have lower levels of debt than unrelated firms. Given their assumption that related firms have higher levels of NOC than unrelated firms, they interprete their findings as supportive for stakeholder theory's prediction of the effect of NOC on capital structure (Barton et al., 1989: 42). Moreover, they find a significantly negative relationship of profit with debt levels, which they interpret to be consistent with stakeholder theory predictions for capital structure differences in large firms (Barton et al., 1989: 40 and 42–43).

However, they emphasize the difficulty in directly measuring NOC and state that it is by no means clear, whether Rumelt's measure is a reasonable proxy for NOC. Despite these limitations of their study they encourage further research to evaluate stakeholder theory's ability to better understand corporate financial phenomena. Particularly, they demand for an effective proxy for the NOC-construct to extend and revise theory (Barton et al., 1989: 43).

5.1.2.2.3 Lowe et al. (1994) and Jordan et al. (1998)

Similar studies, which use some sort of diversification typologies comparable to the categorization scheme of Rumelt (1974), were conducted by Lowe et al. (1994) and Jordan et al. (1998). While the former study analyzes 176 Australian public companies for the 1984–1988 period, Jordan et al. (1998) investigate corporate strategy's importance in the small firm context based on a sample of 275 U.K. firms. Unlike in the studies of larger firms by Barton and Gordon (1988) and Lowe et al. (1994), which provide weak support for a link between corporate strategy and capital structure, Jordan et al. (1998) are unable to show this link in their sample of SMEs. An interesting result of the Jordan et al. (1998) study refers to the relationship between a firm's innovation strategy and its debt level. Drawing from the insight that R&D investment is often firm-specific and lacking collateral value, they hypothesize and report a negative relationship between an innovation strategy and the debt level in small firms (Jordan et al.; 1998: 7–8). Following their explanation these low debt levels *"reflect the market's reluctance to lend, rather than the entrepreneur's reluctance to borrow"* (Jordan et al., 1994: 23). Drawing on Williamson's (1988) arguments this reasoning is of course plausible.

Still, it is worth mentioning that the stakeholder rationale for risk management strongly advises top management not to borrow too extensively from the capital markets. As Jordan et al. (1994: 23) state themselves, the key strategic resource in innovative small firms is often the knowledge embodied in the firm's personnel. Since firm-specific resources often come together with implicit claims attached to (necessarily) incomplete contracts, stakeholders could interpret extensive borrowing as a hazard to their implied future commitments. Hence, low debt levels can indeed be due to reluctant but rational entrepreneurs who incorporate their stakeholders' perspective into their corporate finance decisions.

5.1.2.2.4 Balakrishnan and Fox (1993)

Drawing on the resource-based view, Williamson's (1988) TCE-reasoning on capital structure, and financial signaling models (see, e.g., Spence (1974) and Ross (1977)), Balakrishnan and Fox (1993) empirically investigate the importance of specialized assets and other unique firm characteristics as opposed to industry characteristics in determining the capital structure of the firm. They find that a firm's capital structure is *"closely linked to its business strategy and the nature of the assets and skills required to implement that strategy"* (Balakrishnan and Fox, 1993: 4). Controlling for explanatory financial variables (i.e. risk, non-debt tax shields, uniqueness of assets, advertising intensity and growth opportunities) as well as time, industry, and firm effects they conclude that firm-specific effects are more important in explaining cross-sectional variation in leverage. Based on variance components and regression models they also report that in their sample of 295 single business firms of the U.S. mining and manufacturing industry for the years 1978–1987, certain financial determinants of capital structure are influenced by firm-specific effects (Balakrishnan and Fox, 1993: 4 and 9).

Particularly interesting is their empirical support for assuming that there might be a weakening of the (usually positive) underlying relationship between the redeployability of a firm's assets and its ability to borrow. Balakrishnan and Fox relate this weakening to the reputation of the firm in the capital market for converting R&D-investments into successful projects. That, in turn, reduces the lenders' credit constraints for intangible firm-specific assets (Balakrishnan and Fox, 1993: 13). This explanation is closely related to Zingales' understanding of the firm as *"mutually specialized assets and people"* (Zingales, 1998: 498) because converting firm-specific R&D-investments into rent generating projects is highly dependent on a firm's non-financial stakeholders. Hence, the firm's reputation in the capital market is dependent on the stakeholders' willingness to maintain existing and enter into new business relations with the firm. Therefore, stakeholder-oriented financial decisions on the part of the top-management contribute to increased capital-structure flexibility. The then higher debt level is also acceptable from a stakeholder standpoint if the investments in R&D are reputational in nature and represent a credible commitment for the fulfillment of future implicit claims.

Another interesting aspect of the Balakrishnan and Fox-study is the finding that relative advertising expense is positively and significantly related to leverage (Balakrishnan and Fox, 1993: 11–12). This implies that firms that spend more on reputational assets can take on more debt. With reference to Bhagat et al. (1990), Balakrishnan and Fox argue that image and brand names are intangible assets that may be bought and sold without much transaction costs. Additionally, they allege that corporate investments into customer loyalty represent a guarantee for lenders once these reputational investments have been realized as capital assets. Since brand names are similar to durable goods, they require a high level of maintenance expenditure.

Hence, higher levels of advertising expense can also be regarded as a signal that the firm will stay in the market and thereby increase the firm's ability to borrow (Balakrishnan and Fox, 1993: 12).

5.1.2.2.5 Vicente-Lorente (2001)

Influenced by Bettis (1983), Vicente-Lorente (2001) tackles the capital structure puzzle from the RBV-perspective. He analyzes the interactions between characteristics of resources and capabilites and the financial policy of the firm by developing a theoretical framework exploring the financial effects of a resource-driven strategy (Vicente-Lorente, 2001: 158). Like previous researchers, the author claims that asset characteristcs play a crucial role in capital structure theory insofar as the degree of asset specificy is proposed to be negatively related to the firm's leverage. Further, the author hypothesizes that the degree of opacity of a firm's resources restricts the access to sources of external financing, particularly, to debt capital (Vicente-Lorente, 2001: 162).[76]

He tests his propositions by applying panel data regression models on a final sample of 260 observations of 52 non-financial firms quoted on the Spanish stock exchange from 1990 to 1994. Vicente-Lorente uses four variables to proxy for strategic resources. These are internally expended R&D to total sales as a measure for specific and/or opaque R&D intensity. Second, external R&D expenditures (i.e. R&D acquired by contracting with other firms, universities or research institutions) as a measure of non-specific and/or transparent R&D intensity and third, advertising expenses to net sales used as a proxy for firm-specific assets. The fourth variable is an aggregate measure of human specific capital constructed through factor analysis based on a set of questionnaires sent to human resource managers of the sample firms. Also, the data for the R&D measures and advertising expense are derived from a postal survey. Additionally, the traditional control variables suggested in financial capital structure research are employed.

---

[76] An opaque asset is defined as one that *"due to its nature or to the firm's actions, eludes its imitation by impeding the leakage of any related information to outsiders"* (Vicente-Lorente, 2001: 160). In this context, the competitive advantage of a resource-driven firm is not related to its specific or complementary resources but on the transfer barriers of its strategic assets (Vicente-Lorente, 2001: 160).

As to the control variables, the results are roughly in line with previous evidence (Vicente-Lorente, 2001: 170). Regarding the strategic resources variables, the study finds that the human capital variable is significantly and negatively related to financial leverage measured in terms of market value. However, the effect is insignificant when measuring debt from book values. The internal R&D ratio shows negative and significant effects on leverage, while external R&D has no significant effect. Vicente-Lorente interprets the result as supportive to his propositions, as innovative resources and capabilities generated in conjunction with external partners are less firm-specific and more transparent, and hence have less strategic content than those developed internally (Vicente-Lorente, 2001: 170). The advertising ratio is positively related to market-value leverage on a significant level.

Comparing the results to previous findings, the sign of the internal as well as external R&D ratio is not surprising. The fact that the parameters for external R&D are insignificant, as opposed to the estimates for internal R&D, is noticeable. Given the findings by Kale and Shahrur (2007) who show that firms prefer low debt levels when they have established strategic alliances and joint ventures with their key suppliers and customers (Kale and Shahrur, 2007: 323), Vicente-Lorente's explanation that innovative resources and capabilites built with external partners are less firm-specific seems, at least, to be questionable. The positive and significant effect of advertising intensity on market-valued leverage in the Vicente-Lorente (2001) study is consistent with the results of Balakrishnan and Fox (1993). Equivalently to Balakrishnan and Fox (1993), Vicente-Lorente (2001) claims that firm-specific resources may improve the firm's borrowing capacity, which would postulate a positive relationship between advertising expenditures and leverage (Vicente-Lorente, 2001: 172).

5.1.2.2.6 O'Brien (2003)

O'Brien (2003) builds on the empirical finding that R&D influences capital structure and proposes that low leverage is a strategic priority for firms that are competing on the basis of innovation because it insures uninterrupted R&D-investments, provides funds when necessary to launch new products and ensures acquisitions when beneficial. However, he argues that it is not the absolute R&D intensity of the firm that influences the debt level but the R&D intensity relative to others in the same industry (O'Brien, 2003: 416). This proposition has implications for the pecking order theory of capital structure (see section 5.1.1.2.2 for a detailed discussion of the pecking order model). The assumed negative relationship between profitability and debt will not be as strong for firms following a strategy of innovation. O'Brien argues that innovators will not use an increase in profitability to repay debt but divert it to other uses (O'Brien, 2003: 420). Using panel data techniques on a sample of approximately 91,000 observations of mainly U.S. companies, he shows that firms pursuing an innovative strategy, measured by relative R&D-expenses, have lower debt-ratios.By using an interaction between innovation strategy and profitability, he shows that innovative firms depart from the pecking order model (O'Brien, 2003: 425). Most of his control variables, such as size, profitability, industry market-to-book ratio, and the ratio of tangible assets are in line with previoius research. As opposed to Balakrishnan and Fox (1993) and Vicente-Lorente (2001), this study does not show a statistically significant effect of advertising intensity on leverage (O'Brien, 2003: 425–426). Interestingly, and inconsistent with most of the previous literature as well as stakeholder theory, R&D intensity does not have any significant effect on leverage in the study of O'Brien (2003: 425).

5.1.2.3 Studies considering product/input market interactions

Controversial empirical evidence exists on the hypotheses of Titman (1984) regarding the influence of NFS on the capital structure decision. Empirical evidence for Titman's arguments are, among other results, provided by Opler and Titman (1994), Graham and Harvey (2001), and Istaitieh and Rodríguez (n.d.). Recently, Sarig (1998), Banerjee et al. (2004), Franck and Huyghebaert (2006), Kale and Shahrur (2007), and Berk et al. (2007) contributed to this research stream.

Opler and Titman (1994), for instance, find that highly leveraged firms lose market share to their less leveraged competitors in industry downturns. Moreover, they provide evidence that the decline in sales is more pronounced for highly leveraged firms that are more R&D-intensive (Opler and Titman, 1994: 1016 and 1032).

In a survey, Graham and Harvey (2001) interview 392 U.S. CFOs. They find that high-tech firms are less likely to limit debt in order not to concern non-financial stakeholders, which is clearly contrary to Titman's predictions. On the other hand, they find out that many growth firms claim that customers might not purchase their products if they are worried that the debt level might cause the firm to go out of business. Assuming that growth firms produce unique products, this evidence is consistent with Titman's theory (Graham and Harvey, 2001: 227). Similar results are provided by Brounen et al. (2006), who use the Graham and Harvey questions to describe capital structure policies in European countries. Like the original U.S. survey, Brounen et al. (2006) only find little confirmation for Titman's (1984) theory (Brounen et al., 2006: 1437). However, in their U.K. subsample 34.43% of all firms indicate that worries of customers/suppliers about the amount of debt almost or almost always influence their capital structure decision. The reported value of the French subsample is 31.91%, but only 15.04% in Germany (Brounen et al., 2006: 1415).

For a sample of Spanish manufacturing firms between 1993 and 1999, Istaitieh and Rodríguez (n.d.: 25) provide empirical evidence showing that factors from stakeholder theory affect management's capital structure choice. More specifically, their results show that firms with a high reputation or high client concentration and employees' bargaining power are associated with low leverage.

5.1.2.3.1 Sarig (1998)

Sarig (1998) draws a conclusion regarding the effect of debt on the firm's terms of trade with its stakeholders similar to that by Titman (1984). Arguing from a game-theoretic perspective, Sarig states that any supplier of firm-specific production factors of highly levered firms can achieve better terms than other suppliers of identical but less levered firms (Sarig, 1998: 13). The underlying reason is that a suspension of the firm-specific knowledge may force the firm into bankruptcy (Istaitieh and Rodríguez, n.d.: 15). Hence, the management of a leveraged firm, negotiating on behalf of its shareholders, may reduce debt levels to minimize its vulnerability to threats made by stakeholders to curtail their efforts (Istaitieh and Rodríguez, n.d.: 16). Using the example of one particular stakeholder group, which is the firm's employees, Sarig alleges that shareholders may prefer reducing leverage as employees acquire firm-specific human capital. Moreover, he provides empirical evidence supporting the notion that the bargaining ability of employees is indeed a determinant of firms' leverage (Sarig, 1998: 13).

5.1.2.3.2 Banerjee et al. (2004)

Following Titman (1984) and related literature on the relationship between a firm's stakeholders and its capital structure choice (see, e.g,. Titman and Wessels (1988), Maskimovic and Titman (1991) and Opler and Titman (1994)), Banerjee et al. (2004)

investigate how a firm's financing choices are determined in a supplier-customer relationship. They argue that in a world of incomplete contracts, stakeholders are subject to ex-post bargaining and opportunism after specific investments in the relationship have been made (Banerjee et al., 2004: 6). By looking at bilateral supplier-customer relationships they extend the existing literature, which mainly explored the worker-firm bargaining position (Banerjee et al., 2004: 7). They hypothesize that customer firms that buy higher proportion of its inputs from so-called dependent suppliers would maintain lower debt, especially in industries where specific investments are important, in order to encourage such investments (Banerjee et al., 2004: 12). In their paper, dependent suppliers are defined as suppliers for whom the firm is a major customer. To proxy for that dependence, they use a ratio of total supply from suppliers who record the current firm as one of their principal customers, to cost of goods sold of the customer firm. To account for the degree of specificity in the relationship, different supplier variables from the manufacturing, special manufacturing sector, and non-specialized manufacturing sector are used (Banerjee et al., 2004: 14). Looking at the debt-to-equity-mix of the supplier who is dependent on the principal customer, Banerjee et al. (2004) identify the bilateral bargaining situation as the underlying determinant. Two reasons can explain a low debt level on the part of the supplier. First, following arguments of Titman (1984), rational suppliers may anticipate high stakeholder-driven losses following the loss of a principal customer. Hence, suppliers producing specialized goods will keep leverage low. Second, principal customers may use their bargaining power and impose low debt ratios on supplier-firms in order to protect the value of their firm-specific investments (Banerjee et al., 2004: 8–9). Analyzing a sample of U.S. manufacturing firms for the period from 1979 to 1997 and segment customer data from the *Compustat* database, they show that customer firms in industries producing specialized goods will maintain lower debt ratios if their procurements from dependent suppliers constitute a higher proportion of their costs. Second, their results support the hypothesis that suppliers in specialized industries will maintain lower debt ratios if they depend on relatively few customers for a large proportion of their sales (Banerjee et al., 2004: 26–27). Regarding the low leverage of dependent suppliers, they find that suppliers' voluntarily choose low leverage to avoid direct and indirect costs of financial distress rather than being forced to such a financial policy by their principal customers (Banerjee et al., 2004: 26). Overall, the results of Banerjee et al. (2004) strongly support the arguments of the stakeholder motive for risk management.

5.1.2.3.3 Franck and Huyghebaert (2006)

Franck and Huyghebaert (2006) examine the influence of non-financial stakeholder relationship costs as determinants of the capital structure choice of first-time business start ups before they enter the product markets. They use a sample of first-time business start-ups, since these firms need to build up relationships with NFS from scratch. From a stakeholder perspective, establishing relationships with start-ups is very risky, as such firms are typically characterized by high ex-ante failure risk and large information asymmetries. The authors argue that start-up firms may induce NFS to make relation-specific investments, which is supported by low debt levels. Additionally, start-ups face the high bargaining power of NFS who may try to extract rents from the start-up when negotiating the terms of trade (Franck and Huyghebaert, 2006: 3).

Firstly, Franck and Huyghebaert (2006) hypothesize that the debt ratio of entrepreneurial ventures is negatively related the costs non-financial stakeholders face when the firm is liquidated (Franck and Huyghebaert, 2006: 10). Secondly, they include the aspect of NFS bargaining power in their study which is defined as *"the ability of non-financial stakeholders to appropriate a fraction of the firm's surplus"* (Franck and Huyghebaert, 2006: 10). Factors influencing bargaing power might be the concentration of purchases with a few suppliers, union's strength and customer size. The authors follow Sarig (1998) in considering the impact of bargaining power upon the financing decision before relationships with non-financial stakeholders are defined and postulate a negative relationship between NFS bargaining power and leverage (Franck and Huyghebaert, 2006: 12). Thirdly, the authors conjecture that firms adjust their capital structure to deal with NFS liquidation costs to a larger extent when these stakeholders are in a stronger bargaining position.[77] This last argument is especially important for business start-ups, as these firms have relatively low bargaining power due to a lack of reputation (Franck and Huyghebaert, 2006: 13–14).

The authors perform factor analysis on a set of survey questions to identify a proxy for NFS liquidation costs, customer bargaining power, and employee bargaining power. Their results show that their sample firms scoring high on the NFS liquidation cost variable have unique products and services that are difficult to copy. Firms with a high

[77] The difference between hypothesis one and three is that under hypothesis three, the authors expect not only NFS liquidation costs but also the interaction term between NFS liquidation costs and NFS bargaining power to impact capital structure (Franck and Huyghebaert, 2006: 13).

value for customer bargaining power show a large involvement of customers in the firm's strategic and product market decisions. Firms with high scores on the employee bargaining power proxy face a unionized workfoce that influences day-to-day operations (Franck and Huyghebaert, 2006: 19–20). In a next step, the authors use a cross-sectional OLS regression analysis to estimate the influence of the above-mentioned proxies as well as a set of financial control variables on the capital structure decision of a sample of 209 first-time business start-ups in Belgium. In line with previous literature, they find that their sample firms have significantly lower debt ratios when NFS liquidation costs are high, which is consistent with the predictions of the the stakeholder theory of capital structure as outlined in section 5.1.1.3. Regarding bargaining power they find that only customer bargaining power is significantly negatively related to the debt level. Regarding hypothesis three they find that supplier bargaining power has a negative impact on the relation between NFS liquidation costs and capital structure. However, they do not find significant results for the bargaining power of customers and employees (Franck and Huyghebaert, 2006: 22–25).

5.1.2.3.4 Kale and Shahrur (2007)

The paper by Kale and Shahrur (2007) goes into the same direction as the study by Franck and Huyghebaert (2006). They also investigate the link between a firm's leverage and the characteristics of its suppliers and customers. The authors examine two hypotheses. First, they investigate whether firms dealing with R&D-intensive suppliers and customers choose low leverage as a mechanism to induce their business partners to undertake relations-specific investments. Acknowledging that, additionally to debt, also vertical integration might be used as an incentive to induce relation-specific investments (Williamson, 1985), they expect that the negative relation between debt level and R&D-intensity is weaker when firms integrate vertically through strategic alliances or joint ventures.[78] Second, they consider the relation between a firm's debt level choice and its bargaining position relative to its customers/suppliers (Kale and Shahrur, 2007: 322–326). Their reported results support the arguments of a stakeholder rationale for risk management. They find significant support for their hypothesized negative relation between firm debt levels and the intensity of R&D investments by its suppliers and customers, respectively. Further, they find that leverage is lower when the firm enters into strategic alliances and joint

[78] See also section 3.2.2 for a discussion of vertical integration as a possible mode to reduce incentive problems between firms.

ventures with its suppliers and customers. Regarding the bargaining hypothesis, they find that if a firm faces concentrated supplier or customer industries, it will offset this bargaining disadvantage by increasing debt levels (Kale and Shahrur, 2007. 358–359). The latter finding is consistent with previous research in that field (see, e.g., Bronars and Deere (1991) and Subramaniam (1996)) but inconsistent with the findings of Franck and Huyghebaert (2006) who report a negative relationship between customer bargaining power and debt levels (Franck and Huyghebaert, 2006: 23). This difference between the results of Kale and Shahrur (2007) and Franck and Huyghebaert (2006) might be due to the selection of the sample. While Kale and Shahrur (2007) examine listed firms with already established firm-NFS relations, Franck and Huyghebaert analyze the context of entrepreneurial ventures. Whereas listed firms may have incentives to change their capital structure ex-post the sample firms in the study of Franck and Huyghebaert have to convince NFS to enter into contracting relationships with the entrepreneur (Franck and Huyghebaert, 2006: 24).

5.2 Dividend policy

5.2.1 Theoretical evidence

The discussion about dividend policy in finance literature relies on the classic article of Miller and Modigliani (1961) and Lintner's (1956) empirical study on corporate dividend practices in 28 U.S. companies. Allen and Michaely (1995: 793) regard decisions about the amount of earnings to pay out as dividends as one of the major financial decisions top management faces. The basic question when it comes to dividend payouts is related to the way residual cash is distributed to investors, either through cash dividends or share repurchases (Grullon and Michaely, 2002: 1652). According to the dividend irrelevancy theory of MM (1961), those two means of payback are perfect substitutes given perfect and complete capital markets as well as the firm's investment policy. In a MM world investors are indifferent if and how financial slack is distributed because the total value of the firm is unaffected. If investors desire a different stream of payments they replicate it by appropriate purchases and sales of equity. Since investment and payout decisions are independent from each other, planned investment projects can either be financed internally or by issuing new shares. Thus, there are no rules for firms to follow any systematic dividend policy. However, there are also no penalties imposed by the capital market if they choose to do so (Marsh and Merton, 1987: 2; Allen and Michaely, 1995: 793–802; Schmidt and Terberger, 1999: 235).

Based on MM's insights, other views of dividend policy have emerged in the literature. Some authors claim that dividend policy does affect the firm's cost of capital and hence its total value. Those normative theories in favor of or against higher dividend payouts are based on arguments considering corporate and individual taxes, agency-theory, behavioral theories of individual choice, signaling and transaction cost motives.[79] In their review of micro studies of dividend policy Marsh and Merton (1987) summarize *"that there are a number of conflicting theories of dividend behavior, and the empirical studies to date provide little compelling evidence for one over the others"* (Marsh and Merton, 1987: 3). Out of those theories, both the signaling hypothesis of dividend announcements and the agency-models of dividend policy seem particularly important in the context of the stakeholder rationale for risk management.

5.2.1.1 Asymmetric information - signaling models of dividend policy

Contrary to the view of MM, empirical studies indicate that increases in dividends are viewed as good news by the market, leading to a stock price increase. On the other hand, dividend reductions or even omissions are often followed by a stock price decline (Michaely et al., 1995: 605). Building on the idea of asymmetric information between corporate insiders and external financial stakeholders, dividends can signal investors the management's perception of the firm's future prospects (Benartzi et al., 1997: 1008). This theoretical stream assumes that dividends transmit information about the firm's prospects that cannot be credibly communicated by other means (e.g. annual reports or earnings forecasts). Thus, dividend policy can affect the value of the firm by changing investors' expectations about future earnings. Knowing that firms are reluctant to cut once established dividend levels, this perspective further assumes that investors look beyond the pure announcement of a dividend increase to find out whether it is in fact backed by maintainable higher cash flows in the future or might be financed through costly external sources (Wentges, 2002: 190). However, overall, empirical evidence provides, at best, only weak support to the assertion that dividend changes convey information about future earnings changes (Allen and Michaely, 1995: 824–825; Benartzi, 1997: 1031).

---

[79] For an overview of theories on dividend policy see, e.g., Copeland et al. (2005, chapter 16) or the reviews by Allen and Michaely (1995) and Frankfurter (1999).

5.2.1.2 Agency models of dividend policy

Shareholder-oriented agency arguments about a suggested dividend policy are based on the already discussed papers by Jensen and Meckling (1976), Myers (1977), and Jensen (1986). Dividend policy can contribute to mitigate the conflict between management and stockholders, and bondholders and stockholders, respectively. First, by paying out unnecessary cash, which is otherwise at the discretion of self-interested managers, dividend policy can mitigate the management-stockholder conflict. This is because dividend payouts shift the reinvestment decision back to the shareholders and increase the need for external financing (Lloyd et al., 1985: 20). On the other hand, however, wealth expropriations from bondholders by stockholders can be avoided when both parties agree on restricting dividends ex-ante (Allen and Michaely, 1995: 826–828). The notion of restricting dividend payouts (either through cash or share repurchases) to avoid detrimental effects on bondholders' wealth positions can be extended to all corporate stakeholders. Short-term oriented shareholders might for several reasons (see, e.g., Jensen, 1986) be interested in maximizing their current return on investment and forcing management to distribute excess cash. However, sophisticated stakeholders would recognize or even anticipate such a behavior and its detrimental impact on the current and future financial standing of the firm. Hence, a purely shareholder-driven dividend policy decision will affect the firm's current market value through the value of NOC. As a result, dividend payouts that favor the debtholders' position are also in line with an interpretation of payout policy following stakeholder arguments of corporate finance decisions.

5.2.1.3 A stakeholder-based argument on dividend policy

Unlike the stakeholder theory of capital structure there is no such explicit theory on dividend policy. Stakeholders are usually omitted when discussing payout policies. Hence, also the signaling effect of dividend policy is almost exclusively discussed from an equityholder's point of view. A noticeable exception is Shapiro and Balbirer (2000), who address the impact of a firm's dividend decision on its NFS. Shapiro and Balbirer emphasize that companies relying on intangible assets, such as consumer confidence, should set the dividend at a more conservative and maintainable level (Shapiro and Balbirer 2000: 520). Following their arguments it seems obvious that dividend policy can also affect the value of the firm by changing non-financial stakeholders' expectations of their future income streams related to the firm. This interpretation goes hand in hand with the signaling argument of corporate finance decisions of the stakeholder rationale for risk management (see also section 4.3.2.2.1).

As already presented in section 4.3.2.2 on the stakeholder argument for risk management, non-financial stakeholders favor lower payouts to shareholders because the firm's improved financial standing functions as a buffer for the fulfillment of the firm's implicit contractual promises (Wentges, 2002: 191–193).

5.2.2 Empirical evidence

In their review of dividend policy theories, Allen and Michaely (1995: 833) allege that the empirical evidence on that topic is very mixed. Thus, they are unable to recommend an optimal dividend policy. Nonetheless, an outline of this empirical research is provided at this point.

The most influential piece of empirical research on the dividend behavior of firms was conducted by Lintner (1956: 98), who interviewed and surveyed 28 corporate managers of U.S. non-financial firms. In his classic study he finds that corporate dividends are a real and practical management issue and identifies several common characteristics in the firm's dividend policies in his interviews with corporate managers. First, firms have a long-run payout ratio (i.e. dividends as a proportion of earnings) as a starting point for most payout decisions. Second, managers focus on dividend changes not on absolute levels. Third, managers prefer smoothing dividends rather than increasing them in the case of temporary earnings changes. Related to that is the aspect that managers are reluctant to reduce a once established dividend level. Moreover, dividends are based on long-run sustainable earnings. From an industry perspective it seems interesting that growth companies usually tend to have lower payouts than mature companies (Marsh and Merton, 1987: 5; Brealey and Myers, 2000: 443).

Contrary to Lintner (1956), Charitou and Vafeas (1998) posit that not only current and prior earnings are main determinants for setting dividend policy. Rather, they expect cash flow, which is a more direct liquidity measure, to be a better predictor of dividend changes than the accruals component (Charitou and Vafeas, 1998: 226). Based on the fundamental logic that business organizations cannot, usually, survive in the long-run without generating cash flows from operations, Charitou and Vafeas (1998: 229) name two reasons for why dividend changes are partly determined by the level of cash flow. First, accruals are often manipulated to the managers' advantage because of unfavorable compensation systems. Therefore, accruals are less useful for explaining dividend changes. Second, it is plausible that payout policy is dependent on cash availability (Charitou and Vafeas, 1998: 230). For those reasons they hypothesize that, given earnings, operating cash flows are positively related to dividend changes. However, they make their hypothesis dependent on the magnitude of accruals. They argue that low operating cash flows constrain dividend payout changes, while high operating cash flows do not facilitate such changes. They further hypothesize that the relationship between operating cash flows and dividend changes is positive for firms with low operating cash flows (Charitou and Vafeas, 1998: 231). Empirically analyzing almost 6,000 firm-years observations for the period between 1981 and 1991 from the *Compustat* database they, like prior studies, do not find a significant relationship between dividend changes and operating cash flows. However, they identify that operating cash flows are in fact important in setting payout policy when they are relatively low, acting as a constraint on a firm's payout ability. Moreover, they find support for the notion that cash flows are less important when there is highly competing demand on cash flow by investment projects (Charitou and Vafeas, 1998: 246).

5.2.2.1 Holder et al. (1998)

Holder et al. (1998) examine the influence of NFS on the firm's dividend payout ratio by examining the interaction between dividends and investment. Based on the contributions of Jensen (1983), Titman (1984), Cornell and Shapiro (1987), and Shapiro (1990) they extend the Barton et al. (1989) study on debt policy in high or low-NOC firms to the dividend policy puzzle. They use a proxy for NOC to explain its impact on the dividend payout ratio in a specific year. With reference to Shapiro (1990), Holder et al. (1998: 75) posit that dividend-payout ratios should be lower when NOC becomes higher. They use possible spillover effects as a measure of NOC. This approach is based on the idea of corporate focus that measures a firm's concentration on its core business. A less focused firm is diversified into more business segments and likely to have fewer spillover effects. The stakeholder argument is the following. If stakeholders have implicit claims against division A, the ability of a different line of business, division B, to meet its implicit claims should have relatively little spillover effect on the stakeholder of division A. The more business lines a firm has, the less likely spillover will occur. Hence, firms with low spillover effects (i.e. they are less focused) will then have lower NOC than will firms that have more spillover effects (i.e. are more focused). This is because defaulting on implicit claims is less injurious to a less-focused firm, as compared to a more-focused firm. As stakeholders recognize that focused firms have more to lose when defaulting on implicit claims, they will place higher value on implicit claims for a focused firm (Holder et al., 1998: 75). Thus, NOC should go up and the payout-ratio go down with corporate focus increasing (Holder et al., 1998: 76). Drawing on Comment and Jarrell (1991), they use the maximum proportion of a firm's sales attributable to a certain business line as a measure of a firm's concentration in its core business (Holder et al., 1998: 75). Holder et al. (1998: 76) point out that their measure of NOC is easier to determine than that of Barton et al. (1989), who use strategy categories to account for spillover effects between lines of business. In the Barton et al. (1989) study, firms with a single business line and firms with related business lines are high-spillover firms, while multiple unrelated business lines are low-spillover firms.

Holder et al. (1998) include six non-stakeholder variables based on previous research, which they group into size, agency cost, and transaction cost categories. Larger firms tend to have easier access to capital markets and can therefore afford higher dividend payout-ratios. The hypothesized relationship between firm size and dividend-payout ratio is positive. Following Lloyd et al. (1985) they use the natural log of sales as a size proxy. As ownership by management increases, agency costs decline. Thus, a negative relation between the percentage of shares held by insiders and the dividend-payout ratio is expected. Related to that is the aspect that a more dispersed shareholder structure implies higher agency costs and thus higher dividend payouts. Drawing on Jensen's (1986) free cash flow argument, Holder et al. (1998) hypothesize that there exists a positive relationship between free cash flows and the dividend payout ratio. Holder et al. (1998) use two transaction cost variables. The first is the growth rate of sales and the second the standard deviation of monthly firm returns. The former proxy refers to the fact that high revenue growth creates additional needs of financing, while the latter is explained by higher underwriter charges for high risk firms (Holder et al., 1988: 77).

Using a sample of 477 U.S. firms from the period of 1983 to 1990, Holder et al. (1998) show that more focused firms (i.e. firms that are assumed to have high NOC) indeed have significantly lower payout ratios. Furthermore, the dividend-payout ratio significantly increases with firm size, free cash flow, and the number of shareholders. It significantly decreases, on the other hand, with the standard deviation of firm returns, sales growth, and insider ownership. They conclude that managers may indeed consider the claims of non-financial stakeholders when choosing a target dividend-payout ratio. Thus, their results provide some evidence against the separation of the investment and financing decisions of a firm as stated by MM (Holder et al., 1998: 80). However, their arguments regarding their NOC variable seem questionable. The dependence on cash flows from a single business line implies higher risk of non-payment of implied commitments. From a stakeholder perspective the degree of corporate diversification can also be interpreted as a potential risk factor (Wang et al., 2003: 56; Wentges, 2002: 194). Already Speckbacher and Wentges (2005) argue that managers of more focused firms have good reasons to mitigate the problem of higher (perceived) risk and, therefore, choose a lower dividend-payout ratio (Speckbacher and Wentges, 2005: 22).

Holder et al. admit that their measure for NOC may not be a perfect indicator and encourage further research on other measures of NOC. Moreover, they identify the relationship between the level of NOC and industry/product-characteristics as an area of potential research. Particularly, they propose a contractual perspective of the firm as a starting point for such research (Holder et al, 1998: 81).

5.2.2.2 Brav et al. (2004)

In a recent survey of 384 financial executives in the U.S., Brav et al. (2004: 21) conclude that dividend decisions are still made conservativley as already found by Lintner (1956). Differently to Lintner (1956), Brav et al. (2004) find that the importance of a target for the payout ratio has diminished and financial executives view the target as more flexible nowadays. Additionally, the authors provide evidence that share repurchases are nowadays a very important form of payout, simply because it is a more flexible instrument.[80] This flexibility allows managers to adjust payouts according to investment opportunities, to offset stock option dilution, or to return capital to investors when seemed appropriate (Brav et al., 2004: 21).

---

[80] This view is shared by a majority of finance academics, who perceive dividends to be an unwise mechanism for corporations to distribute funds relative to share repurchases (Welch, 2000: 524–525). For further empirical evidence on the choice between dividends and stock repurchases in a non-MM environment see, e.g., Jagannathan et al. (2000).

Referring to the signaling context of dividend policy, Brav et al. (2004: 15–17) find that corporate executives do in fact consider payout policy as a means of communication with investors. Nevertheless it is rarely thought of as a tool to separate a company from competitors. Brav et al. (2004) state that *"there is no evidence that initiating or increasing payout is viewed consciously as a self-imposed cost to reveal a strong firm's private information about its ability"* (Brav et al., 2004: 17). Therefore they use the term 'convey' instead of the term 'signal' to *"reserve 'signal' for the academic sense of the world (i.e., costly self-imposed action)"* (Brav et al., 2004: 15; original emphasis). The authors ask whether companies use payout policy to show that they can bear costs, in the self-imposed academic sense, to make their company look better than that of competitors. They report that only 4.4 percent of companies agree with this premise, which is the weakest support for any dividend question they pose (Brav et al., 2004: 16). Those findings are interesting from a stakeholder point of view. The results might be due to the way the question was asked since dividend policy can also be used to signal NFS the future financial standing of the firm. NFS might be more interested in the firm's future ability of a particular company to fulfill implicit claims rather than its standing versus its competitors. Furthermore, they report that dividend policy is still very conservative (Brav et al., 2004: 21), implying a low payout ratio. Due to the interrelatedness of dividend policy, cash holdings, and capital structure choice, a low payout-ratio implies a higher amount of liquidity, which is in fact costly to firms. Therefore the term 'signal' might also be useful in a stakeholder context.

5.3 Corporate cash holdings

5.3.1 Theoretical evidence

Brealey and Myers (2000) subsume the problem of a firm's optimal holdings of cash under the ten unsolved problems in finance (Brealey and Myers, 2000: 1014).[81] In an MM world of perfect and complete capital markets, holdings of liquid assets are simply irrelevant. Money can always be raised to finance positive-NPV projects at zero cost (Holmström and Tirole, 2000: 297). Since there is no liquidity premium for cash holdings, there are also no opportunity costs and the total value of the firm is unaffected (Opler et al., 1999: 7). Hence, in an MM world firms should hold no excess

---

[81] *"Obviously, every firm must be able to raise cash on short notice, but we have no good theory of how much cash is enough or how readily the firm should be able to raise it"* (Brealey and Myers, 2000: 1015).

cash at all. However, in a world of imperfect capital markets, firms have substantial amounts of less profitable cash on their balance sheet as a buffer against shocks (Holmström and Tirole, 2000: 295). This fact is supported by several pieces of empirical evidence. In an empirical analysis of corporate cash holdings in publicly held companies in the U.K. for the period between 1984 and 1999, Ozkan and Ozkan (2004: 2116) report a mean cash ratio of 9.9 percent and a median value of 5.9 percent. These values are in line with previous results for U.S. firms. As reported by Opler et al. (1999: 17), the mean cash ratio in their study was 17 percent and 8.1 percent in the investigation of Kim et al. (1998: 351). Bates et al. (2006) even report a 129% increase in the average cash to assets ratio for U.S. industrial firm from 1980 to 2004. In 2004, cash holdings reached a level that covers the outstanding debt for American firms. In other words, average net debt was negative in 2004 in the respective sample (Bates et al., 2006: 2–3).

The traditional literature on corporate cash holdings provides two approaches to explain this phenomenon: the static trade-off theory and the financing hierarchy theory (Opler et al., 1999: 7–14). Additionally, arguments based on corporate hedging theory as well as stakeholder theory can be named.

5.3.1.1 Static trade-off theory

The static trade-off theory asserts that firms trade off various costs and benefits of debt financing when they decide how much cash to hold (Dittmar et al., 2003: 114). The cost of liquid assets is explained by the lower return on this asset class due to a liquidity premium charged by the market. This liquidity premium is related to the term structure of interest rates, since the opportunity costs of holding cash increase with interest rates. Another cost driver for holding cash is taxation. Since interest income from liquid assets is taxed at the corporate and the individual level, investors prefer the firm to repurchase shares with excess cash instead of using it as a buffer (Opler et al., 1999: 10).

The benefits, on the other hand, of holding liquid asset classes lie in avoiding transaction costs for approaching an external capital market (transaction cost motive) and in avoiding foregone investment opportunities due to a shortage in cash (precautionary motive). Those arguments show the close link between the liquidity level of a firm's balance sheet and its ability to fund value-increasing investments when they occur (Almeida et al., 2002: 1). In the following section, the transaction cost motive and the precautionary motive are explained.

The transaction cost motive states that fixed and variable costs accrue when buying and selling financial and real assets in the marketplace. A firm that is short of liquid assets has to raise funds in the capital market, liquidate assets, cut dividends, or reduce investments, or some combination of these actions. Since both, liquidation of assets or going to an incomplete capital market to raise funds is costly, firms will hold cash. Thus, liquid assets have the function of a buffer that assures low opportunity costs in case of cash shortage (Opler et al., 1999: 7–10; Dittmar et al., 2003: 115; Ozkan and Ozkan, 2004: 2106). The marginal cost of being short of funds is related to several characteristics which are interesting from both a stakeholder and a purely financial risk management perspective. First, the costs for converting assets into cash are positively related to their degree of specificity (Williamson, 1988: 589). Hence, firms with mostly relation-specific assets should have higher levels of liquid assets. Second, the volatility of cash flows determines the level of cash holdings (Opler al., 1999: 10). Higher cash flow volatility implies higher probability of cash shortage. As a consequence, a higher cash buffer is required in order to be able to fulfill future implicit claims. Third, cash holdings are also related to the firm's hedging strategy, one being a substitute for the other in order to avoid cash shortages. Using financial hedging can reduce random variation in cash flows, thus reducing the need for such a cash buffer. However, firms for which financial hedging is expensive because they use it infrequently are expected to hold more liquid assets than firms that can do financial hedging at lower cost. The transactions costs for raising funds in the capital market could even be prohibitively high in the case of financial distress. Thus, and fourth, firms that are already in financial distress should have higher cash holdings. Fifth, firms with better growth opportunities are expected to hold more cash because their opportunity costs of foregone investment is higher. This is due to the fact that growth opportunities are generally intangible in nature which have value only as a part of a going concern (Brealey and Myers, 2000: 521; Dittmar et al., 2003: 115; Ozkan and Ozkan, 2004: 2107).

The precautionary motive for holding liquid assets is closely related to agency costs. These costs are driven by information asymmetries between the firm and its bondholders and stockholders, respectively (Opler et al., 1999: 10). Information asymmetries make additional external funds more expensive, since outsiders know less than management. Myers and Majluf (1984: 219–220) argue that in case of such informational asymmetries firms build up financial slack to overcome underinvestment in positive NPV projects. They propose to build up financial slack by either issuing stock in periods when managers' information advantage is small or restricting dividends. Referring to Opler and Titman (1984), Opler et al. (1999) suggest this to firms with high relative R&D expenses since such expenses are a form of investment where information asymmetries are most important. Therefore, firms with higher R&D expenses will hold more liquid assets, ceteris paribus (Opler et al., 1999: 11). It should be pointed out that the ratio of R&D expenses to sales can also be regarded as a driver of the uniqueness of products and services, thus being a proxy for customers' implicit claims with a firm and stakeholders' costs in the event of liquidation (Titman and Wessels, 1988: 5; Bowen et al., 1995: 269).

Information asymmetries also create agency costs of external finance which emerge when the interests of shareholders and debtholders differ. When firms are highly leveraged, there is an incentive for owners not to invest in value enhancing positive-NPV projects, because the benefits will accrue (almost) exclusively to the bondholders. This conflict between a firm's bondholders and stockholders is called the underinvestment problem (Myers (1977) (see also section 4.2.2.3). Since rational bondholders would recognize this expropriation of debt value, they will incorporate it into their pricing decision. Therefore, the firm will suffer losses from these decisions, representing the agency costs of debt (Copeland et al., 2005: 460). Since firms want to avoid situations where agency costs of debt financing are so high that they cannot raise funds to finance their investment activities they will either choose a low level of leverage or hold more liquid assets. This reduces the costs of cash constraints (Opler et al., 1999: 11).

The debtholder–shareholder conflict is similar to the relationship between managers and shareholders. (Opler et al., 1999: 12; Ozkan and Ozkan, 2004: 2109). Excess cash is similar to free cash flow and thus creates the same problems as those described by Jensen (1986: 323–324).[82] Myers and Rajan (1998) describe the problem by saying that *"greater asset liquidity increases the potential for conflict between the manager and*

[82] Harford (1999) shows that firms with high cash holdings tend to make value-decreasing acquisitions. Pinkowitz (2000) finds that cash-rich firms are significantly less likely to be acquired through a takeover and explains that phenomenon by ineffective monitoring of a firm's cash holdings by the market for corporate control. Both studies support Jensen's (1986) entrenchment argument.

the financier over property rights" (Myers and Rajan, 1998: 734). It increases managements' discretionary spending power and creates agency costs of managerial discretion when interests of managers and shareholders are not aligned. There are three reasons why management may prefer holding excess cash. First, because it is risk averse and has its own human capital invested in the firm. Second, management pursues its own objectives. By using cash it can finance activities that would otherwise not be financed by the capital market because it has a negative effect on firm value. Third, management prefers keeping the funds within the firm over distributing cash to shareholders. Since managers have to find ways to spend the funds, this might result in bad investment projects if good projects are not available (Opler et al., 1999: 12). From the arguments above it is evident that agency costs of managerial discretion are less important for firms with valuable growth opportunities because they establish a natural alignment of managers' and investors' interests. Literature about ownership structure offers a solution to overcome these agency costs of managerial discretion. This literature assumes that increased managerial ownership reduces the likelihood of non-value maximizing behavior of management. Thus, a negative relationship between managerial ownership and cash holdings is expected. Additionally, such an obvious alignment of interests could increase the firm's ability to raise funds externally. This minimizes the firms' incentives to accumulate cash. However, it is difficult to specify the exact degree of managerial ownership. When ownership is too little dispersed then management is less subject to external pressures from the capital market. Such entrenched managers would then choose to hold more liquid assets to pursue their own interests (Opler et al., 1999: 13; Ozkan and Ozkan, 2004: 2109–2110).

In summary, the static trade-off theory states that there is an optimal level of cash for a given amount of debt that can be found by comparing the individual firm's benefit and opportunity costs of holding liquid assets. When trading off these benefit and costs, a management acting on the behalf of rational shareholders should also incorporate indirect effects from stakeholder relations into their decision on the level of cash holdings.

5.3.1.2 Financing hierarchy theory

The financing hierarchy view proposes that there is no optimal amount of cash because there is no optimal level of debt. According to the financing hierarchy view, cash and debt are just opposite sides of the same coin and cash is regarded as negative debt

(Dittmar et al. 2003: 116). This means that for a firm it does not make any difference whether it has high debt levels and holds high amounts of cash, or low debt and low cash holdings (Opler et al., 1999: 13). Based on the pecking order theory of financing, the financing hierarchy model regards the cash balance simply as a random outcome of the financing and investment decisions of the firm. For financing their investment projects, firms primarily use internal funds. Not until those internal sources are exhausted firms turn to capital markets to raise debt. As a last resort firms issue new risky equity (Opler et al., 1999: 13). The reason why firms prefer retained earnings over new debt and equity lies in the asymmetric information between managers and corporate outsiders. Since managers want to avoid issuing underpriced shares they prefer debt to equity. Therefore, there is no well-defined target debt-equity mix (Copeland et al., 2005: 602). Hence, from a financing hierarchy perspective holding liquid assets is necessary to finance positive-NPV projects and to avoid informationally sensitive and costly external capital markets.

Unfortunately, the distinction between the financing hierarchy model and the static trade-off model is not as clear-cut as one might want. That implies that many of the determinants of cash holdings suggested by the trade-off and the financing hierarchy theory can be used as proxies for both of them (Opler et al., 1999: 14; Dittmar et al., 2003: 116). One major difference between these two theories affects the predicted relationship between cash level and investment (i.e. capital expenditures and R&D expenses). As explained in the previous subsection, the static trade-off model predicts a positive relationship between these parameters. Since the hierarchy model views cash as the first choice in funding investments it predicts a negative relationship.

5.3.1.3 A corporate hedging based argument on cash holdings

Recently, Acharya et al. (2005) introduced an argument on cash and debt policies that is related to a hedging motive. This argument is based on the assumption that raising funds in the capital markets is often too costly. As shown by Froot et al. (1993) this gives rise to a hedging motive.[83] On this ground, Acharya et al. (2005) build an argument where cash is not simply negative debt as proposed by the financing hierarchy theory.

---

[83] See also section 4.2.2.4.

In the absence of financing frictions, firms' future levels of investments are independent of their current cash policies. Saving is unnecessary, since profitable investment opportunities can be financed through capital markets. The situation is different, however, for constrained firms. Higher cash holdings and lower debt levels increase the future funding capacity of a constrained firm. Acharya et al. (2005) argue that there is a trade-off between the firm's choice between higher cash and lower debt. Higher cash holdings are particularly useful when the firm suffers from low cash flow states. Then the effect of additional cash will be higher than the corresponding effect of lower debt (i.e. greater borrowing capacity). In high cash flow states, however, higher cash balances are assumed to have a lower effect on financing capacity than a corresponding reduction in outstanding debt. Following their argument, the current market value of (risky) debt is largely dependent on the future cash flow state of the firm. Reducing the amount of the firm's outstanding debt by one dollar today increases future debt capacity in good states by more than one dollar. Similarly, reducing outstanding debt by on dollar today raises future debt capacity in bad states by less than one dollar. In contrast, an additional dollar of cash today increases future financing capacity by exactly one dollar, independent of the cash flow state of the firm. Hence, debt reductions are an effective way of boosting investment in high cash flow states (Acharya et al., 2005: 5). The authors use this trade-off to predict how firms allocate free cash flows between cash and repayments of debt. They predict that constrained firms will prefer high cash holdings, as opposed to lower debt levels, if the correlation between cash flows and investment opportunities is low. If the correlation is high, on the other hand, the firm will prefer debt reductions. The basic intuition behind this argument is similar to the hedging motive by Froot et al. (1993). When the correlation between cash flows and investment opportunities is low, hedging needs are high in order to coordinate investment and financing policies. Thus, firms will have a preference towards holding cash. When the correlation between cash flows and profitable investment opportunities is high, on the other hand, then the firm will prefer reducing leverage. That is because a high correlation can be interpreted as a natural hedge that reduces the value of higher cash holdings (Acharya et al., 2005: 6). As a conclusion it can be argued that cash and (negative) debt are not necessarily substitutes when the firm faces financing constraints.

5.3.1.4 A stakeholder-based argument on cash holdings

Unlike Grinblatt and Titman's (1998) stakeholder theory of capital structure (see section 5.1.1.3), no such theory can be found in the literature on corporate cash holdings. An exception is Wentges (2002), who uses stakeholder theory to argue for a conservative liquidity policy, especially for firms with high levels of Net Organizational Capital. His line of argument goes hand in hand with the stakeholder SRRM presented in this work. Higher liquidity reserves, on the one hand, increase management's flexibility to invest in implicit stakeholder claims. On the other hand high cash holdings might be interpreted as a signal to NFS that opportunistic action against their implicit claims will not take place, even in situations of financial difficulties. As specified previously, the benefits of a stakeholder-oriented risk management policy are highest, when the firm enjoys high growth opportunities or large excess tax deductions, follows a differentiation strategy, or depends on intangible assets.[84] Regarding the last point, static trade-off theory and stakeholder arguments on cash holdings come to the same conclusion. Since intangible assets are usually created jointly between the firm and its NFS, these assets are often highly specific in nature. The static trade-off theory suggests holding more cash when converting assets into cash generates higher transaction costs (Williamson, 1988: 598) and the stakeholder-based risk management's argument suggests that NFS need protection of their (sunk) investments when the firm's assets are specific to a high degree. This protection can come in the form of a high cash buffer.

5.3.2 Empirical evidence

5.3.2.1 Kim et al. (1998)

Kim et al. (1998) develop a model of optimal corporate investment in liquid assets based on a trade-off between the costs of holding liquid assets and the benefit of minimizing the need to fund profitable future investment opportunities with costly external sources of finance. Their model predicts that the optimal investment in excess cash increases with the cost of external financing, the variability of future cash flows and the return on future investment opportunities. On the other hand, optimal investment in liquidity is expected to decrease with the return spread between physical assets and liquid assets. They test these predictions using data from U.S. non-financial firms for the period from 1975 to 1994 (Kim et al., 1998: 346–352). Controlling for

---

[84] See also section 4.3.2.3 for this argument.

other variables they find support that liquid asset positions are positively related to market-to-book ratios, earnings volatility and leading economic indicators, and negatively associated with firm size, and a negative return spread between physical and liquid assets holdings (Kim et al., 1998: 355; Almeida et al., 2002: 4).

5.3.2.2 Opler et al. (1999)

Opler et al. (1999) analyze the determinants of corporate cash holdings and particularly the validity of the static trade-off model as well as the financing hierarchy model by using *Compustat* data for U.S. firms for the years from 1971 to 1994 (Opler et al., 1999: 14). Finding evidence in favor of a target adjustment model, they conclude that their results provide support for a static trade-off view of corporate cash holdings. Their results also support the financing hierarchy theory as they report that firms that accumulate excess cash are firms that do well (Opler et al., 1999: 44; Speckbacher and Wentges, 2005: 19). However, Opler et al. (1999) are unable to show that proxies for agency costs have an important impact on cash holdings. They report that the liquidity level decreases significantly for firms with greater access to the capital market, such as large firms and those with good credit ratings (Opler et al., 1999: 44). Particularly interesting from a stakeholder theory standpoint are Opler et al.'s findings that cash holdings increase significantly with firm and industry volatility, market-to-book ratio, and R&D-to-sales ratio (Opler et al., 1999: 27). Unlike Bowen et al. (1995), they use relative R&D expenses as a proxy for costs of financial distress caused by informational asymmetries. Following Opler and Titman (1994), they assume R&D expenses to be a form of investment where information asymmetries are most important. Although Opler et al. (1999) do not argue from a stakeholder theory's perspective, the result that both, cash flow volatility and the market-to-book ratio are positively associated with liquid asset holdings is in accordance with a stakeholder theory of risk management. Their market-to-book ratio could not even be a measure of growth opportunities (as used by Opler et al. (1995)) but also a proxy for NOC since it measures at the same time the size of intangible assets (Speckbacher and Wengtes, 2005: 20).

5.3.2.3 Dittmar et al. (2003)

Dittmar et al. (2003) investigate the determinants of corporate cash holdings in an international context and test whether corporate governance is associated with cash holdings. In short, they find that shareholder rights, and therefore agency costs, are important in determining corporate cash holdings around the world (Dittmar et al. 2003: 113–114). However, they also contribute to the firm level analysis of corporate cash holdings. To separate the influence of shareholder rights on the variation in the firms' cash holdings across countries from firm-specific characteristics, the authors include several control variables. They find that corporate cash holdings are negatively related to firm size, market-to-book ratios, relative R&D expenses, the relative level of cash flows, and negatively associated with relative net working capital (Dittmar et al., 2003: 122).

5.3.2.4 Mikkelson and Partch (2003)

Mikkelson and Partch (2003) analyze the relationship between conservative levels of cash holdings and operating performance. Based on data from the *Compustat* database for the period of 1986–1999, they analyze a sample of 89 publicly traded U.S. non-financial firms to identify the characteristics of corporate cash holdings and to test the consequences of persistent, substantial holdings of cash on corporate performance. Their main objective is to determine whether policies of persistent large cash levels hinder performance. Mikkelson and Partch (2003) also provide evidence on what types of firms tend to hold large amounts of cash over time and how they use that cash. Mikkelson and Partch (2003: 276) find that high cash firms in their sample differ from a comparison group in ways that provide support for the notion that high cash levels are optimal for these firms and foster investment and growth. Firms in their group of high cash are smaller, less levered, have higher market-to-book ratios, and grow faster than firms in the comparison group. Additionally, the firms in the high cash group are characterized by a higher percentage of single-segment firms. Mikkelson and Partch explain the latter characteristic by the inability of single-sourced firms to transfer funds internally among business units (Mikkelson and Partch, 2003: 276 and 282). Regarding the use of excess cash by high cash firms, Mikkelson and Partch (2003: 291–292) find that these firms have extraordinarily high investment expenditures, mainly for R&D, and do not make unusually high total payouts to security holders. Another interpretation for these high R&D expenses offers the stakeholder rationale for risk management. Since firms with single-source cash flows have a higher risk to fail on implicit claims, such firms are expected to maintain high cash levels to always be able to fulfill explicit and implicit stakeholder claims. A regression analysis of operating performance on the characteristics of high cash firms does not uncover evidence of underperformance by firms that retain high cash reserves, which is also consistent with the predictions of SRRM. To account for agency problems, several governance variables (i.e. proportion of insider ownership, outside representation on the board and presence of a controlling founder) are included in the regression whose coefficients, however, are insignificant. Further significant explanatory variables of operating performance are the market-to-book ratio and prior operating performance. Both variables are related positively to performance among high cash firms (Mikkelson and Partch, 2003: 290).

In general the findings of Mikkelson and Partch (2003) are consistent with other empirical studies on the determinants of cash holdings (Opler et al. (1999), Kim et al. (1998) and Ozkan and Ozkan (2004)) and with the stakeholder perspective of risk management. Referring to the work of Minton and Wruck (2001), Mikkelson and Partch (2003: 293) emphasize the importance of further insights into conservative financial policies. Particularly, they encourage further research to *"explore cash holdings, financial leverage, and risk management in combination to more fully understand the motives for and consequences of conservative financial policies"* (Mikkelson and Partch, 2003: 293).

5.3.2.5 Schwetzler and Reimund (2004)

Schwetzler and Reimund analyze the performance effects of persistent excessive cash holdings. In contrast to Mikkelson and Partch (2003), they find a significant operating underperformance of German firms that previously held excessive cash and marketable securities over a three year period (Schwetzler and Reimund, 2004: 23). Schwetzler and Reimund interpret their results in line with Jensen's (1986) agency-based hypothesis of inefficient investment when the firm holds too much cash.

Moreover, the authors report industry-specific median cash holdings. While the average median over all firms is 4.43%, the median cash holdings for the construction (0.0519), engineering (0.0693), pharma & biotech (0.0523), and software (0.0625) industries are way above the average (Schwetzler and Reimund, 2004: 22). These results support the predictions of a stakeholder theory of risk management, since the former two industries are usually engaged in producing unique products and the latter two industries are mainly driven by intangible assets.

5.3.2.6 Ozkan and Ozkan (2004)

Ozkan and Ozkan (2004) investigate the empirical determinants of corporate cash holdings using a sample of 839 U.K. firms from 1984 to 1999. Unlike Opler et al. (1999) they additionally focus on the influence of corporate governance characteristics such as the importance of managerial ownership (e.g. board structure and identity of controlling shareholders). They find support for a non-linear relationship between managerial ownership and cash holdings. They report that the liquidity level falls as managerial ownership increases up to 24 percent and then rises as managerial ownership increases to 64 percent. According to Ozkan and Ozkan (2004), that suggests that the alignment effect of managerial ownership dominates the entrenchment effect (Ozkan and Ozkan, 2004: 2120 and 2130). Furthermore, they find that for U.K. firms, cash holdings significantly increase with growth opportunities (measured by the market-to-book ratio) and decrease with leverage (measured by the debt-to-total-assets ratio). In contrast to Opler et al. (1999) they do not find support for the view that firms with more volatile cash flows hold more cash. Although the estimated coefficient between the liquidity level and cash flow volatility (measured by the standard deviation of cash flow over the average of total assets) is positive, it is insignificant under all specifications (Ozkan and Ozkan, 2004: 2120). Ozkan and Ozkan (2004) do not find support for a negative relationship between firm size (measured by the natural log of assets of a certain base year) and levels of cash. This negative relationship is hypothesized as it can be assumed that larger firms are less likely to experience financial distress, are more diversified and have better external financing opportunities. However, in their regression analysis, the coefficient is positive but insignificant. The authors argue that larger firms might be more successful in generating profits and cash flows, so that they can accumulate more cash holdings (Ozkan and Ozkan, 2004: 2129).

5.3.2.7 Bates et al. (2006)

Bates et al. (2006) investigate the level of cash holdings of U.S. industrial firms for the 1980–2004 period. They find that the average cash to assets ratio climbs from 10.48% to 24.03%. Additionally, they report a sharp secular decrease in net debt which is explained by the rise in cash holdings (Bates et al, 2006: 3). Interesting is the fact that this positive time trend is valid among all firm sizes. A further analysis into the reasons for the cash ratio increase reveals two firm characteristics as major determinants of this trend. First, average industry cash flow risk increases from an average of 7.05% in the 1980s to an average of 15.93% in the 21st century (Bates et al., 2006: 20). The second determinant, which changed dramatically over the last 25 years, is the importance of R&D relative to expenditures. The authors point at potential difficulties in financing R&D investment opportunities when firms face states of financial distress (Bates et al., 2006: 22).

The authors interpret their findings as being supportive of the precautionary motive to hold cash (Bates et al, 2006: 22). However, the findings reported by Bates et al. are also consistent with the perspective of the stakeholder rationale for risk management. Especially when cash flow volatility increases, as reported by Bates et al. (2006: 20), NFS demand higher cash levels in order to specifically invest in the firm. This is of course also true for employees' and other external stakeholders' willingness to engage in firm-specific R&D activities.

5.4 Conservatism in finance and accounting

Interesting empirical findings relating to a firm's financial policy are provided by Minton and Wruck (2001), who investigate a group of firms that follow financial conservatism. In their analysis of more than 5,600 firms for the 1974–1998 period, they define financially conservative firms as those with leverage in the lowest quintile of those listed in the *Compustat* database. They show that conservatively financed firms also have substantial cash balances relative to more leveraged firms and tend to follow a pecking order-style financing strategy. These firms seem to stockpile financial slack or debt capacity. Moreover, and consistent with a prior study by Graham (2000) as well as predictions from stakeholder theory, low leverage firms spend significantly more on R&D and advertising, have superior investment opportunities (measured by the market-to-book ratio), and a lower likelihood of financial distress (measured by the variation of EDITDA to total assets) than control firms (Minton and Wruck, 2001: 1–6). Although Minton and Wruck posit that financial conservatism is not an industry-based phenomenon, they show that the industry's sensivity to financial distress is an important characteristic when deciding on the level of leverage and cash holdings (Minton and Wruck, 2001: 12). Based on logit regressions they predict that firms in the computer industry and in specialty manufacturing are more likely to be financially conservative than other firms. In contrast, retail firms are less likely to be less leveraged (Minton and Wruck, 2001: 14).

Those results are in line with the theoretical analysis of Titman (1984) and the empirical results of Opler and Titman (1994).

The findings by Minton and Wruck (2001) are interesting when drawing on the risk-based stakeholder reasoning for corporate finance decisions. The fact that firms seem to adapt the cash level to the capital structure choice is obvious when considering a firms' stakeholders. Since managers know that the financial image of the firm is a signal of its future financial state, they will prefer a more conservatively looking balance sheet. The market-to-book measure as a proxy for investment opportunities can also bee interpreted as a measure of NOC (Speckbacher and Wentges, 2005: 20). Similarly, their R&D-to-sales measure is also used as proxy for asset specificity in other papers (see, e.g., Titman and Wessels, 1988) or a firm's dependence on implicit claims with corporate stakeholders (Bowen et al., 1995). The finding that low leverage firms have relatively higher advertising spending is also consistent with stakeholder theory when looking at Williamson's argument that investments in advertising have very low redeployability charcteristics (Williamson, 1988: 588).[85] Hence, it is not surprising that these determinants are significantly different for low leverage firms as they are characteristics of firms that heavily rely on implicit claims with NFS when it comes to the value creation process. Additionally, the finding that firms in the computer industry and in speciality manufacturing choose low debt levels is consistent with predictions of the SRRM as these firms impose high costs on their customers when going out of business (see also section 4.3.2.3).

5.5 Concluding remarks

The stakeholder rationale for risk management extends Titman's (1984) initial idea and argues that conservative corporate financial decisions in general can be used as instruments to assure firm-specific investments on the part of important NFS. These non-financial stakeholders can be attracted when the firm reduces total risk instead of systematic risk as suggested traditionally by the CAPM.

Overall, the empirical evidence presented backs the SRRM's conjecture that the firm's corporate finance decisions are determined by the firm-stakeholder relationships.

---

[85] Note that Balakrishnan and Fox (1993) and Vicente-Lorente (2001) interpret advertising expenditures as investments in reputational assets that increase the firm's borrowing capacity, which contradicts Williamson's argument (see also sections 5.1.2.2.4 and 5.1.2.2.5).

Recent studies on the firm's capital structure choice following Titman's (1984) product/input market interactions models strongly support the idea that the debt level is used as an instrument to induce relation-specific investments on the part of NFS. Especially the role of relative R&D expenses as an indicator of relation-specific intangible assets seems to be agreed upon in empirical capital structure literature. The literature combining strategy and capital structure research primarily emphasizes the role of asset characteristics from both a transaction cost and a resource-based perspective and empirically shows that asset structure influences the debt level.

Unlike capital structure research, research on corporate cash holdings is still dominated by financial economics-based reasonings, with strategic and stakeholder aspects only rarely considered as alternative determinants of corporate cash levels. However, traditional corporate finance research provides empirial evidence that strongly supports stakeholder reasonings to be true in this context of corporate finance research. Especially the empirically confirmed positive relationships between market-to-book ratio and relative R&D expenses with the level of cash holdings can be interpreted from a viewpoint of stakeholder theory.

This review of corporate finance literature revealed a general difficulty in empirically measuring the firm-stakeholder relationship. Corporate finance influenced research streams have tended to proxy for stakeholder aspects by using relative R&D and advertising expenses. Strategy scholars on the other hand combined Rumelt's (1974) classification scheme with assumptions about differences in firm-specific levels of NOC to account for stakeholder arguments. In chapter 7 an alternative accounting-based approach is suggested and empirically tested to proxy for the firm-stakeholder relationship.

6 Statistical methodology

This chapter outlines the fundamentals of the statistical methodological framework that is needed for the empirical study presented in chapter 7. After reviewing the basic multiple linear regression model, panel data methodology is discussed.

6.1 Multiple linear regression

The multiple linear regression model is an extension of the simple two-variable regression model assuming that the dependent variable y_i is a linear function of a series of independent variables x_{1i}, x_{2i}, …, x_{ki} where the subscript k denotes the number of regressors and the subscript i denotes the cross-section (e.g. firm, individual, …) (Pindyck and Rubinfeld, 1998: 85).[86] In general, the multiple linear regression model (also called the multiple regression model) can be written as

$$y_i = \beta_0 + \beta_1 x_{1i} + \beta_2 x_{2i} + \beta_3 x_{3i} + \ldots + \beta_k x_{ki} + u_i$$
$$k = 1, 2, \ldots, K \text{ and } i = 1, 2, \ldots, N \qquad (6.1)$$

where β_0 is the intercept, β_1 is the parameter associated with the explanatory variable x_1, β_2 is the parameter associated with variable x_2 and so forth. The variable u_i is the error or disturbance term for the i-th observation. It contains factors other than x_{1i}, x_{2i}, …, x_{ki} that affect y_i. No matter how many regressors k are considered in the model, there will always be factors that cannot be included in the model. These unobserved factors are collectively contained in the error term u_i (Wooldridge, 2006: 76–78). There are several reasons why a disturbance exists (Asteriou, 2006: 27):

Omission of explanatory variables

There might be other factors affecting y_i that have been left out of equation (6.1). This might be possible either because these factors are unknown or these factors cannot be measured directly.

Model specification

Sometimes a model might be misspecified in terms of its structure. It might be that y_t (where the subscript t = 1, 2, …, T, stands for a certain time period) is not affected by

[86] Note that in the multiple regression model dependent variables are also called explained variable or regressand, while the independent variables are also called explanatory variables, control variables, or regressors (Wooldridge, 2006: 77).

x_t, but that it is affected by the value of x in the previous period (i.e. x_{t-1}). If x_t and x_{t-1} are closely related, an estimation of y_t through equation (6.1) leads to discrepancies, which are captured by the error term u. Another reason for misspecification might be that y_t is influenced by interaction effects between two explanatory variables.

Functional misspecification

The relationship between x_i and y_i might be a non-linear relationship, while the multiple general linear regression model assumes a linear relationship.

Measurement errors

If the measurement of one or more variables is not correct, then measurement errors appear in the relationship, which contribute to the disturbance term.

The disturbance term u is also important for understanding the assumptions underlying the multiple regression model. These assumptions can be summarized as follows (Pindyck and Rubinfeld 1998: 86; Asteriou, 2006: 33–34):

1. The relationship between y and x is linear as described in equation (6.1).
2. No exact linear relationship exists between two or more independent variables (i.e. there is no exact multicollinearity between explaining variables).
3. The conditional distribution of the error term u given all x has zero expected mean. This conditional mean assumption implies that x and u are uncorrelated. However, if x and u are correlated the conditional mean is nonzero (Stock and Watson, 2003: 103–105 and 156).
4. The error term has constant variance for all observations.
5. Errors corresponding to different observations are independent and hence uncorrelated (i.e. there is no serial dependence of the error terms).
6. The error term is normally distributed.

Based on these assumptions, the OLS (ordinary least square) estimators are best linear unbiased estimators (BLUE), meaning that they are linear, unbiased, consistent, and efficient (Asteriou, 2006: 34–39). However, violations of these assumptions lead to several problems. The consequences of violations of the most important assumptions are outlined below.

Violation of assumption two leads to the problem of multicollinearity. In this case the OLS estimators cannot be calculated (Asteriou, 2006: 90–92). However, when there exists imperfect multicollinearity between the explanatory variables (i.e. the explanatory variables in the regression equation are correlated, but this correlation is less than one) then it is possible to obtain OLS estimates which are BLUE. Although these estimates are BLUE, imperfect multicollinearity affects the value of the variances and the standard errors. Both tend to be large when there is a relatively high degree of multicollinearity. Moreover, the signs of the estimated coefficients can be the opposite of those expected and the addition or deletion of a few observations might result in substantial changes in the estimated coefficients (Asteriou, 2006: 93–96).

One of the most important problems in econometrics is that in reality the 'true' form or specification of the equation that is estimated is unknown. A common specification error is to estimate an equation that omits one or more influential explanatory variables that belong to the 'true' specification. The problem leads to the omitted variable bias, which violates assumption three, that the expected mean of the error term is zero. Additionally, if the omitted variable is correlated with any of the explanatory variables included in the equation, the error term u is no longer independent of the explanatory variables (Asteriou, 2006: 167–168). In other words, if an omitted variable is a determinant of y, then it is contained in the disturbance term. If it is correlated with any of the x, then the disturbance term is correlated with x. Hence, u and x are correlated and the conditional mean of u given x is nonzero (Stock and Watson, 2003: 145). This results in the OLS estimators of β_1, $\beta_2, \ldots$, β_k to be inconsistent and biased (Asteriou, 2006: 168). The size of the bias is positively related to the correlation between the regressors and the error term. The direction of the bias in the OLS estimators depends on whether x and u are positively or negatively correlated (Stock and Watson, 2003: 145–146).

Violation of assumption four, which says that the variance of the conditional distribution of u_i, given x_i, is constant for all entities, leads to the problem of heteroskedasticity. Homoskedasticity, in contrast, refers to constant variance of the conditional distribution of the disturbance term (Asteriou, 2006: 106). When the assumption of homoskedasticity does not hold, then the OLS estimators are not BLUE. As long as the explanatory variables are not correlated with the error term, the OLS estimators are still unbiased and consistent even in the case of heteroskedasticity. However, heteroskedasticity makes the OLS estimators of the βs inefficient.

Additionally, it affects the variances and the standard errors of the estimated βs in the sense that both are underestimated (Asteriou, 2006: 109). In such a case it is possible to construct an estimator that has a smaller variance than the OLS estimator. This is done by the weighted least squares-method (WLS) where the observations are weighted by the inverse of the square root of the conditional variance of the error term u_i, given x_i (Stock and Watson, 2003: 127). Generally, heteroskedasticity is more likely to appear in a cross-sectional setting than in a time-series framework (Asteriou, 2006: 106).

Assumption five states that the covariances and correlations between different error terms are all zero (i.e. $Cov(u_t, u_s) = 0$ for all $t \neq s$), meaning that the error terms u_t and u_s are independently distributed. However, if this assumption does not hold, then the error terms are not pairwise independent but are pairwise autocorrelated (or serially correlated). Then $Cov(u_t, u_s) \neq 0$ for all $t \neq s$ and an error that occurs in a period t may be carried over to the next period t+1 (Asteriou, 2006: 140). Autocorrelation may be induced by omitted variables. If an omitted variable x_{it} is included in the error term u_t, and the omitted variable exhibits a trend over time, there is autocorrelation among u_t and u_{t-1}, u_{t-2} etc. (Asteriou, 2006: 140). When there is autocorrelation in the error term, the OLS estimations of the regression slopes are still unbiased and consistent, but inefficient and hence not BLUE. Also the estimated variances of the regression coefficients are biased and inconsistent (Asteriou, 2006: 143).

6.2 Panel data

6.2.1 General

Panel data sets consist of a time series for each cross-sectional member in the data set. The key feature of panel data is the fact that the same cross-sectional units (e.g. individuals, firms, countries, etc.) are observed over a certain period of time (Wooldridge, 2006: 10).

Panel data sets can be classified along two dimensions. First, if the sample consists of a constant number of time periods for all cross-sectional units, the data set is 'balanced'. Otherwise, when observations are missing for some of the time periods of the cross-sectional units the panel is 'unbalanced' (Asteriou, 2006: 369).

A second classification, following Stimson (1985), is based on the number of cross-sections as opposed to the number of time periods in the data set. Panel data sets are referred to as cross-sectionally dominant when the number of cross-sections is greater than the number of time points (N>T) or time-serially dominant when the number of time points is greater than the number of cross-sections (T>N) (Stimson, 1985: 918 and 928–929).

6.2.2 The omitted variables problem

The primary motivation of using panel data is that incorporating information related to both cross-section and time-series variables can solve the omitted variable problem (Wooldridge, 2002: 247). Panel data sets allow controlling for individual-specific effects that are correlated with other included independent variables and are either unobservable or left out of the regression model (Hausman and Taylor, 1981: 1377). Ignoring individual or time-specific effects that exist among cross-sectional or time-series units and are not captured by the included explanatory variables might lead to parameter heterogeneity in the model specification. If this heterogeneity is ignored, estimates of parameters might be inconsistent or meaningless (Hsiao, 2003: 8).

The main idea of panel data models is to regard any unobserved factor (also called unobserved component, latent variable or unobserved heterogeneity) affecting the dependent variable as consisting of two effects: those that are constant and those that vary over time (Wooldridge, 2002: 251 and 2006: 461).

6.2.3 The basic linear unobserved effects panel data model

Letting i denote the cross-sectional unit (e.g. individual, firm, city, etc.) and t the time period, a linear panel data model with two time periods and unobserved effects (i.e. omitted variables) that includes only one explanatory variable can be written as (Wooldridge, 2006: 461)

$$y_{it} = \beta_0 + \delta_0 d2_t + \beta_1 x_{it} + a_i + u_{it} \qquad t = 1, 2 \qquad (6.2)$$

The variable $d2_t$ is a dummy variable that equals zero when t = 1 and one when t = 2. Obviously, only T-1 time binary variables can be included in the regression to avoid perfect collinearity among the explanatory variables. This time dummy variable does not change across i, and hence has no i subscript. The parameter δ_0 for the time dummy variable contains the time effect (Stock and Watson, 2003: 284). So, in period one the intercept is β_0 and in period two it is $\beta_0 + \delta_0$. The variable x_{it} may contain observable variables that change across t but not i, variables that change across i but not t, and variables that change across i and t. The variable a_i captures all unobserved, time-constant factors that affect the dependent variable y_{it} and is usually referred to as unobserved component, latent variable, or unobserved heterogeneity.[87] If i indexes firms, then a_i is sometimes called firm effect (Wooldridge, 2002: 251). The error term u_{it} is often referred to as idiosyncratic error, idiosyncratic disturbances, or time-varying error because it represents all unobserved factors that change over time and affect the dependent variable y_{it} (Wooldridge, 2002: 251 and 2006: 461).

Referring to Mundlak (1978), Wooldridge suggests that the key issue regarding a_i is whether or not it is uncorrelated with all observed explanatory variables x_{it}. In modern econometrics, "random effect" therefore stands for zero correlation between the observed explanatory variables and the unobserved effect (i.e. $Cov(x_{it}, a_i) = 0, t = 1, 2, \ldots, T$), while "fixed effect" is synonymous with a_i being allowed to correlate with x_{it} (Wooldridge, 2002: 252).

6.2.4 Methods of estimation

6.2.4.1 Pooled OLS estimation

Equation (6.2) can be estimated by pooling the data and applying OLS. This method, however, has certain drawbacks. These disadvantages of the pooled OLS estimation can be shown by writing equation (6.2) as

$$y_{it} = \beta_0 + \delta_0 d2_t + \beta_1 x_{it} + v_{it} \qquad t = 1, 2 \qquad (6.3)$$

where $v_{it} = a_i + u_{it}$ is the composite error.

As explained in assumption three of the multiple regression model, it is necessary to assume that the unobserved effect a_i is uncorrelated with the explanatory variable x_{it} in order to consistently estimate β. Hence, even if u_{it} is uncorrelated with x_{it}, pooled OLS is biased and inconsistent if a_i and x_{it} are correlated. The resulting bias in pooled OLS is the omitted variable bias discussed above (Wooldridge, 2006: 462). However, in

[87] When the cross-section is a firm, such time-constant factors might, for instance, be managerial quality or structure (Wooldridge, 2002: 248).

most applications the main reason for collecting panel data is to allow the unobserved effect a_i to be correlated with the explanatory variables, which, however, leads to biased and inconsistent estimates. Therefore, other estimation methods are required that generate unbiased, consistent and efficient parameters.

6.2.4.2 First differencing estimation

To be able to allow the unobserved effect a_i to be correlated with the explanatory variables x_{it}, the first-differencing (FD) transformation can be applied. Applying this method differences the data across the years and thereby eliminates the unobserved effect a_i. Although this comes at the cost of losing the first time period for each cross-section, the β_1 parameter does not change by differencing equation (6.2). In a two year context the first-differenced equation is

$$\Delta y_{it} = \delta_0 + \beta_1 \Delta x_i + \Delta u_i \qquad (6.4)$$

where Δ denotes the change from t = 1 to t = 2. When comparing equation (6.4) to equation (6.2) it can be seen that the unobserved effect a_i has been differenced away and the intercept in equation (6.4) is now the change in the intercept from t = 1 to t = 2. In equation (6.4), Δu_i is uncorrelated with Δx_i under the assumption that the idiosyncratic error u_{it} is uncorrelated with the explanatory variable in both time periods. Since the time-constant unobserved effect is differenced away, it is now allowed to be correlated with x_{it} but delivers unbiased and consistent estimates of β_1 when applying OLS (Wooldridge, 2002: 281 and 2006: 463). Equation (6.4) can naturally be extended to data sets with more than two periods.[88]

For more than three time periods the first-differenced equation is

$$\Delta y_{it} = \delta_0 + \delta_3 d3_t + \delta_4 d4_t + \ldots + \delta_T dT_t + \beta_1 \Delta x_{it1} + \ldots + \beta_k \Delta x_{itk} + \Delta u_{it} \qquad (6.5)$$

with t = 2, 3, …, T. Equation (6.5) includes an intercept and T-1 time periods on each unit i for the first-differenced equation to account for secular changes that are not being modeled (Wooldridge, 2006: 471).

[88] For more details on the three and more periods case see Wooldridge (2006: 470–475).

6.2.4.3 Fixed effects estimation

6.2.4.3.1 Estimation with cross-section fixed effects

The fixed effects (FE) estimation is a method for controlling for omitted variables in panel data when these unobserved variables vary across cross-sectional units but do not change over time. The fixed effects transformation is another way, like first differencing, to eliminate the unobserved fixed effect a_i. A model with k explanatory variables can be written as

$$y_{it} = \beta_1 x_{1,it} + \ldots + \beta_k x_{k,it} + a_i + u_{it} \qquad t = 1, 2, \ldots, T. \qquad (6.6)$$

The a_i in the fixed effects regression model can be interpreted as the unknown cross-section specific intercepts as it includes the common intercept β_0 as well as the unobserved variable a_i, which varies across entities. Hence, the slope coefficient is the same for all entities but the intercept of the regression line varies among cross-sections.[89]

The entity-specific intercepts in the fixed effects model also can be expressed by using binary variables to denote the individual entity. When there are more than two cross-sections, additional binary variables are needed to capture all the entity-specific intercepts in equation (6.6) (Stock and Watson, 2003: 278–279).

The fixed effects regression model in equation (6.6) can be written equivalently, by using binary variables, as

$$y_{it} = \beta_0 + \beta_1 x_{1,it} + \ldots + \beta_k x_{k,it} + \gamma_2 D2_i + \gamma_3 D3_i + \ldots + \gamma_n Dn_i + u_{it} \qquad (6.7)$$

where $D1_i$ is a binary variable that equals one when i = 1 and equals zero otherwise. $D2_i$ equals one when i = 2 and zero otherwise, etc. To avoid perfectly multicollinear regressors only N-1 entity-specific dummies can be included.

This shows that there are two equivalent ways to write the fixed effects regression model. In equation (6.6) there are N cross-section-specific intercepts, while in equation

[89] Equation (6.6) focuses exclusively on the cross-section effects. Unlike the basic linear unobserved effects panel data model in equation (6.2), equation (6.6) does not include a time effect. The time effects is explained separately in the following subsection.

(6.7) the model has a common intercept β_0 and N-1 binary regressors. Therefore, in total, equation (6.7) has k + N regressors (the k explanatory variables, the N-1 binary variables and the intercept β_0) (Stock and Watson, 2003: 280).

As the number of entities might be large, regression software packages typically have special routines for OLS estimation of fixed effects regression models. These routines are equivalent to using OLS on the full binary variable regression as shown by equation (6.7), but are faster because they employ some mathematical simplifications. Software packages compute the OLS fixed effects estimator in a two step process (Stock and Watson, 2003: 280–281). First, equation (6.6) is averaged over time for each cross-section i which leads to

$$\overline{y}_i = \beta_1 \overline{x}_{it} + a_i + \overline{u}_i \qquad t = 1, 2, \ldots, T. \qquad (6.8)$$

In equation (6.8) $\overline{y}_i$ is the sum of all y_{it} divided by T, $\overline{x}_{it}$ is the sum of all x_{it} divided by T and $\overline{u}_i$ represents the sum of all u_i divided by T. Since a_i is fixed over time, it appears in equations (6.6) and (6.8). Now equation (6.8) is subtracted from equation (6.6) to arrive at the fixed effects transformed equation (6.9) that can be written as

$$y_{it} - \overline{y}_i = \beta_1(x_{it} - \overline{x}_i) + u_{it} - \overline{u}_i \qquad t = 1, 2, \ldots, T. \qquad (6.9)$$

The difference between y_{it} and $\overline{y}_i$ leads to time-demeaned data on y, and similarly for the difference between x_{it} and $\overline{x}_i$ as well as u_{it} and $\overline{u}_i$. This fixed effects transformation, which is also called within transformation, lets the unobserved time-constant effect a_i disappear. Now the assumption that all u_{it} and $\overline{u}_i$ are uncorrelated with x_{it} and $\overline{x}_i$ for all time periods holds and pooled OLS can be applied to equation (6.9). This method is also known as fixed effects or within estimation (Wooldridge, 2002: 268). The latter name comes from the fact that OLS estimation on equation (6.9) uses the time variation in y and x within each cross-section (Wooldridge, 2006: 486). Because of the time-constant effect, a_i, being transformed away, the fixed effects regression models allows for arbitrary correlation between a_i and the explanatory variables in any time period contrary to assumption three of the multiple linear regression model.

A disadvantage of the fixed effects model is that it ignores all explanatory variables that don't vary over time. Hence, it is not possible to include time-constant factors in the model (Asteriou, 2006: 371). The reason is that there is no way to distinguish the effects of time-constant observables from the time-constant unobservable a_i. When analyzing firms, a time-constant industry classification, for instance, cannot be included in x_{it} unless industry classification changes over time for at least some firms.

6.2.4.3.2 Estimation with time fixed effects

While fixed effects for each cross-section can control for variables that are constant over time but differ across entities, time fixed effects can control for variables that are constant across entities but evolve over time.

Equation (6.6) can be modified by including a time effect s_t as well as a common intercept (Stock and Watson, 2003: 283):

$$y_{it} = \beta_0 + \beta_1 x_{it} + \beta_2 s_t + a_i + u_{it} \qquad (6.10)$$

Equation (6.10) includes the variable $\beta_2 s_t$, which determines y_{it}, but is unobserved and changes over time and is constant across all cross-sections (as indicated by the subscript t). Assuming that s_t is correlated with x_{it}, then omitting s_t from the regression leads to the omitted variable bias. The factor $\beta_2 s_t$ can be eliminated by replacing it by a set of T binary variables, each indicating a different year. These binary variables are referred to as time effects.

Leaving the cross-section fixed effect a_i aside and looking exclusively at the time effects, a time effects regression model with a single explanatory variable and T-1 time effects, indicated by the binary variables $d1_t$, …, dT_t can be written as

$$y_{it} = \beta_0 + \beta_1 x_{it} + \delta_2 d2_t + \ldots + \delta_T dT_t + u_{it} \qquad (6.11)$$

where δ_2, …, δ_T are unknown coefficients. In equation (6.11) $d1_t$ equals 1 if t is the first time period and zero otherwise and $d2_t$ equals 1 if t is the second time period and so forth. The first binary variable, $d1_t$ is excluded to prevent perfect multicollinearity (Stock and Watson, 2003: 283–284).

6.2.4.3.3 Estimation with both cross-section and time fixed effects

If there are omitted variables that are constant over time but vary across cross-sections while others are constant across cross-sections but vary over time, it is appropriate to include both cross-section and time effects in the regression. This is done by including both N-1 cross-section binary variables and T-1 time binary variables together with the intercept. A model with both such effects and a single explanatory variable can be written as

$$y_{it} = \beta_0 + \beta_1 x_{it} + \gamma_2 D2_i + \ldots + \gamma_n Dn_i + \delta_2 d2_t + \ldots + \delta_T dT_t + u_{it} \tag{6.12}$$

where β_0, β_1, $\gamma_2, \ldots, \gamma_n$ and $\delta_2, \ldots, \delta_T$ are unknown coefficients and D2 is a binary variable that equals one when i = 2 and zero otherwise, etc. (Stock and Watson, 2003: 284). The dummy-variable coefficients would measure the change in the cross-section and time-series intercepts with respect to the first cross-section in the first period of time (Pindyck and Rubinfeld, 1998: 252). The combined time and cross-section fixed effects regression model eliminates the omitted variables bias arising from unobserved variables that are constant over time and those that are constant over entities (Stock and Watson, 2003: 284).

6.2.4.4 Random effects estimation

While the fixed effects model delivers unbiased and consistent estimators when the unobserved factor a_i is correlated with each x_{it}, the random effects (RE) model generates unbiased and consistent estimators only when a_i is uncorrelated with each explanatory variable in all time periods (Wooldridge, 2006: 494). If a_i is uncorrelated with the explanatory variables, the slopes coefficients can be estimated by using a single cross-section and there is no need for panel data. However, this would disregard much information in the other time periods. If a pooled OLS is carried out, the estimators are also consistent. Still, the following aspects would be ignored.

When it is assumed that using the composite error term $v_{it} = a_i + u_{it}$, equation (6.6) can be written as

$$y_{it} = \beta_0 + \beta_1 x_{1it} + \ldots + \beta_k x_{kit} + v_{it} \qquad t = 1, 2, \ldots, T. \tag{6.13}$$

Now, a_i is in the composite error term in each time period and the v_{it} can be shown to be serially correlated across time. Therefore, OLS estimation will be incorrect. To account for the serial correlation in v_{it}, a generalized least squares (GLS) estimator needs to be used when applying RE (Wooldridge, 2002: 265 and 2006: 494). The random effect transformation allows for explanatory variables that are constant over time.[90]

6.2.5 Comparison of estimation methods

6.2.5.1 Fixed effects or first differencing

When there are only two time periods, the choice between FE and FD estimation is easy since both methods generate identical results. However, when T>2 the choice between FE and FD depends on the assumptions about the idiosyncratic errors u_{it} (Wooldridge, 2002: 284). For T>2, both FE and FD are unbiased and consistent. Hence, the decision criterion depends on the relative efficiency of the estimators. For samples with large N and small T, however, the FE estimator is more efficient than the FD estimator, when the idiosyncratic errors u_{it} are serially uncorrelated. If u_{it} is substantially positively serially correlated, and hence following close to a random walk, the difference Δu_{it} is serially uncorrelated and an FD model is better (Wooldridge, 2006: 491). However, Wooldridge points out that in many applications the unobserved factors can be expected to be serially correlated and assuming that the u_{it} for all time periods are serially uncorrelated may be too strong. An alternative assumption is that the first differences of the error terms are serially uncorrelated (and have constant variance) (Wooldridge, 2002: 281). As it is difficult to measure whether u_{it} are serially uncorrelated after FE estimation (only the time-demeaned errors $u_{it} - \bar{u}_i$ can be tested, but not the u_{it}) it will be tested whether Δu_{it} obtained from the FD model are serially uncorrelated. If this is the case, first differencing is better. If there is substantial negative serial correlation in Δu_{it}, fixed effects estimation is better (Wooldridge, 2006: 492).

6.2.5.2 Fixed effects or random effects

Referring to Mundlak (1978), Wooldridge (2002) makes the point that the key issue involving the choice between FE and RE is whether or not the unobserved effect a_i is assumed to be uncorrelated with the observed explanatory variables x_{it}. While FE models allow for arbitrary correlation between the unobserved effect a_i and the observed explanatory variables x_{it}, RE models stand for zero correlation between the observed explanatory variables and the unobserved effect (Wooldridge, 2002: 252).

[90] As it can almost always be assumed that the unobserved effect is correlated with the included explanatory variables the random effects approach will not be addressed in detail at this point. For a further discussion see, e.g., Wooldridge (2002: 257–265).

Following Wooldridge (2006), FE models are a more convincing tool for estimating ceteris paribus effects (Wooldridge, 2006: 497). RE models, on the other hand, are used when the key explanatory variable is constant over time. Then RE models or pooled OLS models are preferred over FE. In general, however, RE models, are preferred to pooled OLS because they are more efficient methods of estimation (Wooldridge, 2006: 497).[91]

[91] A foundation for deciding between the fixed and random effects approach is provided by the Hausman test. It is based on the idea that under the hypothesis of no correlation, both OLS and GLS are consistent but OLS is inefficient (Asteriou, 2006: 372). For further details see, e.g., Wooldridge (2002: 288–291), Asteriou (2006: 372–373), or Plasmans (2006: 283–284).

7 Empirical study

7.1 Research gap

Theoretical arguments suggest that stakeholder issues are of serious concern for management when making corporate financial decisions (similar Parsons and Titman, 2007: 50). Hitherto, extant literature has provided only rare direct empirical evidence for these stakeholder issues. Due to the early contributions by Titman (1984), the most advanced research stream is on the firm's capital structure choice, which partially includes stakeholder arguments. As shown in section 4.3, the firm's capital structure decision is only one component in a stakeholder rationale for risk management that takes other corporate financial decisions, such as liquidity and dividend policy, into account. The theoretical arguments as well as the empirical results presented in section 4.3 and chapter 5 are supportive of the concept of a stakeholder reasoning for risk management. However, until now, empirical research on the SRRM has been rare. Lim and Wang (2007), for instance, assert that the stakeholder-oriented stream of risk management literature is, in general, still relatively underdeveloped (Lim and Wang, 2007: 644).

This dissertation aims at providing further empirical evidence on the the firm-NFS relationship as a determinant of corporate finance decisions. It is analyzed whether firms that are more dependent on non-financial stakeholder claims make more conservative financial decisions than firms that are less dependent on such claims. Additionally, it is also analyzed whether there is a difference in the relevance of various stakeholder groups (i.e. customers, suppliers, employees) for the firm's corporate financial decisions. This study concentrates on the capital structure and the cash holdings decisions of non-financial Austrian and German companies.

7.2 Hypotheses

Based on the stakeholder rationale for risk management, the following hypothesis was set up (see also section 4.3.2 for the development of the hypotheses):

> Hypothesis 1: The degree of conservativeness of the firm's financial policies is positively associated with the extent to which the firm is dependent on implicit claims with its non-financial stakeholders, cp.

Based on hypothesis 1, the following two subhypotheses are tested in this study:

> H1.1: The firm's debt level is negatively associated with the extent to which the firm is dependent on implicit claims with its non-financial stakeholders, cp.

> H 1.2: The firm's level of cash holdings is positively associated with the extent to which the firm is dependent on implicit claims with its non-financial stakeholders, cp.

7.3 Data

7.3.1 Data collection

The data to test these hypotheses were obtained from the *Datastream* database in January 2006 and comprise information on the consolidated financial statements of Austrian and German public companies.

A *Datastream* request was made for the complete list of Austrian and German stocks available in the database as of January 25th, 2006 and resulted in an initial sample of 1,048 firms.[92] The following data were downloaded for the respective firms for the period 1998–2004:[93] total liabilities (03351), market capitalization (public) per year end (08004), book value – outstanding shares (05491), total assets (02999), intangible other assets (02649), net sales or revenues (01001), capital expenditures (additions to fixed assets) (04601), operating income (01250), funds from operations (04201), research & development expense (01201), EBITDA (18198), cost of goods sold (01051), salaries & benefits expenses (01084), property, plant & equipment (02301), depreciation, depletion & amortization (01151), depreciation (01148), accumulated depreciation (02401), short term debt & current portion of long term debt (03051), long term debt (03251), accounts payable (03040), pretax income (01401), net income before preferred dividends (01651), interest expense on debt (01251), working capital (03151), short term investments (02008), cash & short term investments (i.e. cash &

---

[92] In order to receive data of the full list of Austrian and German stocks, the *Datastream* request was made for the *Datastream*-lists ALLAS (i.e. All Austrian Equities) and FER1 (i.e. German research stocks from A-K) and FER2 (i.e. German research stocks from L-Z).

[93] *Datastream* field numbers in brackets.

cash equivalents) (02001), cash dividends paid (04551), accounting standards followed (07536).[94]

7.3.2 Sample deletion process

Data were structured in *Microsoft Excel* and stacked by cross-section with all of the sequentially dated observations from 1998 to 2004 for each cross-section grouped together. Five steps were taken to exclude certain firms and to arrive at a net sample size of 597 firms. The steps taken are described below.

The first step aimed at checking the official websites of the Austrian and German stock exchanges[95] to identify companies that have already been delisted but are still included in the *Datastream* sample. In total 210 firms were deleted due to delistings from the Austrian and German stock exchange.

Secondly, the websites of the stock exchanges were screened to identify the country of origin of the respective firm. A dummy variable was introduced to distinguish between firms from Austria/Germany and firms from other countries. In total 24 firms were not of Austrian or German origin and thus excluded from the sample.

Thirdly, the website of each company was checked to find out whether the respective firm went bankrupt within the period 1998 and 2004. A dummy variable was used to distinguish between firms that went insolvent in the respective time period and such that did not. A total of 70 firms were excluded due to insolvency within the respective period.

Step four was taken in order to classify the *Datastream* firms by industry. This classification is based on the NACE Statistical Classification of Economic Activities in the European Community, Rev. 1.1 (2002)[96], which is provided in the *Amadeus* database for each individual firm. In order to assure highest possible accuracy of the industry classification, the NACE codes from *Amadeus* were compared to each company's business description on its website. When necessary, the NACE codes

94 For a definition of the data see the Thomson Worldscope Database Datatype Definitions Guide (2003).

95 See http://www.wienerborse.at/ and http://deutsche-boerse.com/

96 See http://ec.europa.eu/eurostat/ramon/nomenclatures/index.cfm?TargetUrl=LST_NOM_DTL&StrNom=NACE_1_1&StrLanguageCode=EN&IntPcKey=&StrLayoutCode=HIERARCHIC&IntCurrentPage=1

taken from *Amadeus* were revised after screening the firm's website. All firms belonging to the financial services or real estate industry (four-digit NACE codes beginning with 65, 66, 67 and 70) were excluded from the sample. This step reduced the initial sample by 120 firms.

Finally, 27 firms were deleted because either the solvency or the industry status remained unknown even after checking the firms' websites as well as the *Amadeus* database.

The following table shows the reduction of the full sample for each of the five steps for both German and Austrian firms.

	GER	AUT	Total
Initial full sample	909	139	1,048
Step 1: Non tradable	149	61	210
Step 2: No Austrian or German origin	22	2	24
Step 3: Insolvency	70	0	70
Step 4: Financial services or real estate industry	97	23	120
Step 5: Solvency or industry status unknown	21	6	27
Total number of firms (net sample)	550	47	597

Table 1: Sample deletion process

7.3.3 Subsamples based on reported accounting standards

The total number of 597 firms for the period from 1998 to 2004 resulted in a maximum of 4,179 observations per variable. However, firms reported their financial statements according to different accounting standards. To control for differences between these accounting standards, especially between book-value and market-value oriented standards, the Overall sample was split into three subsamples based on the reported accounting standards.

For 932 observations *Datastream* did not report any accounting standard. Hence, data for these observations were excluded from the sample, leaving a maximum of 3,247 available data points. The different accounting standards reported were: "International standards", "IFRS", "International standards and some EEC guidelines", "US standards (GAAP)", "US GAAP reclassified from local standards", "Local standards with some EEC guidelines", "Local standards with EEC and IASC guidelines", and "Local standards". To avoid too many and too small subsamples three groups of accounting standards were built. "Local standards", "Local standards with some EEC guidelines", and "Local standards with EEC and IASC guidelines" were subsumed under "Local Standards", "International standards", "IFRS", and "International standards and some EEC guidelines" were grouped under "IFRS", and "US standards (GAAP)" and "US GAAP reclassified from local standards" were subsumed under "US GAAP".[97] This procedure assures to differentiate between national book-value oriented accounting standards (i.e. the Austrian "Unternehmensgesetzbuch" and German "Handelsgesetzbuch") and international market-value orientied standards (i.e. IAS/IFRS and US GAAP).

Table two below shows that the maximum number of observations was reduced to 3,247 due to non-reporting of any accounting standard. The remaining 3,247 data points represent the Overall sample and were split among the three categories of accounting standards with 1,633 observations falling under the Local Standards category, 1,041 observations in the IFRS category and 573 observations in the US GAAP category.

	Local Standards	IFRS	US GAAP	Overall
Net sample				4,179
No accounting standard defined				932
Number of available observations per accounting standard	1,633	1,041	573	3,247

Table 2: Observations by accounting standard for the sample period 1998-2004

The following table shows the number of different firms, observations, and missing values for each of the subsamples. The difference between the total number of firm illustrated in table one (i.e. 597) and the total number of firms in the Overall sample

[97] Note that German and Austrian firms following their respective local accounting standards are pooled together under "Local Standards". Since, however, the differences between the German and the Austrian accounting rules and regulations is small, distortions from pooling these data are expected to be negligible.

(i.e. 593) illustrated in table three is due to the non-reporting of any accounting standard of four firms.

	Local Standards	IFRS	US GAAP	Overall
Number of different firms per accounting standard	386	286	137	593
Max. number of observations	2,702	2,002	959	4,151
Number of available observations per accounting standard	1,633	1,041	573	3,247
Missing values (in total)	1,069	961	386	904
Missing values (in percent)	39.56%	48.00%	40.25%	21.78%

Table 3: Missing values by accounting standard for the sample period 1998-2004

A detailed overview of the industry allocation based on the NACE classification of economic activity within each of the three subsamples is given in appendix A.

7.4 Variables

A first examination of the descriptive statistics of all variables revealed high values of skewness and kurtosis due to outlier problems. Since, however, least squares procedures are very sensitive to data points that lie far from the true regression line (Pindyck and Rubinfeld, 1998: 7) all variables were winsorized at their 1st and 99th percentiles in order to reduce the effect of outliers (analogously, e.g., Kale and Shahrur, 2007: 333; Dittmar et al., 2003: 119; Opler et al., 1999: 30; Burgstahler and Dichev, 1997: 103).

In the following subsections the construction of the variables used in the capital structure and the cash holdings models is explained.

7.4.1 Capital structure variables

7.4.1.1 Dependent variable

Previous studies use either leverage (i.e. debt over the sum of debt and equity), or gearing (i.e. debt over equity) to empirically measure capital structure. The formula for leverage ensures that the measure is constrained within the range zero to one, while that for gearing guarantees a non-negative value. For both measures zero is the lower limit that signifies the absence of debt (Jordan et al., 1998: 9).

Additionally, a distinction can be made between market and book values of debt and equity when measuring capital structure.[98] However, Bowman (1980) states that the misspecification due to using book value measures is fairly small (Titman and Wessels, 1988: 7; Barton et al., 1989: 40). Moreover, values of the capital structure variables can be calculated as a point-in-time-value at the end of the study period or by an arithmetic average of the annual values over the period of the study. The latter measure is capable of capturing the target capital-structure-mix of the firm that is independent of random year-to-year fluctuations (see, e.g., Barton et al., 1995: 40; Barton and Gordon, 1988: 627; Titman and Wessels, 1988: 8). Most of the previous studies employ several measures to account for both, market and book value of debt.

This study uses a leverage ratio to measure capital structure in terms of book value of debt and market value of equity. The dependent variable is defined as book value of debt proxied by total liabilities (*Datastream* field number 03351) over the sum of market capitalization (public) per year end (08004) to proxy for the market value of equity and book value of debt, again proxied by total liabilities (03351), in percent. Analogously to O'Brien (2003), the ratio is transformed by taking the natural log.[99] Rajan and Zingales (1995) emphasize that using total liabilities in the numerator of the leverage ratio is the broadest definition of leverage. This definition of leverage can be viewed as a proxy for what is left for shareholders in the case of liquidation. Since total liabilities also include items like accounts payable, which may be used primarily for transactions purposes rather than for financing, this definition of leverage may overstate the amount of leverage (Rajan and Zingales, 1995: 1428). In the Rajan and Zingales (1995) study, this proxy for leverage in fact delivered the highest values compared to other definitions of leverage (Rajan and Zingales, 1995: 1430).[100]

---

[98] See, e.g., Barton et al. (1989) and Rajan and Zingales (1995).

[99] Except for a difference in the R-squared, O'Brien reports that his results are identical if an untransformed dependent variable is employed (O'Brien, 2003: 422).

[100] Note that the *Datastream* item 03351 (i.e. total liabilities) employed in the dependent variable includes, among others, current liabilities (03101), which represent debt or other obligations that are due in one year. Hence, also accounts payables are included in the numerator of the leverage ratio employed (Thomson Worldscope Database Datatype Definitions Guide, 2003: 222 and 432). This might result in high leverage ratios as shown by Rajan and Zingales (1995: 1430).

7.4.1.2 Independent financial control variables

Using the above described raw data from *Datastream*, the following financial control variables have been constructed.

Characteristics of assets

Based on Williamson's (1988) redeployability argument on the firm's assets as well as the well known arguments by Jensen and Meckling (1976) and Myers (1977), it is argued that the type of assets owned by a firm affects its capital structure choice (Titman and Wessels, 1988: 3). A positive relationship between the collateral value of assets and the debt ratio is expected. It is usually assumed that intangible assets have a lower redeployability value than tangible assets as these types of assets are more firm-specific than tangible assets. This argument is consistent with a stakeholder-based concept of the firm. Following Titman and Wessels (1988), an asset structure measure is included that is defined as the ratio of intangible assets (02649) over total assets (02999) multiplied by 100.[101] Since the numerator of the *Characteristics of assets* variable is defined as intangible assets instead of tangible assets as in many studies, a negative relation between *Characteristics of assets* and leverage is expected to support the arguments of transaction cost and agency theory.

Growth opportunities

Jensen and Meckling (1976) and Myers (1977) show that equity-controlled firms tend to invest suboptimally to expropriate wealth from the firm's bondholders. The cost associated with this agency relationship is likely to be higher for firms in high growth industries that are more flexible regarding their investment decisions (Titman and Wessels, 1988: 4). Hence, firms with high growth opportunities should choose lower debt ratios. From a static trade-off theory viewpoint, a negative relation between leverage and growth opportunities is expected too. The argument is that growth firms lose more of their value in the case of financial distress (Frank and Goyal, 2005: 37). On the other hand, the pecking order theory predicts that firms with more investments, holding profitability fixed, should accumulate more debt over time. Hence, from this

[101] The *Datastream* item 02649 (i.e. intangible assets) includes, among others, goodwill, patents, copyrights, trademarks, capitalized advertising costs, customer lists, etc. (for the complete definition of this *Datastream* item see the Thomson Worldscope Database Datatype Definitions Guide, 2003: 307). Hence, differences in the treatment of the various types of intangible assets in the national book-value and the international market-value oriented accounting standards may generate regression results that are incomparable across the accounting-specific subsamples. Appendix B illustrates that the mean and median values of *Characteristics of assets* are much lower in the group of firms following book-value oriented Local Standards.

viewpoint, a positive relation between growth and leverage is expected (Frank and Goyal, 2005: 37).

In this study an indicator of growth is included that captures the firm's capital expenditures. This proxy for growth opportunities follows Titman and Wessels (1988: 4) and Vicente-Lorente (2001: 168) and is measured as capital expenditure (04601) divided by total assets (02999) multiplied by 100. Vicente-Lorente argues that a growth proxy based on capital investment expenditure reflects the long-term growth opportunities. Furthermore, it is homogeneous to R&D ratios and, therefore, allows comparative analysis of the effects of tangible and other intangible investments on financial leverage (Vicente-Lorente, 2001: 168).

Another possible indicator of growth opportunities that is used in other studies is the market-to-book ratio. However, this ratio can alternatively be interpreted as a proxy for Net Organization Capital, since it measures at the same time the size of intangible assets (Speckbacher and Wentges, 2005: 20). The market-to-book measure is included as explanatory variable, however, it is interpreted as a proxy for the firm's dependence on the implicit claims with its non-financial stakeholders.

Size

From a trade-off theoretical viewpoint, it is argued that larger firms have easier access to capital markets and borrow at more favourable interest rates. Therefore, a positive relationship between size and leverage is proposed (Ozkan, 2001: 179–180). Another argument in favor of a relationship in this direction can be derived when interpreting size as an inverse proxy for bankrupcty. As large firms are usually more diversified, bankruptcy risk is lower (Rajan and Zingales, 1995: 1451; Frank and Goyal, 2005: 38). Therefore, these firms may have higher leverage. As in other studies, a natural logarithmic transformation of net sales (01001) is used to proxy for the firm's size (see, e.g., Titman and Wessels (1988), and Rajan and Zingales (1995)).

Profitability

According to Myers (1984) and Myers and Majluf's (1984), unusually profitable firms with a slow growth rate will end up with an unusually low leverage ratio compared to its competitors within the same industry, holding investments and dividends fixed. This is because profitable firms prefer retained earnings to finance investments, according to pecking order theory (Ozkan, 2005: 181; Frank and Goyal, 2005: 39). For this reason, profitability should be negatively related to leverage (Vicente-Lorente, 2001: 168). Static trade-off theory, on the other hand, asserts that expected bankruptcy costs are lower and interest tax shields have a higher value for profitable firms (Frank and Goyal, 2005: 39). Therefore, profitable firms should have more debt. The chosen proxy for profitability is defined as EBITDA (18198) as a percentage of total assets (02999) and follows Rajan and Zingales (1995).

The four variables *Characteristics of assets*, *Growth opportunites*, *Size* and *Profitability* used in this study have shown up most consistently as being correlated with leverage in previous studies (Rajan and Zingales, 1995: 1451). Previous studies also show that taxes influence the capital structure decision (see, e.g., DeAngelo and Masulis (1980) and Titman and Wessels (1988)). As in other recent papers (see, e.g., Gaud et al. (2005)), the tax effect is not taken into account in this study. This is due to a lack of data availability regarding taxes, as well as the general difficulty in determining the tax shield, which heavily depends on the choice of the appropriate marginal tax rate (Gaud et al., 2005: 56).

Some papers include some measure of risk as an explanatory variable of debt levels, arguing that the amount of debt is a decreasing function of the volatility of earnings (see, e.g., Titman and Wessels (1988) and Vicente-Lorente (2001)), while others exclude such a measure (see, e.g., Ozkan (2001)). Typically, a minimum number of consecutive firm-year observations are required to construct such a risk proxy (Kale and Shahrur, 2007: 333). The unbalanced panel structure of the subsamples leads to many missing firm observations for consecutive years. Therefore, no volatility measure that relates profit or cash flow to an asset base of the previous year is employed in the models.

The exclusion of a tax and a risk variable might cause an omitted variables problem. It can be assumed that profitability, which is included as a regressor, is correlated with both, the tax shield as well as the volatility of profits. However, the panel data methodology applied in this study controls the omitted variables problem.

7.4.2 Cash holdings variables

7.4.2.1 Dependent variable

Measurements of liquid asset holdings in empirical studies are usually defined as the ratio of cash plus marketable securities to total assets (e.g. Kim et al., 1998: 349). Ozkan and Ozkan (2004: 2121) use this ratio and regress its single year value to several independent variables averaged over a period of the four preceding years. Similarly, Mikkelson and Partch (2003: 283) estimate a regression of this cash-to-assets-ratio on a mixture of independent variables of the same year and on average values of a longer period including the measurement period of the independent variable. Opler et al. (1999) and Dittmar et al. (2003) divide the numerator by total assets minus cash and marketable securities (i.e. net assets). Their main reason for netting out cash from assets is that a firm's profitability is related to assets in place and cash should be measured relative to this (Opler et al., 1999: 15; Dittmar et al., 2003: 118). Opler et al. (1999: 15) report that they also measure liquidity using a cash-to-sales-ratio instead of a cash-to-assets-ratio, which, however, did not affect their main conclusions. Hence, it can be assumed that both proxies for cash are equivalent and do not influence results. Moreover, Dittmar et al. (2003: 121) use a logarithmic transformation of cash and equivalents divided by net assets as do Opler et al. (1999).

Following Dittmar et al. (2003) and Opler et al. (1999), the dependent variable in the cash holdings model is calculated as the natural logarithm of the ratio cash & cash equivalents (02001) in percent of the sum of the book values of total assets (02999) minus cash & cash equivalents (02001).

7.4.2.2 Independent financial control variables

Using the above described raw data from *Datastream*, the following financial control variables have been constructed based on a review of previous empirical studies in the field of cash holdings.

Size

Analogously to Kim et al. (1998), a negative relationship between firm size and the dependent variable is expected (Kim et al., 1998: 349). The underlying argument goes back to the static trade-off model that argues that there are economies of scale in liquid assets, so that larger firms should hold less cash (Opler et al., 1999: 14). The majority of the studies use a logarithmic transformation of total assets to account for size (see, e.g., Opler et al. (1999), Dittmar et al. (2003), and Ozkan and Ozkan (2004)). To assure comparability of the results of this study across the two regression models, firm size is defined equivalently to the measure employed in the capital structure model. The firm size variable is defined as the natural logarithm of net sales (01001).[102]

Cash substitutes

Firms tend to liquidate receivables through factoring or securitization in order to raise liquidity. Moreover, firms may hold liquid assets apart from cash, and by having credit lines available (Opler et al., 2003: 16). Hence, a variable controlling for liquid asset substitutes is included. As in Dittmar et al. (2003: 121) and Opler et al. (1999: 16–17), this measure is defined as the ratio of net working capital to the sum of total assets (02999) minus cash & cash equivalents (02001), with net working capital defined as working capital (03151) less cash & cash equivalents (02001). The ratio of cash substitutes is also defined in percentage points. This variable captures additional sources of liquidity that may act as a complement or substitutes for cash (Dittmar et al., 2003: 119).

Growth opportunities

Arguing from a perspective of agency costs of external finance, growth opportunities are hypothesized to be a determinant of the firm's cash holdings. Again, growth opportunities are proxied by the ratio of the capital expenditure (04601) to total assets (02999) in percent (analogously, Bates et al. 2006: 13 and Opler et al. (1999)). Regarding the relationship between capital expenditure and cash levels, the trade-off theory and the financing hierarchy theory predict different relationships. While the former predicts a positive relationship, given the transaction cost motive, the latter predicts a negative sign (Dittmar et al., 2003: 116; see also section 5.3.1.1).

Leverage/liquidity constraints

With reference to Baskin (1987), Ozkan and Ozkan (2004) argue that the costs of funds used to invest in liquidity increases with the ratio of debt financing. This would imply a reduction in cash holdings with increased leverage (i.e. a negative relationship between these two variables) (Ozkan and Ozkan, 2004: 2108). It is argued that firms with access to debt markets can use borrowing as a substitute for maintaining liquid

---

[102] Note that Dittmar et al. (2003: 126) also use the natural log of sales instead of total assets in the case when sales are employed as the deflator. Moreover, Kim et al. (1998: 349) state that their reported results are the same if they use the natural logarithm of sales to proxy for size.

assets (Kim et al., 1998: 348). Additionally, it is possible that firms finance additional cash holdings through debt (Dittmar et al., 2003: 119), which would imply a positive relationship. Following previous studies (see, e.g., Ozkan and Ozkan (2004), Kim et al. (1998), and Opler et al. (1999)), leverage is measured as the ratio of book value of total liabilities (03351) over the book value of total assets (02999) in percentage points.

Dividend payments

Taking transaction cost theory as a starting point, the amount of dividend a firm currently pays influences its ability to raise funds, as the firm could easily cut back dividend payments. Hence, dividend paying firms are expected to hold less cash (Dittmar et al., 2003: 115). Firms that do not pay dividends have to use the possibly expensive external capital markets to raise funds (Opler et al., 1999: 9). As in Opler et al. (1999: 15) and Bates et al. (2006: 14), a dividend dummy is included that equals one when a cash dividend is paid in the respective year and zero otherwise.

Other studies include the R&D expense-to-sales ratio in their regression models based on the argument that this ratio measures the potential for financial distress costs (Opler et al., 1999: 16; Bates et al., 2006: 14). In this study, the financial distress costs are captured by the independent stakeholder variables, which are explained below. The customer variable is defined similarly to the R&D expense-to-sales ratio as R&D expense over total assets in percent.

Usually a risk measure is considered as an explanatory variable when modelling cash holdings (see, e.g., Kim et al. (1998), Opler et al. (1999), Schwetzler and Reimund (2004), Ozkan and Ozkan (2004), and Bates et al. (2006)). Ozkan and Ozkan (2004), for instance, proxy for risk by the standard deviation of cash flow divided by average total assets. Since a firm's cash flow is influenced partly by the level of net working capital, which is an element of the *Cash substitutes* variable, a correlation between the *Cash substitutes* variable and a cash flow-based risk variable can be assumed. However, as in the capital structure model the missing consecutive firm-year observations in the panel of the accounting-specific subsamples make it impossible to include a consistent and comparable volatility measure. Again, panel data methodology controls for this omitted variables problem.

7.4.3 Stakeholder variables

The importance of implicit and explicit contractual relations and claims between the firm and its stakeholders was explained throughout this work. The independent stakeholder variables that are used in this work are proxies for the extent to which the firm is dependent on implicit claims with NFS. Hence, these variables are identical for both models.

7.4.3.1 An accounting-based approach of measuring implicit stakeholder claims

A review of the existing literature reveals two concepts aiming at measuring a firm's dependence on implicit claims with its key stakeholders. One is used by Holder et al. (1998) and Barton et al. (1989), who use NOC as a determinant of capital structure and dividend policy decisions. Their proxies are based on Rumelt's (1974) diversification strategy-based proxy for NOC (see also sections 5.2.2.1 and 5.1.2.2.2).

The second concept is applied by Bowen et al. (hereafter BDS) (1995) and Matsumoto (2002) in an accounting context. These two papers investigate to what extent management's incentives regarding the firm's accounting decisions and earnings announcements are contingent on the relevance of corporate stakeholders' implicit claims to the firm. As mentioned in section 2.3.2, the BDS (1995) and Matsumoto (2002) approach of measuring stakeholder theory is rooted in stakeholder-based accounting research on earnings management. Like the stakeholder rationale for risk management, this stream of accounting literature is founded on the work of Cornell and Shapiro (1987). A review of the studies by BDS (1995) and Matsumoto (2002) sets the basis for developing variables that proxy for the firm's dependence on the implicit claims with its NFS.

7.4.3.1.1 Bowen et al. (1995)

In their 1995 paper, Bowen et al. analyze the firm's incentives to choose income-increasing accounting methods drawing on stakeholder and reputational arguments. In contrast to measuring stakeholder dependence through a strategy-based proxy for NOC like in the papers by Barton et al. (1989) and Holder et al. (1998), BDS (1995) use a different approach. They heavily draw on arguments of Cornell and Shapiro (1987) and Maksimovic and Titman (1991) that a firm's financial image is relevant to stakeholders' assessment of the firm's current and expected future reputation for fulfilling implicit commitments. In short, BDS (1995) use stakeholder theory as an argument for earnings management (Roberts and Mahoney, 2004: 406). They hypothesize that a firm has incentives to choose long-run income-increasing accounting methods when the firm is more dependent on implicit claims of NFS. Already BDS (1995) discuss two critical linkages underlying their hypothesis. First, the relation between the terms of trade and a firm's reputation for fulfilling implicit claims and, second, the link between its reputation and reported accounting numbers. While the former association is based on strong theoretical arguments[103], BDS admit that the latter is more tenuous as it is based on anecdotal evidence (Bowen et al, 1995: 261).

BDS (1995) empirically find that a firm's management has higher incentives to choose long-run income-increasing accounting methods when the firm is more dependent on implicit claims of different non-financial stakeholders. This is based on the notion that stakeholders are likely to use accounting data to help assess the firm's reputation for fulfilling its implicit commitments. As they find that a firm should do earnings management to increase the market value of the firm by overstating its profitability, their argument implicitly assumes that at least some stakeholders are unlikely or unable to completely adjust these reported numbers for differences in accounting methods (Bowen et al., 1995: 261 and 291). The essence of BDS (1995) is that management uses accounting information opportunistically in order to influence stakeholders' assessment of the value of the firm's implicit claims (Roberts and Mahoney, 2004: 407). Recently, Roberts and Mahoney (2004) have addressed that contradiction inherent in the argument by BDS (1995). As a consequence, this rather means that managers may convince stakeholders of the firm's trustworthiness by intentionally misleading them through earnings management (Roberts and Mahoney, 2004: 411).

The intention of the stakeholder-based risk management literature, however, is to create trustworthiness on the part of NFS through conservative financial decisions. This literature on the stakeholder reasoning for risk management assumes that non-financial stakeholders assess the firm's financial conditions on the basis of parameters such as capital structure, dividend payments, and cash-holdings, which are less likely to be subject to window-dressing. It is assumed that non-financial stakeholders

[103] As shown in this work, the theoretical foundation for this link has even been strengthened through the contributions of the stakeholder rationale for risk management.

recognize the detrimental effect of non-conservative financial decisions on the fulfillment of implicit commitments.

Although the final conclusion of the BDS (1995) paper (i.e. to pretend a high value of the firm's implicit claims through earnings management) differs substantially from the SRRM, BDS' approach to measure the ties between the firm and its non-financial stakeholders through accounting data seems promising for usage in the context of this study. Therefore, the implicit claims variables used by BDS (1995) are discussed before presenting the stakeholder proxies employed in this study.

Customers

BDS (1995) account for implicit relations with customers by using two empirical proxies. First, and referring to Titman and Wessels (1988), they suggest uniqueness of a firm's products to measure the costs stakeholders suffer in the event of liquidation. Hence, it is postulated that R&D expense scaled by firm size is a valid proxy for customers' implicit claims (Bowen et al., 1995: 269). Extending the proxy used by Titman and Wessels (1988), they include a dummy variable in order to indicate membership of firms to the construction and/or manufacturing industry. This is based on the insight that particularly buyers of durable products are purchasing implicit claims related to specified quality and availability of continuing parts and service over a product's lifetime (Bowen et al. 1995: 269).

Suppliers

The relation between a firm and its suppliers is determined by the terms of payment and continuing demand for the suppliers' products. BDS (1995: 270) underline the significance of implicit claims with suppliers of inventory for the firm. Thus, they use cost of goods sold adjusted for the change in the LIFO reserve as a proxy. Consistent with R&D expense the measure is scaled by firm size. However, even Bowen et al. (1995: 270) admit that it is a poor proxy for manufacturing firms, because much of their cost of goods sold is internally generated. A more general problem refers to firms that are heavily dependent on intangible assets. For those firms this inventory-based proxy seems to be inadequate.

Employees

BDS (1995: 270) use two measures to cover the extent to which firms depend on implicit claims with their employees. They hypothesize that the extent to which firms depend on implicit claims with their employees is likely to vary with the level of labor intensity. Thus, they use labor intensity as one minus the ratio of gross property, plant, and equipment scaled by firm size. Moreover, and referring to previous research, they interpret a firm's defined benefit pension plans as implied commitments. BDS (1995: 271) use a dummy variable to account for the existence of such a pension plan. It is worth noting that the R&D variable used to account for customer relations can also be interpreted as an indicator of implicit claims of employees (Bowen et al., 1995: 270 and 288).

Short-term creditors

A single variable is used to cover creditor relations. It is assumed that lenders depend on implicit claims related to timely payment, the amount of future borrowing, as well as the duration of the relationship. Hence, these implicit claims with a firm's short-term creditors are considered by the amount of short-term notes payable reported on the balance sheet scaled by firm size (Bowen et al., 1995: 271).

All stakeholders

Bowen et al. (1995) include a scaled advertising expenditure ratio as an overall proxy for the influence of all four stakeholder groups. Based on a literature review they assert that advertising expenditures are likely to be used to build and protect reputation (Bowen et al., 1995: 271–272 and 288).

There are, of course, certain drawbacks related to Bowen et al's implicit claims variables. According to BDS (1995: 269), their stakeholder variables do not only represent implicit claims, but also broad firm characteristics that might be subject to alternative interpretations. Second, each variable is not always uniquely associated with a single type of stakeholder group but with a wider class of key stakeholders (Bowen et al., 1995: 268). Third, the authors admit that implicit claims in general are *"difficult to analyze both conceptually and empirically"* (Bowen et al., 1995: 292). However, the results for each of their implicit claims variables are consistent with the predicted hypotheses in at least one of the named income-increasing accounting decisions. Additionally, the implicit claims variables provided significant explanatory power incremental to the control variables (Bowen et al., 1995: 288 and 292).

7.4.3.1.2 Matsumoto (2002)

A similar study has been conducted by Matsumoto (2002) who uses BDS' (1995) implicit claim variables to analyze the effect of the firm's implicit stakeholder claims on the likelihood that the firm meets or exceeds expectations at the earnings announcement. More general, he hypothesizes that 1) a firm's ownership structure, 2) the reliance on stakeholders' implicit claims and, 3) the value relevance of earnings influences management's incentive to avoid negative earnings surprises (Matusumo, 2002: 484). Regarding the second point, the underlying argument is equivalent to the BDS (1995) study. Meeting or exceeding analysts' earnings expectations contributes to the financial image stakeholders have of the firm and influences the terms of trade they have with the firm (Matsumoto, 2002: 490). To test this relationship, Matusomo (2002: 493) uses the three proxy variables from BDS with the highest explanatory power. Those are a dummy variable accounting for membership in the durable goods industry, a R&D expenditure variable, and a labor intensity measure. Controlling for alternative explanatory variables, Matsumoto's results provide evidence that firms with greater reliance on implicit claims with their stakeholders, higher transient institutional ownership, and higher value-relevance of earnings are more likely to take actions to meet or exceed analysts' forecasts at the earnings announcement (Masumoto, 2002:511). However, he also points to the already known measurement problem regarding stakeholder dependency. Similar to BDS (1995) he notes that the level of implicit claims with stakeholders is inherently unobservable and proxies are subject to alternative interpretations (Matsumoto, 2002: 493).

7.4.3.2 Independent stakeholder variables employed in this study

This study aims at contributing to identify the influence of non-financial stakeholders' implicit claims on corporate financial decisions. As emphasized by previous researchers, stakeholder theory in general is difficult to analyze empirically (Franck and Huyghebaert, 2006: 2). The variables to proxy for implicit claims of non-financial stakeholder groups used in this study are based on previous empirical contributions, particularly by BDS (1995) and Matsumoto (2002).

Stakeholder variables are included that proxy for the firm's relationship with its customers, suppliers and employees. Additionally, the market-to-book ratio, a general proxy for all non-financial stakeholder groups and an industry dummy variable are included in the regression models.[104] These variables are based on the *Datastream* raw data and are described below.

Customers

Following BDS (1995), a customer variable is included and defined as research & development expense (01201) over total assets (02999) multiplied by 100. This variable is similar to the classic uniqueness-variable used in corporate financial research, which is typically defined as research and development expenses over sales (e.g. Titman and Wessels, 1995: 5) and measures the costs imposed on customers when the firm goes out of business or approaches a state of financial distress. Following theoretical arguments and previous empirical findings, relative R&D expenses are assumed to be negatively related to leverage and positively related to the level of cash holdings.

Suppliers

As suggested by BDS (1995), the supplier variable is calculated as cost of goods sold (01051) over total assets (02999) in percentage points.[105] Due to data limitations no adjustment for the LIFO reserve is employed, as originally suggested by BDS (1995). It is assumed that cost of goods sold is negatively related to leverage and positively related to the level of cash holdings.

Employees

Following BDS (1995), Matsumoto (2002) and Miller and Chen (2003; see also section 4.3.3.2), the proxy to account for the firm-employees relation is defined as 1 minus the ratio of property, plant and equipment (02301) over total assets (02999) and is scaled in percent. The argument behind this proxy is that the extent to which firms depend on implicit claims with their employees is likely to vary with their levels of labor intensity. This means that a firm with high labor intensity depends more on implicit claims with employees than a firm with high capital intensity (BDS, 1995:

[104] Since the focus of this study lies on non-financial stakeholders, the BDS variable accounting for short-term creditors is omitted from the analysis. Moreover, BDS (1995) use the ratio of advertising expense to total assets as an explanatory variable and interpret it as a general stakehoder proxy. This is based on the argument that advertising expenditure is a form of firm-specific investment that is used to build and protect reputation. Due to data limitations a ratio based on advertising expense cannot be employed in this study.

[105] Miller and Chen (2003) also use relative cost of goods sold (COGS) to proxy for the firm-stakeholders relations. They argue that *"suppliers and employees involved in operations are the key stakeholders whose compensation makes up COGS"* (Miller and Chen, 2003: 362).

270). Hence, labor intensity is assumed to be negatively related to leverage and positively related to cash holdings.

Market-to-book ratio

As mentioned earlier, market-to-book ratio is often used in empirical studies to proxy for growth opportunities. Alternatively, following Speckbacher and Wentges (2005: 20), it may also be interpreted as a proxy for intangible assets. As argued in this dissertation, intangible assets are mainly built in conjunction between the firm and its NFS, who invest specifically into the firm. Therefore, the market-to-book measure is used to proxy for the firm's dependence on the implicit claims with its non-financial stakeholders in this study. It is expected that the market-to-book ratio is negatively related to leverage and positively to cash holdings. The measure is defined as total liabilities (03351) plus market capitalization per year end (08004) over total assets (02999) as in previous papers (e.g. Opler et al., 1999: 17, Dittmar et al. 2003: 118, Ozkan 2001: 180).

Industry

As laid down in section 4.3.2.3, certain industry characteristics call for considering non-financial stakeholders in the firm's risk management strategy. Hence, and following Titman and Wessels (1988), a dummy variable is included to identify industries that are especially prone to terms of trade effects of financial distress. Based on the two-digit NACE industry classification, any firm belonging to the following industries, indicated in table four, has an industry dummy variable of one. If the firm belongs to any other industry category the dummy is zero. Following the literature on the stakeholder rationale for risk management, these industries are both, dependent on intangible assets and generate high liquidation costs for NFS when entering a state of financial distress. Hence, an industry dummy of one should be negatively related to the leverage and positively related to the level of cash holdings.

NACE industry definition	NACE code
Manufacture of machinery and equipment	29
Manufacture of motor vehicles, trailers and semi-trailers	34
Manufacture of other transport equipment	35
Air transport	62
Computer and related activities	72
Research and development	73
Other business activities (i.e. services)	74

Table 4: Industry dummy variable

7.5 FD and FE model specifications

Panel data methodology is the method of choice when it is assumed that there exist unobserved effects a_i that are correlated with the observed independent variables. Possible omitted variables are discussed above together with the variables that are included in the models. The existence of an omitted variables problem rules out using an RE model, as explained in chapter 6. Moreover, pooled OLS delivers biased and inconsistent estimators, as pointed out by Wooldridge (2006: 462). Hence, FD and FE panel data regression models are set up for explaining corporate capital structure and cash holdings, respectively. As explained in section 6.2.5.1, the choice between the two models is based on the residuals Δu_{it} of the first differences model. If these residuals do not show signs of substantial negative autocorrelation, the FD model is appropriate. However, if there is significant negative autocorrelation among the residuals of the FD model (i.e. an autocorrelation coefficient close to -0.5), the FE model should be preferred.

Despite the methodological problems discussed in chapter 6, extant literature reports OLS as well as FE and RE panel data models and disregards FD models. Therefore this study will follow the literature and report the results of FE estimations in order to assure comparability of the estimations. In case the residuals Δu_{it} of the first differences model FD model indicate that an FD model should be preferred over the FE model, the differences of the results between two models are indicated in the appendix. In order to allow for reliable interpretation of significance levels, heteroscedasticity-robust standard errors are calculated when estimating the models.[106] The specification of the models is described below.

Due to the downturn of the world economy at the beginning of this decade and the massive decline of the global stock markets between 2000 and 2001, the data of the sample period 1998–2004 might be too heterogeneous from a macroeconomic perspective, which might influence the estimated results. In order to assure a more homogenous data basis, the period from 2002 to 2004 is chosen to test the models.

7.5.1 Capital structure models

Based on chapter 6, FD and FE models are established for explaining capital structure. Following equation (6.5) the FD capital structure model is defined as

$$\Delta \text{nlog leverage}_{it} = \text{Intercept} + \delta_1 \text{ Year03}_t + \delta_2 \text{ Year04}_t + \beta_1 \, \Delta\text{Characteristics of assets}_{it} + \beta_2 \, \Delta\text{Growth opportunities}_{it} + \beta_3 \, \Delta\text{nlog Size}_{it} + \beta_4 \, \Delta\text{Profitability}_{it} + \beta_5 \, \Delta\text{Customers}_{it} + \beta_6 \, \Delta\text{Suppliers}_{it} + \beta_7 \, \Delta\text{Employees}_{it} + \beta_8 \, \Delta\text{Market-to-book ratio}_{it} + \beta_9 \text{ Industry}_{it} + \Delta u_{it}$$

with t = 1, 2, …, T.

The FE capital structure model is defined as

$$\text{nlog leverage}_{it} = \text{Intercept} + \beta_1 \text{ Characteristics of assets}_{it} + \beta_2 \text{ Growth opportunities}_{it} + \beta_3 \text{ nlog Size}_{it} + \beta_4 \text{ Profitability}_{it} + \beta_5 \text{ Customers}_{it} + \beta_6 \text{ Suppliers}_{it} + \beta_7 \text{ Employees}_{it} + \beta_8 \text{ Market-to-book ratio}_{it} + \beta_9 \text{ year03} + \beta_{10} \text{ year04} + a_i + u_{it}$$

with t = 1, 2, …, T.

Since time constant variables cannot be included in an FE model, the industry dummy used in the FD model is excluded from the FE model.

---

[106] *EViews* 5.1 offers several versions of heteroskedasticity robust standard errors. These are based on White (1980) and variants of the Panel Corrected Standard Error (PCSE) methodology developed by Beck and Katz (1995). In this study, the PCSE methodology for usage in a time-series cross-section data setting is employed (EViews, 2004: 853–855 and 887).

7.5.2 Cash holdings models

As in section 7.5.1 FD and FE models are established for explaining cash holdings. The FD cash holdings model is defined as

$$\Delta\text{nlog Cash holdings}_{it} = \text{Intercept} + \delta_1 \text{ Year03}_t + \delta_2 \text{ Year04}_t + \beta_1 \Delta\text{Cash substitutes}_{it} + \beta_2 \Delta\text{Leverage/liquidity constraints}_{it} + \beta_3 \Delta\text{nlog Size}_{it} + \beta_4 \Delta\text{Growth opportunities}_{it} + \beta_5 \Delta\text{Dividend payments}_{it} + \beta_6 \Delta\text{Customers}_{it} + \beta_7 \Delta\text{Suppliers}_{it} + \beta_8 \Delta\text{Employees}_{it} + \beta_9 \Delta\text{Market-to-book ratio}_{it} + \beta_{10} \text{ Industry}_{it} + \Delta u_{it}$$

with t = 1, 2, …, T.

The FE cash holdings model is defined as

$$\text{nlog Cash holdings}_{it} = \text{Intercept} + \beta_1 \text{ Cash substitutes}_{it} + \beta_2 \text{ Leverage/liquidity constraints}_{it} + \beta_3 \text{ nlog Size}_{it} + \beta_4 \text{ Growth opportunities}_{it} + \beta_5 \text{ Dividend payments}_{it} + \beta_6 \text{ Customers}_{it} + \beta_7 \text{ Suppliers}_{it} + \beta_8 \text{ Employees}_{it} + \beta_9 \text{ Market-to-book ratio}_{it} + \beta_{10} \text{ Year03} + \beta_{11} \text{ Year04} + a_i + u_{it}$$

with t = 1, 2, …, T.

Since time constant variables cannot be included in an FE model, the industry dummy used in the FD model is excluded from the FE model.

7.6 Results and discussion

7.6.1 Univariate descriptive results

In the following two sections the univariate results of the dependent variables are discussed. A complete overview of the descriptive statistics of all variables employed in the models for the period from 2002 to 2004 is given in appendix B.

7.6.1.1 Univariate descriptive results of corporate capital structure

An analysis of the levels of leverage for the period from 2002 to 2004 reveals some variation among the accounting-specific subsamples, as indicated in table five. It shows the distribution of leverage across the four samples. Across the accounting-specific subsamples, the mean (median) leverage lies at 48.99% (56.40%) for the US GAAP firms, at 61.17% (74.90%) for the IFRS observations and 73.59% (85.04) for the Local standards group. In the Overall sample mean leverage is 62.60%, while the median lies at 76.75%.

	Leverage in %			
	Local Standards	**IFRS**	**US GAAP**	**Overall**
Mean	73.59	61.17	48.99	62.60
Median	85.04	74.90	56.40	76.75

Table 5: Leverage ratios in percent across all subsamples

Previous studies reported lower leverage ratios for U.S. and U.K. firms. In a recent study, Kale and Shahrur (2007) report a mean market leverage ratio of 18.7% and a median value of 13.2% for the sample period from 1984 to 2003 (Kale and Shahrur, 2007: 334). Ozkan (2001) reports a mean leverage ratio of 16.8% for a sample of U.K. firms for the period from 1984 to 1996 (Ozkan, 2001: 195). The reason for the difference in the leverage ratios to previous studies may be related to the differing definitions employed in these studies. In their international comparison of capital structure across countries, Rajan and Zingales (1995) report mean and median values for the ratio of total liablities to total assets (with the value of equity measured in terms of market value) of 44% for U.S. and around 40% for U.K. firms. For Germany they report a mean leverage ratio of 56% and a median of 60%. When measuring leverage as the ratio of debt (i.e. short term plus long term debt) to total assets, the mean value for the U.S. firms falls to 24% and the median to 20% (Rajan and Zingales, 1995: 1430). While this study uses total liabilities to proxy for leverage, Ozkan (2001) and Kale and Shahrur (2007) use total debt (Ozkan, 2001: 185; Kale and Shahrur, 2007: 332).[107] Therefore and given the findings of Rajan and Zingales (1995), their leverage ratios can be expected to lie below those found in this study.[108]

Recently, Gaud et al. (2005) have investigated the capital structure of Swiss companies between 1991 and 2000. Using the *Worldscope* database and defining leverage as the ratio of total debt (as do Ozkan (2001) and Kale and Shahrur (2007)) to total assets,

[107] Whereas Kale and Shahrur (2007) use *Compustat* data, the univariate leverage ratios in the study by Ozkan (2001) are directly comparable to this study as he uses *Datastream* data.

[108] While total debt only covers short and long term debt, total liabilities of non-financial companies additionally captures provisions for risk and charges, deferred taxes, deferred income, other liabilities, deferred tax liability in untaxed reserves and pension/post retirement benefits (Thomson Worldscope Database Datatype Definitions Guide, 2003: 428 and 432).

where total assets are the sum of the book value of debt plus the market value of equity at the end of the year, they report similar leverage ratios as found in this study. Without controlling for different accounting standards, they report a mean ratio leverage of 40.2% for the year 2000 and an average value of 49.5% for the period from 1991 to 2000 (Gaud et al., 2005: 59). This is closer to the results reported in this study, even when measuring the numerator of the leverage ratio in terms of total debt instead of total liabilities.

A more general reason for the above differences in reported leverage ratios of German and Austrian firms might lie in the firms' traditionally preferred sources of finance. Usually, firms in German speaking countries prefer debt finance from banks over equity funding from the capital markets as in the Anglo-saxon countries.

Given all that, the leverage ratios reported in this study do not seem to be unreasonably high.

7.6.1.2 Univariate descriptive results of corporate cash holdings

As reported in table six below, the distribution of the levels of cash holdings is also dispersed across the four samples. The mean (median) value in the Overall sample is 9.23% (9.73%). Somewhat noticeable are the higher levels of cash holdings for the US GAAP firms. While the mean cash ratio for the Local standards group lies at 5.48% (5.61%) and at 11.71% (10.77%) for the IFRS group, it reaches 21.41% (19.50%) in the group of US GAAP firms.

	Cash holdings in %			
	Local Standards	**IFRS**	**US GAAP**	**Overall**
Mean	5.48	11.71	21.41	9.23
Median	5.61	10.77	19.50	9.73

Table 6: Cash ratios in percent across all subsamples

Although the US GAAP group in this sample reports slightly higher values than usually reported in previous studies, these results are generally in line with comparable studies and with Bates et al.'s (2006) evidence of increasing cash ratios (see also section 5.3.2.7),

Using *Datastream* data on publicly traded U.K. firms from 1995 to 1999, Ozkan and Ozkan (2004) report a mean cash ratio of 9.9% and a median value of 5.9%. For U.S. firms, Kim et al. (1998) report mean and median values of the cash ratio of 8.1% and 4.7% respectively (Kim et al., 1998: 351). However, the results of Ozkan and Ozkan (2004) and Kim et al. (1998) are not directly comparable to those of this study. Both papers measure relative cash as the ratio of total cash and equivalents to total assets (Ozkan and Ozkan, 2004: 2117; Kim et al., 1998: 349) while this study uses net assets in the denominator (see also section 7.4.2.1).

The univariate descriptive results of Opler et al. (1999) and Dittmar et al. (2003), on the other hand, are directly comparable to those reported here as their definition of the cash ratio is equivalent to the definition in this study. In their analysis of firm year data from 1971 to 1994 of U.S.-based publicly traded firms, Opler et al. (1999) report a mean ratio of 17%, which is similar to the 21.41% found in this study for the sample firms reporting according to US GAAP. The median cash ratio in Opler et al.'s study is 6.5% (Opler et al., 1999: 17). In their international comparison of corporate cash holdings, Dittmar et al. (2003) report median country cash ratios of 8.4% for Austria, 7.3% for Germany, 8.1% for the U.K. and 6.4% for the U.S (Dittmar et al., 2003: 118–120), which also consistent with the results illustrated in table six.

7.6.2 Multivariate results

A preliminary analysis of the correlation matrix of the stakeholder variables (see appendix C) reveals that both *Customers* and *Employees* are negatively correlated with leverage and positively related to cash holdings in the Overall sample as well as in the accounting-specific subsamples as predicted by the stakeholder rationale for risk management. *Suppliers*, however, does not show the expected signs in any of the accounting-based subsamples. The sole exception is the IFRS subsample, where *Suppliers* is positively related to cash holdings. The *Market-to-book ratio* is negatively related to leverage in all subsamples and positively related to cash holdings in the IFRS, US GAAP, and the Overall sample. These findings support the assumption that the firm-stakeholder relationship influences the firms' corporate finance decisions in the way argued by the SRRM.

7.6.2.1 Multivariate analysis of corporate capital structure

Table seven presents the multivariate results of the fixed effects capital structure model for the three accounting-specific subsamples and the Overall sample for the period from 2002 to 2004.

Dependent variable		nlog Leverage			
Estimation method		Fixed Effects			
Sample period		2002 - 2004			
	Expected sign	Local Standards	IFRS	US GAAP	Overall
Characteristics of assets	-	-0.0006	0.0099 **	0.0091 *	0.0056 ***
		(0.729)	(0.039)	(0.075)	(0.001)
Growth opportunities	-/+	-0.0094	0.0046	-0.0152	-0.0014
		(0.109)	(0.474)	(0.332)	(0.613)
nlog Size	+	0.1127 *	0.1494	0.0364	-0.0924
		(0.080)	(0.135)	(0.695)	(0.187)
Profitability	+/-	-0.0047 *	-0.0071 ***	-0.0008	-0.0041 ***
		(0.065)	(0.000)	(0.820)	(0.000)
Customers	-	0.0188	0.0336 ***	0.0093	-0.0021
		(0.136)	(0.002)	(0.666)	(0.751)
Suppliers	-	-0.0008	-0.0025	0.0006	0.0019 **
		(0.712)	(0.195)	(0.217)	(0.031)
Employees	-	-0.0034 **	-0.0025 *	-0.0008	-0.0019 **
		(0.044)	(0.065)	(0.741)	(0.043)
Market-to-book ratio	-	-0.6749 ***	-0.6701 ***	-0.5014 ***	-0.5634 ***
		(0.000)	(0.000)	(0.000)	(0.000)
Year 03		-0.0589 ***	0.0104	-0.1637 ***	-0.0651 ***
		(0.002)	(0.657)	(0.001)	(0.000)
Year 04		-0.0645 ***	-0.0070	-0.1371 ***	-0.0604 ***
		(0.000)	(0.819)	(0.000)	(0.000)
Effects specification		Cross-section fixed	Cross-section fixed	Cross-section fixed	Cross-section fixed
Coef covariance method		Cross-section SUR	Cross-section SUR	Cross-section SUR	Cross-section SUR
Cross-sections included		28	106	62	176
Total panel observations		66	222	143	431
R^2		96.09%	96.33%	94.40%	93.78%
Adjusted R^2		90.93%	92.35%	88.80%	89.08%
S.E. of regression		7.37%	13.60%	20.70%	17.64%
F-statistic		18.6119 ***	24.2009 ***	16.8580 ***	19.9564 ***
Probability (F-statistic)		(0.000)	(0.000)	(0.000)	(0.000)
Autocorr. of residuals at lag 1 in FD model		0.0602	0.0320	-0.3298 **	-0.2724 ***
		(0.793)	(0.810)	(0.027)	(0.000)

* $p < 0.1$; ** $p < 0.05$; *** $p < 0.01$ (p-values in parentheses)
All variables are winsorized at the 1st and 99th percentiles

Table 7: Fixed effects estimation of the capital structure model

Table seven shows that the number of firms and cross-sections included in the estimations varies considerably between the accounting standards. Generally, the numbers of observations and cross-sections that are used for computing the regression depends on the missing values for each variable. Usually, *EViews* employs casewise exclusion, meaning that only those observations are included for which the dependent variable and all of the independent variables have non-missing data (EViews, 2004:

127). Appendix B shows the available number of observations for each variable for the period from 2002 to 2004.[109]

Moreover, table seven illustrates that the R-squared and the adjusted R-squared in all samples are very high. This is usually the case in an FE model because a dummy variable is included for each cross-sectional unit, which explains much of the variation in the data (Wooldridge, 2006: 490).

The stakeholder variables *Customers*, *Suppliers*, *Employees* and *Market-to-book ratio* are of primary interest in the regression model, as they proxy for the firm's dependence on implicit stakeholder claims. The relationship between *nlog Leverage* and *Market-to-book ratio* shows the expected negative sign and is highly significant at the 1% level in the overall sample as well as in all accounting-specific subsamples. This is consistent with prior research by, e.g., O'Brien (2003) and Rajan and Zingales (1995), who find identical results. Consistent with the SRRM, firms whose market value exceeds its book value, which is an indicator for the existence of intangible assets not reflected in the firm's accounting data, choose lower leverage.

Employees is slightly negatively related to *nlog Leverage* in all samples. It is significant at the 5% level in the Overall sample and at the 5% and 1% levels in the Local Standards and the IFRS subsamples, respectively. This evidence conforms to the empirical predictions of Berk et al.'s (2007: 25) capital structure model as it shows that labor intensive firms choose lower debt ratios.

Suppliers is significantly positively related to *nlog Leverage* at the 5% level in the Overall sample, which is contrary to the theoretical expectations. This result indicates that firms with high values for relative cost of goods sold prefer higher leverage. In the three accounting-specific subsamples the regression coefficients of *Suppliers* are insignificant.

Customers is insignificant in the Overall, the Local Standards and the US GAAP samples. An exception is the IFRS firms where this variable is positive and highly significant at the 1% level. This is interesting insofar, as the relative R&D expenses

---

[109] The same applies to the corporate cash holdings models in the next section.

are almost exclusively negatively related to debt levels in previous studies, as shown in chapter 5.

Regarding the traditional financial control variables, *Profitability* is significantly negatively related to leverage in the Overall sample and in the Local standards and IFRS subsamples. In the US GAAP subsample the coefficient for profitability is negative but highly insignificant. This negative relationship is consistent with prior studies (see, e.g., Rajan and Zingales (1995), Barton and Gordon (1988), Titman and Wessels (1988), and O'Brien (2003)) and with the pecking order theory, as firms seem to use profits to repay debt.

Previous research found ambiguous results regarding the relationship between size and debt ratios. While Vicente-Lorente (2001) does not find any significant relationship between size and leverage, O'Brien (2003) reports that leverage increases with firm size. Rajan and Zingales (1995) also find a significantly positive relationship between size and leverage in the U.S., Japan, France and Canada but a negative and strongly significant relationship for Germany (Rajan and Zingales, 1995: 1453). In this sample, *Size* is significantly related to leverage at the 10% level in the Local standards subsample where it shows the expected positive relationship, which is supportive for the trade-off theory of debt and the empirical implications of Berk et al.'s (2007: 4) capital structure model. In all other samples, however, *Size* is insignificant, which does not give much support for the hypothesized relationship.

Growth opportunities, proxied by relative capital expenditures, is expected to be negatively related to the debt level following agency and static trade-off arguments, while pecking order theory predicts a positive relationship. In this study the variable is insignificant in all samples tested.

Transaction cost theory would expect the *Characteristics of assets* variable to be negatively related to leverage as redeployability of intangible assets is lower than for non-specific tangible assets. However, the significant relationships in the Overall sample as well as in the IFRS and US GAAP subsamples show the opposite direction, indicating that firms with high intangible assets borrow more. This is surprising for two reasons. First, previous research, e.g., by Rajan and Zingales (1995) and O'Brien (2003), found evidence for the underlying theory. Second, given that *Characteristics of assets* reflects the level of intangible assets of the firm, it should show the same sign as *Market-to-book ratio*, which is also a proxy for the level of intangible assets. A reason for the latter phenomenon might be that the *Market-to-book ratio* reflects the (higher) level of intangible assets as valued by the capital markets while *Characteristics of assets* reflects the firm's (lower) book value of intangible assets.

As to the two year dummy variables for 2003 and 2004, the regression results show that debt levels are significantly lower than in the base year in the Overall sample as well as in the Local standards and the US GAAP samples.

As indicated by the positive and insignificant autocorrelation coefficients at lag one of the residuals in the first differences models, the true capital structure models for Local standards and IFRS is a first differences model instead of an FE model presented above. The results of the FD models are qualitatively similar to the FE model (see appendix D). The main differences between the two models are the coefficients for *Size,* which are higher and strongly significant in both subsamples. The *Industry dummy*, which cannot be included in the FE model, is significant at the 1% level in the Local standards sample and at the 10% level in the IFRS sample. Interestingly, it shows the expected negative sign in the Local standards but a positive sign in the IFRS sample.

7.6.2.2 Multivariate analysis of corporate cash holdings

Table eight presents the multivariate results of the fixed effects cash holdings model for the three accounting-specific subsamples and the Overall sample for the period from 2002 to 2004.

Dependent variable		nlog Cash holdings			
Estimation method		Fixed Effects			
Sample period		2002 - 2004			
	Expected sign	Local Standards	IFRS	US GAAP	Overall
Cash substitutes	-	-0.0191 **	-0.0155 ***	-0.0083 ***	-0.0147 ***
		(0.032)	(0.001)	(0.000)	(0.000)
Leverage/liquidity constraints	+/-	-0.0169	-0.0287 ***	-0.0220 ***	-0.0306 ***
		(0.475)	(0.000)	(0.001)	(0.000)
nlog Size	-	-0.4128	-0.9841 ***	0.0587	-0.4473 ***
		(0.167)	(0.001)	(0.670)	(0.000)
Growth opportunities	+/-	-0.0303	0.0111	-0.0326	-0.0266
		(0.548)	(0.577)	(0.213)	(0.158)
Customers	+	-0.0197	0.0126	0.0168	-0.0204 ***
		(0.819)	(0.358)	(0.147)	(0.001)
Suppliers	+	-0.0033	0.0085 ***	-0.0026 **	0.0033 ***
		(0.564)	(0.000)	(0.032)	(0.000)
Employees	+	0.0002	0.0146 *	0.0213 ***	0.0101 ***
		(0.964)	(0.093)	(0.000)	(0.000)
Market-to-book ratio	+	-1.3719 *	0.4729 ***	0.3787 *	0.3457 ***
		(0.083)	(0.000)	(0.079)	(0.000)
Year 03		0.3146 ***	-0.0428	0.0635	0.0862 ***
		(0.001)	(0.657)	(0.254)	(0.000)
Year 04		0.7203 ***	0.2143 **	0.2537 ***	0.2785 ***
		(0.000)	(0.012)	(0.005)	(0.000)
Dividend Dummy	-	0.0245	-0.2425	-0.0706	0.0689
		(0.938)	(0.225)	(0.779)	(0.684)
Effects specification		Cross-section fixed	Cross-section fixed	Cross-section fixed	Cross-section fixed
Coef covariance method		Cross-section SUR	Cross-section SUR	Cross-section SUR	Cross-section SUR
Cross-sections included		27	107	66	179
Total panel observations		64	226	155	448
R^2		94.90%	91.16%	93.97%	91.89%
Adjusted R^2		87.64%	81.59%	88.10%	85.95%
S.E. of regression		54.10%	53.33%	48.35%	53.59%
F-statistic		13.0733 ***	9.5233 ***	16.0070 ***	15.4650 ***
Probability (F-statistic)		(0.000)	(0.000)	(0.000)	(0.000)
Autocorr. of residuals at lag 1 in FD model		-0.3636	-0.3689 ***	-0.1089	-0.1779 ***
		(0.100)	(0.000)	(0.297)	(0.004)

* $p < 0.1$; ** $p < 0.05$; *** $p < 0.01$ (p-values in parentheses)
All variables are winsorized at the 1st and 99th percentiles

Table 8: Fixed effects estimation of the cash holdings model

Table eight illustrates that the R-squared and the adjusted R-squared are very high for all tested samples, as expected for an FE model (Wooldridge, 2006: 490).

Beginning with the interpretation of the stakeholder variables, the *Market-to-book ratio* for the Overall sample is positive and significant at the 1% level, indicating that firms with high intangible assets prefer larger liquidity buffers. This is the expected result, given the stakeholder rationale for risk management's implications for corporate finance decision and consistent with previous studies (see, e.g., Kim et al. (1998), Dittmar et al. (2003), Opler et al. (1999), and Ozkan and Ozkan (2004)). The estimations for the US GAAP and the IFRS subsamples are equivalent to the Overall sample, however, with the coefficient in the US GAAP sample being significant only at the 10% level. Interestingly, the regression coefficient of the *Market-to-book ratio* in the sample for Local standards firms is highly negative. While the regression coefficients in the other three subsamples lie within the range of 0.3457 and 0.4729 and are consistent with predictions of stakeholder theory, the ß coefficient in the Local standards sample is -1.37 and significant at the 10% level. This would suggest that a Local standards firm reduces its level of cash holdings with an increasing *Market-to-book ratio*.

The *Employees* ratio is positive in all four subsamples as predicted and significant at the 1% level in the Overall and the US GAAP samples and significant at the 10% level in the IFRS subsample. The regression coefficient in the subsample of Local standards, however, is insignificant. This suggests that firms in all these samples increase their level of cash holdings with an increase in their level of labor intensity. This is in conformity with the SRRM as the employees' request for stable financing and a low risk profile becomes more important when the firm's dependence on implicit stakeholder claims, as indicated by its labor intensity, increases.

The results for the Suppliers variable is contradictory. While *Suppliers* is positively and highly significantly related to the level of cash holdings in the Overall and in the IFRS samples, as expected by the SRRM, the regression coefficient is negative and insignificant for the Local standards firms and negative and significant for US GAAP firms.

Customers is highly significant in the Overall sample but with a negative sign, which is inconsistent with stakeholder-theoretical arguments and the precautionary motive for holding cash. In all other accounting-specific subsamples the *Customers* coefficient is insignificant.

As to the financial control variables, *Growth opportunities*, measuring relative capital expenditure, is insignificant in the Overall as well as in all accounting-specific subsamples.

As found in previous studies (see, e.g., Kim et al. (1998), Dittmar et al. (2003), Opler et al. (1999), and Ozkan and Ozkan (2004)), *Cash substitutes* is significantly and negatively related to the level of cash holdings, confirming the prediction that working capital is used as a substitute for readily available cash.

As empirically found by Dittmar et al. (2003), *Size* is strongly significant in the Overall sample with a negative sign as predicted by the static trade-off theory, indicating that larger firms hold less cash. As to the accounting-specific subsamples, only the firms in the IFRS subsample show a significant and negative relationship, while the coefficients are insignificant in all other subsamples.

Leverage/liquidity constraints indicates that the debt level is negatively related to the level of corporate cash holdings, confirming the findings of Kim et al. (1998) and Ozkan and Ozkan (2004). This supports the idea that the costs of funds invested in liquidity increase with leverage as argued by Baskin (1987).

The regression coefficient of the 2004 dummy variable indicates a positive and significant impact on cash holdings in that year. For the 2003 dummy variable the estimation results show a significantly positive effect only in the Overall sample and the Local standards subsample while there is an insignifcant effect in the remaining two subsamples. The *Dividend Dummy* shows contradictory signs but is insignificant in all samples.

The autocorrelation coefficients at lag one of the residuals in the first differences cash holdings models for the Overall sample and the US GAAP subsample are only slightly negative, indicating that in fact an FD model should be preferred over the FE model. The results of the FD models are provided in appendix E. Comparing the results of the FD cash holdings model for the US GAAP subsample with the FE model shows that all variables except for *Cash substitutes* and *Leverage/liquidity constraints* are insignificant with similar coefficients as in the FE model. In the Overall sample, *Cash substitutes*, *Leverage/liquidity constraints*, and *Size* are negatively related to cash holdings as in the FE model but at lower significance levels. The stakeholder variables *Suppliers*, *Employees*, and *Market-to-book ratio* are positive and significant as in the FE model but also at lower levels of significance. Additionally, the coefficients of *Market-to-book ratio* drops from 0.3457 to 0.1884 in the FD model, while the *Suppliers* coefficient increases from 0.0033 to 0.0051.

8 Conclusions and suggestions for future research

This dissertation develops the interdisciplinary approach of the stakeholder rationale for risk management. It shows that the stakeholder rationale for risk management is grounded in instrumental stakeholder theory, neo-institutional economic theories of the firm, and traditional financial approaches to risk management. Moreover, it is strongly related to the resource-based view that explains how non-financial stakeholders of the firm might promote value generation and lead to superior firm performance. It is theoretically shown that incorporating non-financial stakeholders into the firm's risk management strategy is in line with the predominant shareholder value perspective.

The stakeholder rationale for risk management contributes to the corporate finance literature by explaining conservative corporate financial decisions and by addressing the questions if and why shareholders might be in favor of such financial policies.

The empirical study addresses the question if the degree of conservativeness of the firm's financial policies is positively associated with the extent to which the firm is dependent on implicit claims with its non-financial stakeholders. The investigation shows that sample firms, which are valued highly relative to their book values by the capital markets, prefer lower debt and higher cash levels. This supports the notion that capital markets are aware of the fact that conservative financial policies contribute to shareholder value generation when the firm is more dependent on relation-specific investments on the part of non-financial stakeholders.

The evidence regarding the group-specific stakeholder variables is mixed. It shows that the sample firms value employees as an essential stakeholder group. The results presented provide support for the assumption that the firm's dependence on human capital is a strong determinant of the capital structure choice and the level of cash holdings. This result is consistent with the empirical predictions of the capital structure model of Berk et al. (2007), who assert that labor-intensive firms should have lower leverage than capital-intensive firms. From a viewpoint of the stakeholder rationale for risk management it can be argued that firms acknowledge that employees, compared to customers and suppliers, have the lowest possiblity to diversify the risk related to their firm-specific investments and therefore adjust their corporate finance decisions. The evidence regarding the firm's suppliers is too mixed to give clear proof that this stakeholder group significantly influences capital structure and liquidity policies. This finding is in line with the results of Bowen et al., who report low explanatory power of this variable (Bowen et al., 1995: 288). Since other papers identify the firm-supplier relations as an important determinant of corporate finance decisions (see, e.g., Banerjee et al. (2004) and Kale and Shahrur (2007)), a possible explanation may be that the *Suppliers* variable employed is an inappropriate proxy for the implicit relations between the firm and its suppliers.[110] Relative R&D-expense, the classic stakeholder proxy used in empirical corporate finance literature, does not show up as a determinant of either capital structure choice or the level of cash holdings. The *Customers* variable is insignificant in almost all subsamples. In the case the coefficient of *Customers* is significant, the sign is contrary to the predicted one. Surprisingly, and contrary to many previous studies, relative R&D expenses do not explain conservative financial decisions for the sample firms. This is astonishing since the negative relationship between R&D intensity and the firm's debt position is a broadly accepted regularity (Vicente-Lorente, 2001: 167). It might be the case, however, that this regularity does not hold for Austrian and German firms. Evidence supportive to these assumptions is provided by Brounen et al. (2006: 1415 and 1437), who report that only 15.04% of their German sample firms take customers' and suppliers' worries about the debt level into consideration when it comes to the capital structure decision. Further research should go in this direction to find out whether R&D intensity is also an important determinant of corporate finance decisions in German-speaking countries.

Overall, this empirical investigation provides partial support for the stakeholder rationale for risk management's hypothesis that the firm's degree of dependence on implicit stakeholder claims is positively related to conservative financial policies that lower the firm's risk profile and induce non-financial stakeholders to make value-enhancing relation-specific investments. However, mixed evidence among the accounting-specific subsamples is found. Several reasons might be responsible for these results.

From a methodological point of view it needs to be addressed that the fixed effects estimation controls for the firm-specific unobserved effects a_i only. There might also

---

[110] Unlike Austrian and German firms, the Statement of Financial Accounting Standards (SFAS) no. 14 and 131 require U.S. firms to disclose the identity of any customer that contributes at least 10% to the firm's revenues (Banerjee et al., 2004: 10; Kale and Shahrur, 2007: 331). This information enables Banerjee et al. (2004) and Kale and Shahrur (2007) to develop more sophisticated variables to proxy for the firm-supplier relation when analyzing the capital structure of their U.S. sample firms. For more details on the construction of their variables see the respective papers.

exist unobserved effects that vary both across entities and over time and influence the decisions on capital structure and cash holdings (e.g., management's attitude towards risk, ownership structure, product portfolio, etc.). These types of omitted variables, a_{it}, are not controlled for by the fixed effects estimation procedure applied.

Using the data set as a point of reference, the difference between European and U.S. company data needs to be emphasized. Unlike firms in the U.S., Austrian and German listed companies may report their financials statements according to either local or international accounting standards. Given the fact that these standards differ substantially, accounting ratios, which are prevalently used in empirical corporate finance research, are not comparable across the standards. In the last few years, many Austrian and German companies switched from local to, and between international standards (i.e. IAS/IFRS or U.S. GAAP). This fact created two general problems. First, it generated a highly unbalanced panel set for each observed accounting standard. Second, ratios were not allowed to be based on accounting data of different years because the standards for the same cross-section potentially varied across the time-series. Therefore, it was impossible to include a risk proxy in the regression models, capturing the volatility of earnings or cash flows, which would have been an interesting and important explanatory variable in the context of this work.

Another aspect refers to the length and quality of the data used. The empirical models set up in this work are tested on firm financial statement and capital market data from 2002 to 2004. Data from 1998 to 2001 were left unused in order to create a more homogeneous time-series within the data set as to the macroeconomic and capital market conditions in the countries analyzed. A longer time series with fewer shifts in accounting standards (i.e. a more balanced data set) would generally be advantageous for such panel estimations.

A major finding of this study is that accounting standards seem to play an important role when investigating the determinants of corporate finance decisions. This is especially true for studies on samples of European firms because these firms may choose between different accounting standards that are incomparable with each other. Hence, futures studies on corporate financial issues should consider these different standards when using accounting-based proxies.

This dissertation partially provides supportive empirical evidence for including stakeholder arguments in corporate finance and risk management. Like previous studies, one of the major problems lies in finding a way to proxy for stakeholder theory in general and for the implicit firm-stakeholder relations in particular. More research needs to be devoted to this apparent problem in empirical stakeholder-oriented corporate finance research.

Another natural extension of this research would be to examine the performance implications of the firm-stakeholder relationships together with conservative financial decisions.

Appendix A
(Industry classification of all samples for the 1998-2004 period)

Accounting standard classification: Local Standards						
			Firms		Observations	
category	NACE industry definition	NACE code	total #	in %	total #	in %
AA	Agriculture, hunting and related service activities	01	1	0.3%	7	0.4%
AA	Forestry, logging and related service activities	02	0	0.0%	0	0.0%
BA	Fishing, fish farming and related service activities	05	0	0.0%	0	0.0%
CA	Mining of coal and lignite; extraction of peat	10	0	0.0%	0	0.0%
CA	Extraction of crude petroleum and natural gas; service activities incidental to oil and gas extraction, excluding surveying	11	0	0.0%	0	0.0%
CA	Mining of uranium and thorium ores	12	0	0.0%	0	0.0%
CB	Mining of metal ores	13	0	0.0%	0	0.0%
CB	Other mining and quarrying	14	2	0.5%	8	0.5%
DA	Manufacture of food products and beverages	15	20	5.2%	113	6.9%
DA	Manufacture of tobacco products	16	0	0.0%	0	0.0%
DB	Manufacture of textiles	17	4	1.0%	16	1.0%
DB	Manufacture of wearing apparel; dressing and dyeing of fur	18	11	2.8%	63	3.9%
DC	Tanning and dressing of leather; manufacture of luggage, handbags, saddlery, harness and footwear	19	0	0.0%	0	0.0%
DD	Manufacture of wood and of products of wood and cork, except furniture; manufacture of articles of straw and plaiting materials	20	5	1.3%	31	1.9%
DE	Manufacture of pulp, paper and paper products	21	7	1.8%	32	2.0%
DE	Publishing, printing and reproduction of recorded media	22	5	1.3%	19	1.2%
DF	Manufacture of coke, refined petroleum products and nuclear fuel	23	1	0.3%	7	0.4%
DG	Manufacture of chemicals and chemical products	24	17	4.4%	62	3.8%
DH	Manufacture of rubber and plastic products	25	9	2.3%	40	2.4%
DI	Manufacture of other non-metallic mineral products	26	16	4.1%	85	5.2%
DJ	Manufacture of basic metals	27	4	1.0%	17	1.0%
DJ	Manufacture of fabricated metal products, except machinery and equipment	28	6	1.6%	18	1.1%
DK	Manufacture of machinery and equipment n.e.c.	29	31	8.0%	136	8.3%
DL	Manufacture of office machinery and computers	30	4	1.0%	19	1.2%
DL	Manufacture of electrical machinery and apparatus n.e.c.	31	6	1.6%	31	1.9%
DL	Manufacture of radio, television and communication equipment and apparatus	32	10	2.6%	29	1.8%
DL	Manufacture of medical, precision and optical instruments, watches and clocks	33	6	1.6%	31	1.9%
DM	Manufacture of motor vehicles, trailers and semi-trailers	34	15	3.9%	56	3.4%
DM	Manufacture of other transport equipment	35	3	0.8%	13	0.8%
DN	Manufacture of furniture; manufacturing n.e.c.	36	6	1.6%	30	1.8%
DN	Recycling	37	0	0.0%	0	0.0%
EA	Electricity, gas, steam and hot water supply	40	12	3.1%	60	3.7%
EA	Collection, purification and distribution of water	41	1	0.3%	7	0.4%
FA	Construction	45	9	2.3%	37	2.3%
GA	Sale, maintenance and repair of motor vehicles and motorcycles; retail sale of automotive fuel	50	1	0.3%	7	0.4%
GA	Wholesale trade and commission trade, except of motor vehicles and motorcycles	51	23	6.0%	114	7.0%
GA	Retail trade, except of motor vehicles and motorcycles; repair of personal and household goods	52	8	2.1%	37	2.3%
HA	Hotels and restaurants	55	3	0.8%	11	0.7%
IA	Land transport; transport via pipelines	60	0	0.0%	0	0.0%
IA	Water transport	61	3	0.8%	21	1.3%
IA	Air transport	62	1	0.3%	2	0.1%
IA	Supporting and auxiliary transport activities; activities of travel agencies	63	3	0.8%	10	0.6%
IA	Post and telecommunications	64	4	1.0%	12	0.7%
JA	Financial intermediation, except insurance and pension funding	65	0	0.0%	0	0.0%
JA	Insurance and pension funding, except compulsory social security	66	0	0.0%	0	0.0%
JA	Activities auxiliary to financial intermediation	67	0	0.0%	0	0.0%
KA	Real estate activities	70	0	0.0%	0	0.0%
KA	Renting of machinery and equipment without operator and of personal and household goods	71	3	0.8%	17	1.0%
KA	Computer and related activities	72	30	7.8%	64	3.9%
KA	Research and development	73	2	0.5%	7	0.4%
KA	Other business activities	74	71	18.4%	286	17.5%
LA	Public administration and defence; compulsory social security	75	0	0.0%	0	0.0%
MA	Education	80	0	0.0%	0	0.0%
NA	Health and social work	85	6	1.6%	32	2.0%
OA	Sewage and refuse disposal, sanitation and similar activities	90	0	0.0%	0	0.0%
OA	Activities of membership organizations n.e.c.	91	0	0.0%	0	0.0%
OA	Recreational, cultural and sporting activities	92	16	4.1%	43	2.6%
OA	Other service activities	93	1	0.3%	3	0.2%
PA	Activities of households as employers of domestic staff	95	0	0.0%	0	0.0%
PA	Undifferentiated goods producing activities of private households for own use	96	0	0.0%	0	0.0%
PA	Undifferentiated services producing activities of private households for own use	97	0	0.0%	0	0.0%
QA	Extra-territorial organizations and bodies	99	0	0.0%	0	0.0%
			386	**100%**	**1633**	**100%**

Accounting standard classification: IFRS						
			Firms		Observations	
category	NACE industry definition	NACE code	total #	in %	total #	in %
AA	Agriculture, hunting and related service activities	01	0	0.0%	0	0.0%
AA	Forestry, logging and related service activities	02	0	0.0%	0	0.0%
BA	Fishing, fish farming and related service activities	05	0	0.0%	0	0.0%
CA	Mining of coal and lignite; extraction of peat	10	0	0.0%	0	0.0%
CA	Extraction of crude petroleum and natural gas; service activities incidental to oil and gas extraction, excluding surveying	11	0	0.0%	0	0.0%
CA	Mining of uranium and thorium ores	12	0	0.0%	0	0.0%
CB	Mining of metal ores	13	0	0.0%	0	0.0%
CB	Other mining and quarrying	14	1	0.3%	2	0.2%
DA	Manufacture of food products and beverages	15	3	1.0%	9	0.9%
DA	Manufacture of tobacco products	16	0	0.0%	0	0.0%
DB	Manufacture of textiles	17	3	1.0%	14	1.3%
DB	Manufacture of wearing apparel; dressing and dyeing of fur	18	4	1.4%	21	2.0%
DC	Tanning and dressing of leather; manufacture of luggage, handbags, saddlery, harness and footwear	19	0	0.0%	0	0.0%
DD	Manufacture of wood and of products of wood and cork, except furniture; manufacture of articles of straw and plaiting materials	20	0	0.0%	0	0.0%
DE	Manufacture of pulp, paper and paper products	21	3	1.0%	10	1.0%
DE	Publishing, printing and reproduction of recorded media	22	4	1.4%	7	0.7%
DF	Manufacture of coke, refined petroleum products and nuclear fuel	23	0	0.0%	0	0.0%
DG	Manufacture of chemicals and chemical products	24	13	4.5%	66	6.3%
DH	Manufacture of rubber and plastic products	25	5	1.7%	20	1.9%
DI	Manufacture of other non-metallic mineral products	26	8	2.8%	35	3.4%
DJ	Manufacture of basic metals	27	4	1.4%	15	1.4%
DJ	Manufacture of fabricated metal products, except machinery and equipment	28	2	0.7%	9	0.9%
DK	Manufacture of machinery and equipment n.e.c.	29	22	7.7%	76	7.3%
DL	Manufacture of office machinery and computers	30	2	0.7%	8	0.8%
DL	Manufacture of electrical machinery and apparatus n.e.c.	31	5	1.7%	15	1.4%
DL	Manufacture of radio, television and communication equipment and apparatus	32	10	3.5%	35	3.4%
DL	Manufacture of medical, precision and optical instruments, watches and clocks	33	13	4.5%	41	3.9%
DM	Manufacture of motor vehicles, trailers and semi-trailers	34	9	3.1%	35	3.4%
DM	Manufacture of other transport equipment	35	3	1.0%	10	1.0%
DN	Manufacture of furniture; manufacturing n.e.c.	36	0	0.0%	0	0.0%
DN	Recycling	37	0	0.0%	0	0.0%
EA	Electricity, gas, steam and hot water supply	40	7	2.4%	37	3.6%
EA	Collection, purification and distribution of water	41	0	0.0%	0	0.0%
FA	Construction	45	6	2.1%	19	1.8%
GA	Sale, maintenance and repair of motor vehicles and motorcycles; retail sale of automotive fuel	50	0	0.0%	0	0.0%
GA	Wholesale trade and commission trade, except of motor vehicles and motorcycles	51	18	6.3%	77	7.4%
GA	Retail trade, except of motor vehicles and motorcycles; repair of personal and household goods	52	1	0.3%	2	0.2%
HA	Hotels and restaurants	55	1	0.3%	3	0.3%
IA	Land transport; transport via pipelines	60	0	0.0%	0	0.0%
IA	Water transport	61	0	0.0%	0	0.0%
IA	Air transport	62	2	0.7%	12	1.2%
IA	Supporting and auxiliary transport activities; activities of travel agencies	63	4	1.4%	13	1.2%
IA	Post and telecommunications	64	5	1.7%	20	1.9%
JA	Financial intermediation, except insurance and pension funding	65	0	0.0%	0	0.0%
JA	Insurance and pension funding, except compulsory social security	66	0	0.0%	0	0.0%
JA	Activities auxiliary to financial intermediation	67	0	0.0%	0	0.0%
KA	Real estate activities	70	0	0.0%	0	0.0%
KA	Renting of machinery and equipment without operator and of personal and household goods	71	2	0.7%	8	0.8%
KA	Computer and related activities	72	48	16.8%	172	16.5%
KA	Research and development	73	6	2.1%	18	1.7%
KA	Other business activities	74	48	16.8%	154	14.8%
LA	Public administration and defence; compulsory social security	75	0	0.0%	0	0.0%
MA	Education	80	0	0.0%	0	0.0%
NA	Health and social work	85	2	0.7%	8	0.8%
OA	Sewage and refuse disposal, sanitation and similar activities	90	0	0.0%	0	0.0%
OA	Activities of membership organizations n.e.c.	91	0	0.0%	0	0.0%
OA	Recreational, cultural and sporting activities	92	21	7.3%	69	6.6%
OA	Other service activities	93	1	0.3%	1	0.1%
PA	Activities of households as employers of domestic staff	95	0	0.0%	0	0.0%
PA	Undifferentiated goods producing activities of private households for own use	96	0	0.0%	0	0.0%
PA	Undifferentiated services producing activities of private households for own use	97	0	0.0%	0	0.0%
QA	Extra-territorial organizations and bodies	99	0	0.0%	0	0.0%
			286	**100%**	**1041**	**100%**

Accounting standard classification: US GAAP						
			Firms		Observations	
category	NACE industry definition	NACE code	total #	in %	total #	in %
AA	Agriculture, hunting and related service activities	01	0	0.0%	0	0.0%
AA	Forestry, logging and related service activities	02	0	0.0%	0	0.0%
BA	Fishing, fish farming and related service activities	05	0	0.0%	0	0.0%
CA	Mining of coal and lignite; extraction of peat	10	0	0.0%	0	0.0%
CA	Extraction of crude petroleum and natural gas; service activities incidental to oil and gas extraction, excluding surveying	11	0	0.0%	0	0.0%
CA	Mining of uranium and thorium ores	12	0	0.0%	0	0.0%
CB	Mining of metal ores	13	0	0.0%	0	0.0%
CB	Other mining and quarrying	14	0	0.0%	0	0.0%
DA	Manufacture of food products and beverages	15	0	0.0%	0	0.0%
DA	Manufacture of tobacco products	16	0	0.0%	0	0.0%
DB	Manufacture of textiles	17	0	0.0%	0	0.0%
DB	Manufacture of wearing apparel; dressing and dyeing of fur	18	0	0.0%	0	0.0%
DC	Tanning and dressing of leather; manufacture of luggage, handbags, saddlery, harness and footwear	19	0	0.0%	0	0.0%
DD	Manufacture of wood and of products of wood and cork, except furniture; manufacture of articles of straw and plaiting materials	20	1	0.7%	3	0.5%
DE	Manufacture of pulp, paper and paper products	21	1	0.7%	5	0.9%
DE	Publishing, printing and reproduction of recorded media	22	1	0.7%	1	0.2%
DF	Manufacture of coke, refined petroleum products and nuclear fuel	23	0	0.0%	0	0.0%
DG	Manufacture of chemicals and chemical products	24	9	6.6%	40	7.0%
DH	Manufacture of rubber and plastic products	25	0	0.0%	0	0.0%
DI	Manufacture of other non-metallic mineral products	26	0	0.0%	0	0.0%
DJ	Manufacture of basic metals	27	0	0.0%	0	0.0%
DJ	Manufacture of fabricated metal products, except machinery and equipment	28	2	1.5%	9	1.6%
DK	Manufacture of machinery and equipment n.e.c.	29	8	5.8%	40	7.0%
DL	Manufacture of office machinery and computers	30	1	0.7%	3	0.5%
DL	Manufacture of electrical machinery and apparatus n.e.c.	31	3	2.2%	17	3.0%
DL	Manufacture of radio, television and communication equipment and apparatus	32	6	4.4%	28	4.9%
DL	Manufacture of medical, precision and optical instruments, watches and clocks	33	16	11.7%	71	12.4%
DM	Manufacture of motor vehicles, trailers and semi-trailers	34	3	2.2%	17	3.0%
DM	Manufacture of other transport equipment	35	0	0.0%	0	0.0%
DN	Manufacture of furniture; manufacturing n.e.c.	36	1	0.7%	4	0.7%
DN	Recycling	37	0	0.0%	0	0.0%
EA	Electricity, gas, steam and hot water supply	40	1	0.7%	5	0.9%
EA	Collection, purification and distribution of water	41	0	0.0%	0	0.0%
FA	Construction	45	0	0.0%	0	0.0%
GA	Sale, maintenance and repair of motor vehicles and motorcycles; retail sale of automotive fuel	50	0	0.0%	0	0.0%
GA	Wholesale trade and commission trade, except of motor vehicles and motorcycles	51	2	1.5%	8	1.4%
GA	Retail trade, except of motor vehicles and motorcycles; repair of personal and household goods	52	3	2.2%	11	1.9%
HA	Hotels and restaurants	55	0	0.0%	0	0.0%
IA	Land transport; transport via pipelines	60	0	0.0%	0	0.0%
IA	Water transport	61	0	0.0%	0	0.0%
IA	Air transport	62	0	0.0%	0	0.0%
IA	Supporting and auxiliary transport activities; activities of travel agencies	63	3	2.2%	14	2.4%
IA	Post and telecommunications	64	3	2.2%	16	2.8%
JA	Financial intermediation, except insurance and pension funding	65	0	0.0%	0	0.0%
JA	Insurance and pension funding, except compulsory social security	66	0	0.0%	0	0.0%
JA	Activities auxiliary to financial intermediation	67	0	0.0%	0	0.0%
KA	Real estate activities	70	0	0.0%	0	0.0%
KA	Renting of machinery and equipment without operator and of personal and household goods	71	0	0.0%	0	0.0%
KA	Computer and related activities	72	39	28.5%	144	25.1%
KA	Research and development	73	6	4.4%	31	5.4%
KA	Other business activities	74	18	13.1%	75	13.1%
LA	Public administration and defence; compulsory social security	75	0	0.0%	0	0.0%
MA	Education	80	0	0.0%	0	0.0%
NA	Health and social work	85	0	0.0%	0	0.0%
OA	Sewage and refuse disposal, sanitation and similar activities	90	1	0.7%	5	0.9%
OA	Activities of membership organizations n.e.c.	91	0	0.0%	0	0.0%
OA	Recreational, cultural and sporting activities	92	8	5.8%	24	4.2%
OA	Other service activities	93	1	0.7%	2	0.3%
PA	Activities of households as employers of domestic staff	95	0	0.0%	0	0.0%
PA	Undifferentiated goods producing activities of private households for own use	96	0	0.0%	0	0.0%
PA	Undifferentiated services producing activities of private households for own use	97	0	0.0%	0	0.0%
QA	Extra-territorial organizations and bodies	99	0	0.0%	0	0.0%
			137	**100%**	**573**	**100%**

Accounting standard classification: Overall sample						
			Firms		Observations	
category	NACE industry definition	NACE code	total #	in %	total #	in %
AA	Agriculture, hunting and related service activities	01	1	0.2%	7	0.2%
AA	Forestry, logging and related service activities	02	0	0.0%	0	0.0%
BA	Fishing, fish farming and related service activities	05	0	0.0%	0	0.0%
CA	Mining of coal and lignite; extraction of peat	10	0	0.0%	0	0.0%
CA	Extraction of crude petroleum and natural gas; service activities incidental to oil and gas extraction, excluding surveying	11	0	0.0%	0	0.0%
CA	Mining of uranium and thorium ores	12	0	0.0%	0	0.0%
CB	Mining of metal ores	13	0	0.0%	0	0.0%
CB	Other mining and quarrying	14	2	0.3%	10	0.3%
DA	Manufacture of food products and beverages	15	20	3.4%	122	3.8%
DA	Manufacture of tobacco products	16	0	0.0%	0	0.0%
DB	Manufacture of textiles	17	5	0.8%	30	0.9%
DB	Manufacture of wearing apparel; dressing and dyeing of fur	18	13	2.2%	84	2.6%
DC	Tanning and dressing of leather; manufacture of luggage, handbags, saddlery, harness and footwear	19	0	0.0%	0	0.0%
DD	Manufacture of wood and of products of wood and cork, except furniture; manufacture of articles of straw and plaiting materials	20	5	0.8%	34	1.0%
DE	Manufacture of pulp, paper and paper products	21	8	1.3%	47	1.4%
DE	Publishing, printing and reproduction of recorded media	22	6	1.0%	27	0.8%
DF	Manufacture of coke, refined petroleum products and nuclear fuel	23	1	0.2%	7	0.2%
DG	Manufacture of chemicals and chemical products	24	27	4.6%	168	5.2%
DH	Manufacture of rubber and plastic products	25	11	1.9%	60	1.8%
DI	Manufacture of other non-metallic mineral products	26	18	3.0%	120	3.7%
DJ	Manufacture of basic metals	27	5	0.8%	32	1.0%
DJ	Manufacture of fabricated metal products, except machinery and equipment	28	6	1.0%	36	1.1%
DK	Manufacture of machinery and equipment n.e.c.	29	41	6.9%	252	7.8%
DL	Manufacture of office machinery and computers	30	6	1.0%	30	0.9%
DL	Manufacture of electrical machinery and apparatus n.e.c.	31	11	1.9%	63	1.9%
DL	Manufacture of radio, television and communication equipment and apparatus	32	18	3.0%	92	2.8%
DL	Manufacture of medical, precision and optical instruments, watches and clocks	33	28	4.7%	143	4.4%
DM	Manufacture of motor vehicles, trailers and semi-trailers	34	17	2.9%	108	3.3%
DM	Manufacture of other transport equipment	35	5	0.8%	23	0.7%
DN	Manufacture of furniture; manufacturing n.e.c.	36	6	1.0%	34	1.0%
DN	Recycling	37	0	0.0%	0	0.0%
EA	Electricity, gas, steam and hot water supply	40	16	2.7%	102	3.1%
EA	Collection, purification and distribution of water	41	1	0.2%	7	0.2%
FA	Construction	45	9	1.5%	56	1.7%
GA	Sale, maintenance and repair of motor vehicles and motorcycles; retail sale of automotive fuel	50	1	0.2%	7	0.2%
GA	Wholesale trade and commission trade, except of motor vehicles and motorcycles	51	33	5.6%	199	6.1%
GA	Retail trade, except of motor vehicles and motorcycles; repair of personal and household goods	52	9	1.5%	50	1.5%
HA	Hotels and restaurants	55	3	0.5%	14	0.4%
IA	Land transport; transport via pipelines	60	0	0.0%	0	0.0%
IA	Water transport	61	3	0.5%	21	0.6%
IA	Air transport	62	2	0.3%	14	0.4%
IA	Supporting and auxiliary transport activities; activities of travel agencies	63	6	1.0%	37	1.1%
IA	Post and telecommunications	64	8	1.3%	48	1.5%
JA	Financial intermediation, except insurance and pension funding	65	0	0.0%	0	0.0%
JA	Insurance and pension funding, except compulsory social security	66	0	0.0%	0	0.0%
JA	Activities auxiliary to financial intermediation	67	0	0.0%	0	0.0%
KA	Real estate activities	70	0	0.0%	0	0.0%
KA	Renting of machinery and equipment without operator and of personal and household goods	71	5	0.8%	25	0.8%
KA	Computer and related activities	72	84	14.2%	380	11.7%
KA	Research and development	73	12	2.0%	56	1.7%
KA	Other business activities	74	102	17.2%	515	15.9%
LA	Public administration and defence; compulsory social security	75	0	0.0%	0	0.0%
MA	Education	80	0	0.0%	0	0.0%
NA	Health and social work	85	7	1.2%	40	1.2%
OA	Sewage and refuse disposal, sanitation and similar activities	90	1	0.2%	5	0.2%
OA	Activities of membership organizations n.e.c.	91	0	0.0%	0	0.0%
OA	Recreational, cultural and sporting activities	92	29	4.9%	136	4.2%
OA	Other service activities	93	2	0.3%	6	0.2%
PA	Activities of households as employers of domestic staff	95	0	0.0%	0	0.0%
PA	Undifferentiated goods producing activities of private households for own use	96	0	0.0%	0	0.0%
PA	Undifferentiated services producing activities of private households for own use	97	0	0.0%	0	0.0%
QA	Extra-territorial organizations and bodies	99	0	0.0%	0	0.0%
			593	**100%**	**3247**	**100%**

Appendix B
(Descriptive statistics of all samples for the 2002-2004 period)

Accounting standard classification: Local Standards

Variables winsorized at 1st and 99th percentiles; Sample period: 2002 - 2004

	nlog Leverage	nlog Cash holdings	nlog Size	Profitability
Mean	4.30	1.70	11.21	6.87
Median	4.44	1.73	11.61	9.39
Maximum	4.60	8.10	17.32	44.62
Minimum	2.05	-4.02	5.27	-70.77
Std. Dev.	0.41	1.87	2.24	14.57
Skewness	-2.78	0.00	-0.45	-1.72
Kurtosis	12.18	3.55	3.07	8.75
Observations	425	694	688	680

	Characteristics of assets	Cash substitutes	Leverage/liquidity constraints	Growth opportunities
Mean	6.23	9.32	60.37	4.61
Median	2.19	9.60	62.93	3.24
Maximum	52.60	68.49	119.78	37.90
Minimum	0.00	-72.56	2.30	0.00
Std. Dev.	9.59	25.30	24.85	5.14
Skewness	2.35	-0.29	-0.31	2.59
Kurtosis	8.48	2.97	2.67	12.57
Observations	691	616	682	670

	Customers	Suppliers	Employees	Market-to-book ratio
Mean	3.23	96.44	19.70	0.81
Median	2.01	84.80	28.08	0.80
Maximum	21.57	391.04	99.76	2.21
Minimum	0.00	0.05	-156.67	0.20
Std. Dev.	3.66	69.90	55.28	0.27
Skewness	2.22	1.33	-0.58	1.06
Kurtosis	9.79	5.60	2.66	6.54
Observations	98	654	629	430

Accounting standard classification: IFRS

Variables winsorized at 1st and 99th percentiles; Sample period: 2002 - 2004

	nlog Leverage	nlog Cash holdings	nlog Size	Profitability
Mean	4.11	2.46	12.07	5.28
Median	4.32	2.38	11.77	9.36
Maximum	4.59	6.08	17.59	42.34
Minimum	1.95	-1.72	7.95	-103.38
Std. Dev.	0.52	1.42	2.13	19.49
Skewness	-1.71	-0.03	0.50	-2.40
Kurtosis	5.55	2.68	2.57	11.30
Observations	446	686	686	670

	Characteristics of assets	Cash substitutes	Leverage/liquidity constraints	Growth opportunities
Mean	15.13	0.62	55.27	4.30
Median	9.58	2.40	58.88	3.18
Maximum	70.67	58.41	123.90	30.53
Minimum	0.01	-105.21	-9.91	0.00
Std. Dev.	15.02	26.99	23.58	4.10
Skewness	1.31	-0.90	-0.35	2.20
Kurtosis	4.29	4.72	2.92	10.15
Observations	685	688	681	692

	Customers	Suppliers	Employees	Market-to-book ratio
Mean	4.60	91.32	47.44	0.97
Median	2.68	81.44	58.88	0.88
Maximum	40.32	378.06	99.19	3.64
Minimum	0.00	3.73	-74.35	0.25
Std. Dev.	5.97	63.94	41.32	0.41
Skewness	2.39	1.46	-0.81	2.20
Kurtosis	10.33	5.70	2.80	11.00
Observations	335	675	674	451

Accounting standard classification: US GAAP

Variables winsorized at 1st and 99th percentiles; Sample period: 2002 - 2004

	nlog Leverage	nlog Cash holdings	nlog Size	Profitability
Mean	3.89	3.06	11.68	-0.27
Median	4.03	2.97	11.43	7.77
Maximum	4.59	6.62	18.25	33.46
Minimum	1.93	-1.19	6.67	-106.55
Std. Dev.	0.60	1.47	2.18	23.96
Skewness	-1.31	-0.08	0.80	-1.84
Kurtosis	4.24	3.29	3.44	6.68
Observations	208	305	302	276

	Characteristics of assets	Cash substitutes	Leverage/liquidity constraints	Growth opportunities
Mean	15.00	-2.25	47.98	3.87
Median	12.01	3.44	47.35	2.76
Maximum	55.50	53.18	132.05	18.58
Minimum	0.00	-132.94	0.33	0.00
Std. Dev.	13.61	33.74	24.63	3.58
Skewness	0.87	-1.69	0.38	1.54
Kurtosis	3.11	6.55	3.05	5.31
Observations	307	303	303	313

	Customers	Suppliers	Employees	Market-to-book ratio
Mean	8.66	66.72	56.51	0.94
Median	6.42	56.75	67.88	0.85
Maximum	45.40	293.14	99.13	4.78
Minimum	0.00	0.00	-39.82	0.24
Std. Dev.	8.94	54.90	33.44	0.55
Skewness	1.67	1.65	-0.96	3.49
Kurtosis	5.87	6.26	3.05	20.60
Observations	229	295	288	211

Accounting standard classification: Overall sample

Variables winsorized at 1st and 99th percentiles; Sample period: 2002 - 2004

	nlog Leverage	nlog Cash holdings	nlog Size	Profitability
Mean	4.14	2.22	11.66	4.99
Median	4.34	2.27	11.65	9.13
Maximum	4.60	6.21	17.62	42.77
Minimum	1.45	-3.34	5.67	-103.38
Std. Dev.	0.53	1.65	2.19	18.68
Skewness	-1.95	-0.31	0.16	-2.23
Kurtosis	6.90	3.17	3.11	10.26
Observations	1082	1672	1672	1628

	Characteristics of assets	Cash substitutes	Leverage/liquidity constraints	Growth opportunities
Mean	11.31	3.44	56.37	4.37
Median	5.59	5.77	59.05	3.11
Maximum	68.85	62.43	128.99	32.84
Minimum	0.00	-111.81	-2.62	0.00
Std. Dev.	13.23	27.52	24.69	4.54
Skewness	1.48	-0.89	-0.12	2.50
Kurtosis	4.69	4.69	2.71	12.36
Observations	1685	1607	1666	1678

	Customers	Suppliers	Employees	Market-to-book ratio
Mean	5.85	89.23	38.08	0.90
Median	3.40	77.08	49.35	0.85
Maximum	43.84	373.05	99.50	4.78
Minimum	0.00	0.02	-122.30	0.20
Std. Dev.	7.24	65.48	48.39	0.43
Skewness	2.17	1.40	-0.87	3.27
Kurtosis	8.51	5.53	3.09	22.28
Observations	663	1620	1592	1096

Appendix C

(Correlation matrices of all samples for the 2002-2004 period)

Local standards

Variables winsorized at 1st and 99th percentiles; Sample period 2002 - 2004

No.	Variable	1	2	3	4	5	6	7	8	9	10	11	12
1	nlog Leverage	1.000	-0.150	-0.103	0.103	-0.107	-0.506	-0.296	0.718	-0.078	0.103	-0.330	-0.093
2	Characteristics of assets		1.000	-0.126	0.106	0.200	0.097	-0.255	-0.056	0.354	-0.322	0.396	0.163
3	Growth opportunities			1.000	0.372	0.347	-0.011	-0.072	-0.059	0.088	0.004	-0.390	0.143
4	nlog Size				1.000	0.510	0.063	-0.079	0.308	0.249	-0.120	-0.098	0.467
5	Profitability					1.000	0.081	0.056	0.074	0.240	0.021	-0.110	0.338
6	nlog Cash holdings						1.000	0.348	-0.392	0.092	-0.239	0.462	-0.047
7	Cash Substitutes							1.000	-0.471	0.117	0.379	0.247	-0.310
8	Leverage/Liquidity constraints								1.000	0.092	-0.175	-0.267	0.580
9	Customers									1.000	-0.154	-0.005	0.273
10	Suppliers										1.000	-0.154	-0.335
11	Employees											1.000	-0.042
12	Market-to-book ratio												1.000

IFRS

Variables winsorized at 1st and 99th percentiles; Sample period 2002 - 2004

No.	Variable	1	2	3	4	5	6	7	8	9	10	11	12
1	nlog Leverage	1.000	-0.029	0.114	0.265	-0.294	-0.528	-0.217	0.704	-0.318	0.143	-0.392	-0.688
2	Characteristics of assets		1.000	-0.303	-0.145	-0.021	-0.024	-0.167	-0.127	0.157	-0.196	0.338	-0.073
3	Growth opportunities			1.000	0.191	0.181	-0.203	-0.021	0.133	-0.105	0.002	-0.450	0.009
4	nlog Size				1.000	0.321	-0.278	0.109	0.501	-0.233	-0.062	-0.305	0.135
5	Profitability					1.000	-0.102	0.322	-0.150	-0.006	-0.037	-0.066	0.326
6	nlog Cash holdings						1.000	-0.186	-0.541	0.342	0.032	0.408	0.196
7	Cash Substitutes							1.000	-0.255	-0.031	-0.033	-0.001	0.105
8	Leverage/Liquidity constraints								1.000	-0.382	0.130	-0.352	-0.048
9	Customers									1.000	-0.241	0.267	0.107
10	Suppliers										1.000	0.067	-0.030
11	Employees											1.000	0.186
12	Market-to-book ratio												1.000

US GAAP

Variables winsorized at 1st and 99th percentiles; Sample period 2002 - 2004

No.	Variable	1	2	3	4	5	6	7	8	9	10	11	12
1	nlog Leverage	1.000	0.187	0.238	0.332	0.028	-0.512	-0.126	0.712	-0.471	0.371	-0.254	-0.508
2	Characteristics of assets		1.000	-0.196	0.114	-0.097	-0.379	-0.033	0.154	-0.077	0.044	0.351	-0.078
3	Growth opportunities			1.000	0.243	0.282	-0.317	0.073	0.216	-0.227	-0.025	-0.579	-0.064
4	nlog Size				1.000	0.477	-0.542	0.186	0.490	-0.358	0.160	-0.296	0.191
5	Profitability					1.000	-0.309	0.469	0.029	-0.332	0.015	-0.130	0.056
6	nlog Cash holdings						1.000	-0.281	-0.478	0.410	-0.187	0.310	0.151
7	Cash Substitutes							1.000	-0.345	-0.354	0.005	0.115	-0.188
8	Leverage/Liquidity constraints								1.000	-0.319	0.434	-0.323	0.121
9	Customers									1.000	-0.364	0.134	0.314
10	Suppliers										1.000	0.035	-0.017
11	Employees											1.000	-0.042
12	Market-to-book ratio												1.000

Overall sample

Variables winsorized at 1st and 99th percentiles; Sample period 2002 - 2004

No.	Variable	1	2	3	4	5	6	7	8	9	10	11	12
1	nlog Leverage	1.000	-0.036	0.142	0.267	-0.071	-0.536	-0.152	0.726	-0.361	0.260	-0.361	-0.564
2	Characteristics of assets		1.000	-0.232	-0.017	-0.061	-0.041	-0.173	-0.105	0.135	-0.153	0.395	-0.048
3	Growth opportunities			1.000	0.239	0.238	-0.196	-0.045	0.139	-0.108	-0.004	-0.441	-0.011
4	nlog Size				1.000	0.413	-0.299	0.097	0.441	-0.251	-0.003	-0.265	0.175
5	Profitability					1.000	-0.171	0.318	0.028	-0.201	-0.005	-0.126	0.177
6	nlog Cash holdings						1.000	-0.135	-0.550	0.299	-0.148	0.443	0.149
7	Cash Substitutes							1.000	-0.267	-0.121	0.011	0.042	-0.063
8	Leverage/Liquidity constraints								1.000	-0.338	0.262	-0.372	0.048
9	Customers									1.000	-0.269	0.219	0.182
10	Suppliers										1.000	-0.043	-0.040
11	Employees											1.000	0.074
12	Market-to-book ratio												1.000

Appendix D
(FD capital structure model results of Local Standards/IFRS firms)

Dependent variable		Δnlog Leverage	
Estimation method		First Differences	
Sample period		2002 - 2004	
	Expected sign	Local Standards	IFRS
ΔCharacteristics of assets	-	-0.0020	0.0081 ***
		(0.510)	(0.007)
ΔGrowth opportunities	-/+	-0.0032	-0.0100
		(0.256)	(0.171)
Δnlog Size	+	0.1879 ***	0.2008 **
		(0.002)	(0.063)
ΔProfitability	+/-	-0.0050 **	-0.0078 ***
		(0.013)	(0.000)
ΔCustomers	-	0.0100	0.0187
		(0.194)	(0.106)
ΔSuppliers	-	-0.0018 *	-0.0017
		(0.052)	(0.291)
ΔEmployees	-	-0.0039 ***	-0.0037 **
		(0.003)	(0.011)
ΔMarket-to-book ratio	-	-0.6421 ***	-0.6791 ***
		(0.000)	(0.000)
Year 03		-0.0584 ***	-0.0388
		(0.001)	(0.268)
Year 04		-0.0048	-0.0451
		(0.844)	(0.107)
Industry Dummy	-	-0.0673 ***	0.0420 *
		(0.001)	(0.078)
Coef covariance method		Cross-section SUR	Cross-section SUR
Cross-sections included		25	72
Total panel observations		54	142
R^2		82.21%	68.30%
Adjusted R^2		77.55%	65.61%
S.E. of regression		8.60%	17.08%
F-statistic		17.6448 ***	17.6448 ***
Probability (F-statistic)		(0.000)	(0.000)
Autocorr. of residuals at lag 1 in FD model		0.0602	0.0320
		(0.793)	(0.810)

* p < 0.1; ** p < 0.05; *** p < 0.01 (p-values in parentheses)
All variables are winsorized at the 1st and 99th percentiles

Appendix E
(FD cash holdings model results of US GAAP/Overall sample firms)

Dependent variable		Δnlog Cash holdings	
Estimation method		First Differences	
Sample period		2002 - 2004	
	Expected sign	US GAAP	Overall
ΔCash substitutes	-	-0.0112 ***	-0.0065 *
		(0.000)	(0.091)
ΔLeverage/liquidity constraints	+/-	-0.0232 ***	-0.0173 *
		(0.001)	(0.080)
Δnlog Size	-	-0.0292	-0.3419 **
		(0.877)	(0.032)
ΔGrowth opportunities	+/-	-0.0319	-0.0103
		(0.218)	(0.575)
ΔCustomers	+	-0.0230	-0.0109
		(0.396)	(0.341)
ΔSuppliers	+	0.0012	0.0051 *
		(0.738)	(0.068)
ΔEmployees	+	0.0106	0.0111 ***
		(0.211)	(0.002)
ΔMarket-to-book ratio	+	0.1260	0.1884 *
		(0.438)	(0.077)
Year 03		0.0142	0.0077
		(0.929)	(0.928)
Year 04		0.0315	0.1074
		(0.820)	(0.200)
Industry Dummy	+	-0.1725	-0.0883
		(0.228)	(0.314)
Dividend Dummy	-	-0.0063	-0.0587
		(0.966)	(0.440)
Coef covariance method		Cross-section SUR	Cross-section SUR
Cross-sections included		59	154
Total panel observations		132	371
R^2		16.16%	10.00%
Adjusted R^2		7.71%	6.98%
S.E. of regression		73.74%	76.34%
F-statistic		1.9119 **	3.3133 ***
Probability (F-statistic)		(0.039)	(0.000)
Autocorr. of residuals at lag 1 in FD model		-0.1089	-0.1779 ***
		(0.297)	(0.004)

* $p < 0.1$; ** $p < 0.05$; *** $p < 0.01$ (p-values in parentheses)
All variables are winsorized at the 1st and 99th percentiles

References

Aabo, T. (2004). Stakeholder versus Shareholder Satisfaction in Corporate Risk Management. EFMA 2004 Basel Meeting Paper. Available on the internet on: http://ssrn.com/abstract=487602.

Aaker, D.A. and Jacobson, R. (1990). The Risk of Marketing: The Roles of Systematic, Uncontrollable and Controllable Unsystematic, and Downside Risk. In Bettis, R.A. and Thomas, H. (eds.). *Risk, Strategy, and Management*. pp. 137–160. JAI Press Inc., Greenwich.

Acharya, V.V., Almeida, H. and Campello, M. (2005). Is Cash Negative Debt? A Hedging Perspective on Corporate Financial Policies. CEPR Working Paper. Version as of February, 2005. Available on the internet on: http://cepr.org/pubs/dps/DP4886.asp.

Akerlof, G.A. (1970). The Market for "Lemons": Quality Uncertainty and the Markt Mechanism. *The Quarterly Journal of Economics* 84: 488–500.

Alchian, A.A. (1965). Some Economics of Property Rights. *Il Politico* 30: 816–829. Reprinted in Alchian, A.A. (ed.). *Economic Forces at Work*. pp. 127–149. Liberty Press, Indianapolis.

Alchian, A.A. and Demsetz, H. (1972). Production, Information Costs, and Economic Organization. *American Economic Review* 62: 777–795.

Alchian, A.A. and Woodward, S. (1988). The Firm is Dead; Long Live the Firm. A Review of Oliver E. Williamson's *The Economic Institutions of Capitalism*. *Journal of Economic Literature* 26: 65–79.

Allayannis, G., Rountree, B. and Weston, J.P. (2005). Earnings Volatility, Cash Flow Volatility, and Firm Value. Working Paper. Version as of December, 2005. Available on the internet on: http://faculty.fuqua.duke.edu/seminarscalendar/Rountree.doc

Allen, F. and Michaely, R. (1995). Dividend Policy. In Jarrow, R., Maksimovic, V. and Ziemba, W.T. (eds.). *Handbooks in Operations Research and Management Science*. pp. 793–837. Elsevier, Amsterdam et al.

Allen, F. and Santomero, A.M. (1998). The Theory of Financial Intermediation. *Journal of Banking & Finance* 21: 1461–1485.

Almeida, H., Campello, M. and Weisbach, M.S. (2002). Corporate Demand for Liquidity. *NBER Working Paper* Nr. 9253. Available on the internet on: http://www.nber.org/papers/w9253.

Amit, R. and Wernerfelt, B. (1990). Why Do Firms Reduce Business Risk? *Academy of Management Journal* 33: 520–533.

Asher, C.C., Mahoney, J.M. and Mahoney, J.T. (2005). Towards a Property Rights Foundation for a Stakeholder Theory of the Firm. *Journal of Management and Governance* 9: 5–32.

Asteriou, D. (2006). Applied Econometrics. A Modern Approach using EViews and Microfit. Palgrave Macmillan, New York.

Atkinson, A.A., Waterhouse, J.H. and Wells, R.B. (1997). A Stakeholder Approach to Strategic Performance Measurement. *SLOAN MANAGEMENT REVIEW* Spring: 25–37.

Balakrishnan, S. and Fox, I. (1993). Asset Specificity, Firm Heterogeneity and Capital Structure. *Strategic Management Journal* 14: 3–16.

Banerjee, S., Dasgupta, S. and Kim, Y. (2004). Buyer-Supplier Relationships and the Stakeholder Theory of Capital Structure. SSRN Working Paper. Version as of September, 2004.

Barclay, M.J. and Smith, C.W. (1999). The Capital Structure Puzzle: Another Look at the Evidence. *Journal of Applied Corporate Finance* 12: 8–20

Barney, J.R. (1986). Strategic Factor Markets: Expectations, Luck and Business Strategy. *Management Science* 42: 1231–1241.

Barney, J.R. (1991). Firm Resources and Sustained Competitive Advantage. *Journal of Management* 17: 99–120.

Barney, J.R. (1996). The Resource-based Theory of the Firm. *Organization Science* 7: 469.

Barney, J.R. (2001). Resource-based *Theories* of Competitive Advantage: A Ten-year Retrospective on the Resource-based View. *Journal of Management* 27: 643–650.

Barney, J.R. and Hesterly, W. (1996). Organizational Economics: Understanding the Relationship between Organizations and Economic Analysis. In: Clegg, S., Hardy, C. and Nord, W.R. (eds.). *Handbook of Organization Studies*. pp. 115–147. Sage, Thousand Oaks.

Barney, J.R., Wright, M. and Ketchen, D.J. (2001). The Resource-based View of the Firm: Ten Years after 1991. *Journal of Management* 27: 625–641.

Barton, S.L. and Gordon, P.J. (1987). Corporate Strategy: Useful Perspective for the Study of Capital Structure? *Academy of Management Review* 12: 67–75.

Barton, S.L. and Gordon, P.J. (1988). Corporate Strategy and Capital Structure. *Strategic Management Journal* 9: 623–632.

Barton, S.L., Hill, N.C., and Sundaram, S. (1989). An Empirical Test of Stakeholder Theory Predictions of Capital Structure. *Financial Management* (Spring): 36–44.

Bartram, S.M. (2000). Corporate Risk Management as a Lever for Shareholder Value Creation. *Financial Markets, Institutions and Instruments* 9: 279–324.

Baskin, J. (1987). Corporate Liquidity in Games of Monopoly Power. *The Review of Economics and Statistics* 69: 312-319.

Bates, T.W., Kahle, K.M., and Stulz, R.M. (2006). Why Do U.S. Firms Hold so Much More Cash than They Used to? NBER Working Paper No. 12534. Version as of August, 2006. Available on the internet on: http://www.nber.org/papers/w12534.

Beck, N. and Katz, J.N. (1995). What to Do (and Not to Do) with Time-series Cross-section Data. American Political Science Review 89: 634–647.

Benartzi, S., Michaley, R. and Thaler, R. (1997). Do Changes in Dividends Signal the Future or the Past? *The Journal of Finance* 52: 1007–1034.

Berk, J.B., Stanton, R. and Zechner, J. (2007). Human Capital, Bankruptcy and Capital Structure. NBER Working Paper No. W13014. Version as of January, 2007. Available on the internet on: http://ssrn.com/abstract=978405.

Berman, S.L., Wicks, A.C., Kotha, S. and Jones, T.M. (1999). Does Stakeholder Orientation Matter? The Relationship between Stakeholder Management Models and Firm Financial Performance. *Academy of Management Journal* 42: 488–506.

Bessembinder, H. (1991). Forward Contracts and Firm Value: Investment Incentive and Contracting Effects. *Journal of Financial and Quantitative Analysis* 26: 519–532.

Bettis, R. (1983). Modern Financial Theory, Corporate Strategy and Public Policy: Three Conundrums. *The Academy of Management Review* 8: 406–415.

Bhagat, S., Shleifer, A. and Vishny, R.W. (1990). Hostile Takeovers in the 1980s: The Return to Corporate Specialization. *Brookings Papers: Microeconomics*. Brookings Institute, Washington, D.C.

Black, F. (1972). Capital Market Equilibrium with Restricted Borrowing. *Journal of Business* 45: 444–454.

Black, F., Jensen, M. and Scholes, M. (1972). The Capital Asset Pricing Model: Some Empirical Tests. In Jensen, M. (ed.). *Studies in the Theory of Capital Markets*. pp. 79–124. Praeger, New York.

Blair, M.M. (2005). Closing the Theory Gap: How the Economic Theory of Property Rights Can Help Bring "Stakeholders" Back into Theories of the Firm. *Journal of Management and Governance* 9: 33–39.

Blazenko, G.W. (1987). Managerial preference, Asymmetric Information, and Financial Structure. *The Journal of Finance* 42: 839–862.

Boatright, J.R. (2002). Contractors as Stakeholders: Reconciling Stakeholder Theory with the Nexus-of-contracts Firm. *Journal of Banking & Finance* 26: 1837–1852.

Bolton, P. and Scharfstein, D.S. (1990). A Theory of Predation Based on Agency Problems in Financial Contracting. *The American Economic Review* 80: 93–106.

Bowen, R.M., Johson, M., Shevlin, T. and Shores, D. (1992). Determinants of the Timing of Quarterly Earnings Announcements. *Journal of Accounting, Auditing & Finance* 7: 395–422.

Bowen, R.M., DuCharme, L. and Shores, D. (1995). Stakeholders' Implicit Claims and Accounting Method Choice. *Journal of Accounting and Economics* 20: 255–295.

Bowman, J. (1980). The Importance of a Market Value Measurement of Debt in Assessing Leverage. *Journal of Accounting Research* 18: 242–254.

Bowman, R.G. (1979). The Theoretical Relationship Between Systematic Risk and Financial (Accounting) Variables. *The Journal of Finance* 34: 617–630.

Brander, J.A. and Lewis, T.R. (1986). Oligopoly and Financial Structure: The Limited Liability Effect. *The American Economic Review* 76: 956–970.

Brav, A. Graham, J.R., Campbell R. H., and Michaely, R. (2004). Payout policy in the 21st century. Working Paper, Version as of June 14, 2004.

Brealey R.A. and Myers, S.C. (2000). Principles of corporate finance. 6th International Edition. Irwin McGraw-Hill. Boston etc.

Breeden, D. and Viswanathan, S. (1996). Why Do Firms Hedge? An Asymmetric Information Model. Working Paper, Duke University.

Brennan, M.J. (1995). Corporate Finance Over the Past 25 Years. *Financial Management* 24: 9–22.

Bronars, S.G. and Deere, D.R. (1991). The Threat of Unionization, the Use of Debt, and the Preservation of Shareholder Wealth. *The Quarterly Journal of Economics* 106: 231–254.

Brounen, D., Jong, Abe de and Koedijk, K. (2006). Capital Structure Policies in Europe: Survey Evidence. *Journal of Banking & Finance* 30: 1409–1442.

Burgstahler, D. and Dichev, I. (1997). Earnings Management to Avoid Earnings Decreases and Losses. *Journal of Accounting & Economics* 24: 99–126.

Carroll, A.B. (1989). Business and Society: Ethics and Stakeholder Management. South-Western, Cincinnati.

Carroll, A.B. and Näsi, J. (1997). Understanding Stakeholder Thinking: Themes from a Finnish Conference. *Business Ethics* 6: 46–51.

Charitou, A. and Vafeas, N. (1998). The Associations between Operating Cash Flow and Dividend Changes: An Empirical Investigation. *Journal of Business Finance & Accounting* 25: 225–249.

Chatterjee, S., Lubatkin. M.H. and Schulze, W.S. (1999). Toward a Strategic Theory of Risk Premium: Moving Beyond CAPM. *Academy of Management Review* 24: 556–567.

Clarkson, M.B.E. (1994). A Risk Based Model of Stakeholder Theory. *Proceedings of the Second Toronto Conference on Stakeholder Theory*. Toronto: Centre for Corporate Social Performance & Ethics, University of Toronto.

Clarkson, M.B.E. (1995). A Stakeholder Framework for Analyzing and Evaluating Corporate Social Performance. *The Academy of Management Review* 20: 92–117.

Cochrane, J.H. (1999). New Facts in Finance. NBER Working Paper. Version as of June, 1999. Available on the internet on: http://www.nber.org/papers/w7169.

Coff, R.W. (1999). When Competitive Advantage Doesn't Lead to Performance: The Resource-based View and Stakeholder Bargaining Power. *Organization Science* 10: 119–133.

Combs, J.G. and Ketchen, D. (1999). Explaining Interfirm Cooperation and Performance: Toward a Reconciliation of Predictions from the Resource-Based View and Organizational Economics. *Strategic Management Journal* 20: 867–888.

Connor, K.R. (1991). A Historical Comparison of Resource-Based Theory and Five Schools of Thought Within Industrial Organization Economics: Do We Have a New Theory of the Firm? *Journal of Management* 17: 121–154.

Connor, K.R. and Prahalad, C.K. (1996). A Resource-based Theory of the Firm: Knowledge Versus Opportunism. *Organization Science* 7: 477–501.

Copeland, T.E., Weston, J.F. and Shastri, K. (2005). Financial Theory and Corporate Policy. 4th Edition. Pearson Addison Wesley.

Cornell, B. and Shapiro, A.C. (1987). Corporate Stakeholders and Corporate Finance. *Financial Management* 16: 5–14.

Cornell, B., Landsman, W. and Shapiro, A. (1989). Cross-Sectional Regularities in the Response of Stock Prices to Bond Rating Changes. *Journal of Accounting, Auditing & Finance* 4: 460–479.

Cragg, W. (2002). Business Ethics and Stakeholder Theory. *Business Ethics Quarterly* 12: 113–142.

Cuijpers, R., Moers, F., and Peek, E. (2005). Firm-Level Reporting Incentives and Accounting Properties: Stakeholder- versus Shareholder-Oriented Governance Structures. SSRN Working Paper. Version as of May, 2005. Available on the internet on: http://ssrn.com/abstract=648522.

Das, T.K. and Teng, B. (1996). Risk Types and Inter-Firm Alliance Structures. *Journal of Management Studies* 33: 827–843.

DeAngelo, H. and Masulis, R. (1980). Optimal Capital Structure under Corporate and Personal Taxation. *Journal of Financial Economics* 8: 3–29.

Deephouse, D.L. and Wiseman, R.M. (2000). Comparing Alternative Explanations for Accounting Risk-return Relations. *Journal of Economic Behavior & Organization* 42: 463–482.

DeMarzo, P.M. and Duffie, D. (1995). Corporate Incentives for Hedging and Hedge Accounting. *The Review of Financial Studies* 8: 743–771.

Demsetz, H. (1997). The Firm in Economic Theory: A Quiet Revolution. *American Economic Review* 87: 426–429.

Dierickx, I. and Cool, K. (1989). Asset Stock Accumulation and Sustainability of Competitive Advantage. *Management Science* 35: 1504–1511.

Dittmar, A., Mahrt-Smith, J. and Servaes, H. (2003). International Corporate Governance and Corporate Cash Holdings. *Journal of Financial and Quantitative Analysis* 38: 111–133.

Donaldson, T. and Preston, L. (1995). The Stakeholder Theory of the Corporation: Concepts, Evidence and Implications. *Academy of Management Review* 20: 65–91.

Eisenhardt, K.M. (1989). Agency Theory: An Assessment and Review. *Academy of Management Review* 14: 57–74.

EViews (2004). EViews 5 User's Guide. Quantitative Micro Software, LLC. Irvine.

Fama, E.F. (1978). The Effects of a Firm's Investment and Financing Decisions on the Welfare of Its Security Holders. *The American Economic Review* 68: 272–284.

Fama, E.F. and French, K.R. (1992). The Cross-Section of Expected Stock Returns. *The Journal of Finance* 47: 427–465.

Fama, E.F. and French, K.R. (1993). Common risk factors in the returns on bonds and stocks. *Journal of Financial Economics* 33: 3–56.

Fama, E.F. and French, K.R. (1995). Size and Book-to-Market Factors in Earnings and Returns. *The Journal of Finance* 50: 131–155.

Fama, E.F. and French, K.R. (1996). Multifactor Explanations of Asset Pricing Anomalies. *The Journal of Finance* 51: 55–84.

Fama, E.F. and French, K.R. (2002). Testing Trade-Off and Pecking Order Predictions About Dividends and Debt. *The Review of Financial Studies* 15: 1–33.

Fama, E.F. and French, K.R. (2004). The Capital Asset Pricing Model: Theory and Evidence. *Journal of Economic Perspectives* 18: 25–46.

Fama, E.F. and MacBeth, J. (1973). Risk, Return and Equilibrium: Empirical Tests. *Journal of Political Economy* 81: 607–636.

Fatemi, A. and Luft, C. (2002). Corporate Risk Management, Costs and Benefits. *Global Finance Journal* 13: 29–38.

Fenn, G.W., Post, M. and Sharpe, S.A. (2002). Does Corporate Risk Management Create Shareholder Value. In Jameson, R. (ed.): *Financial Risk and the Corporate Treasury*. pp. 1–31. Risk Publications, London.

Franck, T. and Huyghebaert, N. (2006). Non-Financial Stakeholder Relationship Costs as a Determinant of Capital Structure: Empirical Evidence from First-Time Business Start-Ups. EFA 2006 Zurich Meetings Paper. Version as of April, 2006. Available on the internet on http://ssrn.com/abstract=909201.

Frank, M.Z. and Goyal, V.K. (2005). Trade-off and Pecking Order Theories of Debt. Working Paper. Version as of February, 2005. Forthcoming in Espen Eckbo, B. (ed.). *Handbook of Corporate Finance: Empirical Corporate Finance*. Elsevier/North-Holland.

Frankfurter, G. M. (1999). What is the Puzzle in "The Dividend Puzzle"? *Journal of Investing* 8: 76–85.

Freeman, R.E. (1984). Strategic Management: A Stakeholder Approach. Pitman. Boston.

Freeman, R.E. and Gilbert Jr., D.R. (1987). Managing Stakeholder Relationships. In Sethi, S.P. and Falbe, C.M. (eds.). *Business and Society: Dimensions of Conflict and Cooperation*. Lexington Books, New York.

Freeman, R.E. and McVea, J. (2001). A Stakeholder Approach to Strategic Management. In Hitt, M.A., Freeman, R.E. and Harrison, J.S. (eds.). *The Blackwell Handbook of Strategic Management*. pp. 189–207. Blackwell Publishers, Oxford.

Freeman, R.E. and Reed, D.L. (1983). Stockholders and Stakeholders: A New Perspective on Corporate Governance. *California Management Review* 25: 88–106.

Freeman, R.E. (2000). Business Ethics at the Millenium. *Business Ethics Quarterly* 10: 169–180.

Froot, K.A., Scharfstein, D.S., and Stein, J.C. (1989). LDC debt: Foregiveness, Indexation, and Investment Incentives. *The Journal of Finance* 44: 1335–1350.

Froot, K.A., Scharfstein, D.S., and Stein, J.C. (1993). Risk Management: Coordinating Corporate Investment and Financing Policies. *The Journal of Finance* 48: 1629–1658.

Froot, K.A., Scharfstein, D.S., and Stein, J.C. (1994). A Framework for Risk Management. *HARVARD BUSINESS REVIEW* 48: 91–102.

Furubotn, E.G. and Pejovich, S. (1972). Property Rights and Economic Theory: A Survey of Recent Literature. *Journal of Economic Literature* 10: 1137–1162.

Gaud, P., Jani, E., Hoesli, M. and Bender, A. (2005). The Capital Structure of Swiss Companies: An Empirical Analysis Using Dynamic Panel Data. *European Financial Management* 11: 51-69.

Gay, G.D. and Nam, J. (1998). The Underinvestment Problem and Corporate Derivatives Use. *Financial Management* 27: 53–69.

Géczy, C., Minton, B.A. and Schrand, C. (1997). Why Firms Use Currency Derivatives. *The Journal of Finance* 52: 1323–1354.

Glaum, M. (2002). The Determinants of Selective Hedging – Evidence from German Non-financial Corporations. Working Paper. Version as of August, 2002. Available on the internet on: http://wiwi.uni-giessen.de/dl/det/Glaum/2515/.

Goldberg, V.P. (1976). Regulation and Administered Contracts. *Bell Journal of Economics* 7: 426–452.

Graham, J.R. (2000). How Big Are the Tax Benefits of Debt. *The Journal of Finance* 55: 1901–1941.

Graham, J.R. (2003). Taxes and Corporate Finance. Working Paper. Version as of September, 2003. Forthcoming in Espen Eckbo, B. (ed.): *Handbook of Corporate Finance: Empirical Corporate Finance*. Elsevier/North-Holland.

Graham, J.R. and Harvey, C.R. (2001). The Theory and Practice of Corporate Finance: Evidence From the Field. *Journal of Financial Economics* 60: 187–243.

Grandori, A. (2005). Neither Stakeholder Nor Shareholder 'Theories': How Property Right and Contract Theory can Help in Getting Out of the Dilemma. *Journal of Management and Governance* 9: 41–46.

Grinblatt, M. and Titman, S. (1998). Financial Markets and Corporate Strategy. Irwin/McGraw-Hill. Boston et al.

Grossman, S.J. and Hart, O.D. (1986). The Costs and Benefits of Ownership: A Theory of Vertical and Lateral Integration. *The Journal of Political Economy* 94: 691–719.

Grullon, G. and Michaely, R. (2002). Dividends, Share Repurchases, and the Substitution Hypothesis. *The Journal of Finance* 57: 1649–1684.

Harford, J. (1999). Corporate Cash Reserves and Acquisitions. *The Journal of Finance* 54: 1969–1997.

Harris, M. and Raviv, A. (1990). Capital Structure and the Informational Role of Debt. *The Journal of Finance* 45: 321–349.

Harris, M. and Raviv, A. (1991). The Theory of Capital Structure. *The Journal of Finance* 46: 297–355.

Harrison, J. (2006). Stakeholder Theory and the Resource-Based View of Competitiveness. Working Paper presented at the Strategic Management Society 26th Annual Conference in Vienna.

Hart, O. (1989). An Economist's Perspective on the Theory of the Firm. *Columbia Law Review* 89. Reprinted in Buckley, P.J. and Michie, J. (eds). *Firms, Organizations and Contracts.* 1st edition, 1999. pp. 199–218. Oxford University Press. Oxford.

Hart, O.D. (1991). Incomplete Contracts and the Theory of the Firm. In Williamson, O.E. and Winter, S.G. (eds.) *The Nature of the Firm*. pp. 138–158. Oxford University Press, Oxford.

Hart, O.D. (1995). Corporate Governance: Some Theory and Implications. *The Economic Journal* 105: 678–689.

Hart, O. and Moore, J. (1990). Property Rights and the Nature of the Firm. *The Journal of Policital Economy* 98: 1119–1158.

Haushalter, G.D. (2000). Financing Policy, Basis risk, and Corporate Hedging: Evidence from Oil and Gas Producers. *The Journal of Finance* 55: 107–152.

Hausman, J.A. and Taylor, W.E. (1981). Panel Data and Unobservable Individual Effects. *Econometrica* 49: 1377–1398.

Hill, C.W.L. and Jones, T.M. (1992). Stakeholder-Agency Theory. *Journal of Management Studies* 29: 131–154.

Hillman, A.J. and Keim, G.D. (2001). Shareholder Value, Stakeholder Management, and Social Issues: What's the Bottom Line? *Strategic Management Journal* 22: 125–139.

Holder, M.E., Langrehr, F.W. and Hexter, J.L. (1998). Dividend Policy Determinants: An Investigation of the Influences of Stakeholder Theory. *Financial Management* 27: 73–82.

Holmström, B. and Tirole, J. (2000). Liquidity and Risk Management. *Journal of Money, Credit, and Banking* 32: 296–319.

Holmstrom, B. and Tirole, J. (1989). The Theory of the Firm. In: Schmalensee, R. and Willig, R.D. (eds). *Handbook of Industrial Organization.* Vol. 1: 61–133. North Holland, Amsterdam.

Hoskisson, R.E., Hitt, M.A., Wan, W.P. and Yiu, D. (1999). Theory and Research in Strategic Management. Swings of a Pendulum. *Journal of Management* 25: 417–456.

Hsiao, Cheng (2003). Analysis of Panel Data. 2nd Edition. Cambridge University Press, Cambridge.

Hyun-Han, S. and Stulz, R.M. (2000). Shareholder Wealth and Firm Risk. Dice Center Working Paper No. 2000-19. Version as of December 2000. Available on the internet on: http://ssrn.com/abstract=254271.

Istaitieh, A. and Rodríguez, J.M. (n.d.). Stakeholder Theory, Market Structure and the Firm's Capital Structure: An Empirical Evidence. SSRN Working Paper. Available on the internet on: http://ssrn.com/abstract=413661

Istaitieh, A. and Rodríguez-Fernández, J.M. (2006). Factor-product Markets and Firm's Capital Structure: A Literature Review. *Review of Financial Economics* 15: 49–75.

Jagannathan, M., Stephens, C. and Weisbach, M. (2000). Financial Flexibility and the Choice between Dividends and Stock Repurchases. *Journal of Financial Economics* 57: 355–384.

Jaggia, P.B. and Thakor, A.V. (1994). Firm-specific Human Capital and Optimal Capital Structure. *International Economic Review* 35. 283–308.

Jansson, E. (2005). The Stakeholder Model: The Influence of the Ownership and Governance Structures. *Journal of Business Ethics* 56: 1–13.

Jensen, M.C. (1972). Capital Markets: Theory and Evidence. *Bell Journal of Economics and Management Science* 3: 357–398.

Jensen, M.C. (1983). Organization Theory and Methodology. *Accounting Review* (April): 319–339.

Jensen, M.C. (1986). Agency Costs of Free Cash Flow, Corporate Finance, and Takeovers. *American Economic Review* (May): 323–329.

Jensen, M.C. (2001). Value Maximization, Stakeholder Theory, and the Corporate Objective Function. *Bank of America Journal of Applied Corporate Finance* 3: 8–21.

Jensen, M.C. (2002). Value Maximization, Stakeholder Theory, and the Corporate Objective Function. *Business Ethics Quarterly* 12: 235–256.

Jensen, M.C. and Meckling, W.H. (1976). Theory of the Firm: Managerial Behavior, Agency Costs and Ownership Structure. *Journal of Financial Economics* 3. Available on the internet on: http://papers.ssrn.com/sol3/papers.cfm?abstract_id=94043.

Jones, T.M. and Wicks, A.C. (1999). Convergent Stakeholer Theory. *Academy of Management Review* 24: 206–221.

Jordan, J., Lowe, J., and Taylor, P. (1998). Strategy and Financial Policy in UK Small Firms. *Journal of Business Finance & Accounting* 25: 1–27.

Kale, J.R. and Shahrur, H. (2007). Corporate Capital Structure and the Characteristics of Suppliers and Customers. *Journal of Financial Economics* 83: 321–365.

Kim, C.S., Mauer, D.C. and Sherman, A.E. (1998). The Determinants of Corporate Liquidity: Theory and Evidence. *The Journal of Financial and Quantitative Analysis* 33: 335–359.

Kim, J. and Mahoney, J.T. (2002). Resource-Based and Property Rights Perspectives on Value Creation: The Case of Oil Field Unitization. *Managerial and Decision Economics* 23: 225–245.

Kim, J. and Mahoney, J.T. (2005). Property Rights Theory, Transaction Costs Theory, and Agency Theory: An Organizational Economics Approach to Strategic Management. *Managerial and Decision Economics* 26: 223–242.

Klein, B. (1993). Vertical Integration as Organizational Ownership: The Fisher Body-General Motors Relationship Revisited. In Williamson, O.E. and Winter, S.G. (eds.). *The Nature of the Firm*. pp. 213–226. Oxford University Press, New York.

Klein, B., Crawford, R. and Alchian, A. (1978). Vertical Integration, Appropriable Rents and the Competitive Contracting Process. *Journal of Law and Economics* 21: 297–326.

Kochhar, R. (1997). Strategic Assets, Capital Structure, and Firm Performance. *Journal of Financial and Strategic Decisions* 10: 23–36.

Kraus, A. and Litzenberger, R.H. (1973). A State-Preference Model of Optimal Financial Leverage. *The Journal of Finance* 28: 911–922.

Kreps, D.M. (1990). Corporate Culture and Economic Theory. In Alt, J.E. and Shepsle, K.A. (eds.). *Perspectives on Policital Economy*. pp. 90–143. Cambridge University Press, Cambridge.

Leland, H.E. and Pyle, D.H. (1977). Informational Asymmetries, Financial Structure, and Financial Intermediation. *The Journal of Finance* 32: 371–387.

Levy, H. (1978). Equilibrium in an Imperfect Market: A Constraint on the Number of Securities in the Portfolio. *The American Economic Review* 68: 643–658.

Lim, S.S. and Wang, H.C. (2007). The Effect of Financial Hedging on the Incentives for Corporate Diversification: The Role of Stakeholder Firm-specific Investments. *Journal of Economic Behavior & Organization* 62: 640–656.

Lintner, J. (1965). The Valuation of Risky Assets and the Selection of Risk Investments in Stock Portfolios and Capital Budgets. *The Review of Economics and Statistics* 47: 13–37.

Lloyd, W.P., Jahera, J.S. and Page, D.E. (1985). Agency Costs and Dividend-Payout Ratios. *Quarterly Journal of Business and Economics* (Summer): 19–29.

Lockett, A. and Thompson, S. (2001). The resource-based view and economics. *Journal of Management* 27: 723–754.

Lowe, J., Naughton, T. and Taylor, P. (1994). The Impact of Corporate Strategy on the Capital Structure of Australian Companies. *Managerial and Decision Economics* 15: 245–257.

Lubatkin, M. and Chatterjee, S. (1994). Extending Modern Portfolio Theory into the Domain of Corporate Diversification: Does it Apply? *Academy of Management Journal* 37: 109–136.

Lubatkin, M. and Schulze, B. (2003). Risk, Strategy, and Finance: Unifying Two World Views. *Long Range Planning* 36: 7–8.

Madhok, A. and Tallman, S.B. (1998). Resources, Transactions and Rents: Managing Value through Interfirm Collaborative Relationships. *ORGANIZATION SCIENCE* 9: 326–339.

Mahoney, J.T. (2001). A Resource-based Theory of Sustainable Rents. *Journal of Management* 27: 651–660.

Maksimovic, V. and Titman, S. (1991). Financial Policy and Reputation for Product Quality. *The Review of Financial Studies* 4: 175–200.

Markides, C. and Williamson, P.J. (1996). Corporate Diversification and Organizational Structure: A Resource-based View. *Academy of Management Journal* 39: 340–367.

Markowitz, H. (1952). Portfolio Selection. *The Journal of Finance* 7: 77–91.

Markowitz, H. (1959). Portfolio Selection: Efficient Diversifications of Investments. Cowles Foundation Monograph No. 16. John Wiley & Sons, Inc., New York.

Marsh, T.A. and Merton, R.C. (1987). Dividend Behavior for the Aggregate Stock Market. *Journal of Business* 60: 1–40.

Marshall, A. (1936). Principles of Economis. 8th edition. Macmillan, London.

Matsumoto, D.A. (2002). Management's Incentives to Avoid Negative Earnings Surprises. *The Accounting Review* 77: 483–514.

Mayers, D. and Smith, C.W. (1982). On the Corporate Demand for Insurance. *Journal of Business* 55: 281–296.

Mayers, D. and Smith, C.W. (1990). On the Corporate Demand for Insurance: Evidence from the Reinsurance Market. *Journal of Business* 63: 19–40.

Mian, S.L. (1996). Evidence on Corporate Hedging Policy. *Journal of Financial and Quantiative Analysis* 31: 419–439.

Michaley, R., Thaler, R.H. and Womack, K.L. (1995). Price Reactions to Dividend Initiations and Omissions: Overreaction or Drift? *The Journal of Finance* 50: 573–608.

Mikkelson, W.H. and Partch, M.M. (2003). Do Persistent Large Cash Reserves Hinder Performance? *Journal of Financial and Quantitative Analysis* 38: 275–294.

Milgrom, P. and Roberts, J. (1992). Economics, Organization and Management. Prentice-Hall International.

Miller, K.D. (1998). Economic Exposure and Integrated Risk Management. *Strategic Management Journal* 19: 497–514.

Miller, K.D. and Chen, W. (2003). Risk and Firms' Costs. *STRATEGIC ORGANIZATION* 1: 355–382.

Miller, M. (1977). Debt and Taxes. *The Journal of Finance* 32: 261–275.

Miller, M. and Modigliani, F. (1961). Dividend Policy, Growth and the Valuation of Shares. *Journal of Business* 34: 411–433.

Minton, B.A. and Schrand, C. (1999). The Impact of Cash Flow Volatility on Discretionary Investment and the Cost of Debt and Equity Financing. *Journal of Financial Economics* 54: 423–460.

Minton, B. A. and Wruck, K. H. (2001). Financial Conservatism: Evidence on Capital Structure from Low Leverage Firms. Version as of July 9, 2001. AFA 2002 Atlanta; Dice Ctr. Working Paper No. 2001–6. Available on the internet on: http://ssrn.com/abstract=269608.

Mitchell, R.K., Agle, B.R. and Wood, DJ. (1997). Toward a Theory of Stakeholder Identification and Sallience: Defining the Principle of Who and What Really Counts? *Academy of Management Review* 22: 853–886.

Modigliani, F. and Miller, M.H. (1958). The Cost of Capital, Corporation Finance, and the Theory of Investment. *American Economic Review* 48: 261–297.

Modigliani, F. and Miller, M.H. (1963). Corporate Income Taxes and the Cost of Capital: A Correction. *The American Economic Review* 53: 433–443.

Mundlak, Y. (1978). On the Pooling of Time Series and Cross Section Data. *Econometrica* 46: 69–85.

Myers, S.C. (1977). Determinants of Corporate Borrowing. *Journal of Financial Economics* 5: 147–175.

Myers, S.C. (1984). The Capital Structure Puzzle. *The Journal of Finance* 39: 575–592.

Myers, S.C. (2001). Capital Structure. *The Journal of Economic Perspectives* 15: 81–102.

Myers, S.C. and Majluf, N.S. (1984). Corporate Financing and Investment Decisions When Firms Have Informations Investors Do Not Have. *Journal of Financial Economics* 13: 187–221.

Myers, S.C. and Rajan, R.G. (1998). The Paradox of Liquidity. *The Quarterly Journal of Economics* 108: 733–771.

Nance, D.R., Smith, C.W., and Smithson, C.W. (1993). On the Determinants of Corporate Hedging. *The Journal of Finance* 48: 267–284.

Naylor, T.H: and Tapon, F. (1982). The Capital Asset Pricing Model: An Evaluation of its Potential as a Strategic Planning Tool. *Management Science* 28: 1166–1173.

Noteboom, B., Berger, H. and Noorderhaven, N.G. (1997). Effects of Trust and Governance on Relational Risk. *Academy of Management Journal* 40: 308–338.

O'Brien, J.P. (2003). The Capital Structure Implications of Pursuing a Strategy of Innovation. *Strategic Management Journal* 24: 415–431.

Opler, T.C. and Titman, S. (1994). Financial Distress and Corporate Performance. *The Journal of Finance* 49: 1015–1040.

Opler, T.C., Pinkowitz, L., Stulz, R., and Williamson, R. (1999). The Determinants and Implications of Corporate Cash Holdings. *Journal of Financial Economics* 52: 3–46.

Ozkan, A. (2001). Determinants of Capital Structure and Adjustment to Long Run Target: Evidence from UK Company Panel Data. *Journal of Business Finance & Accounting* 28: 175-198.

Ozkan, A. and Ozkan, N. (2004). Corporate Cash Holdings: An Empirical Investigation of UK Companies. *Journal of Banking & Finance* 28: 2103–2134.

Parsons, C. and Titman, S. (2007). Capital Structure and Corporate Strategy. SSRN Working Paper. Version as of Janurary, 2007. Available on the internet on: http://ssrn.com/abstract=983553.

Peavy, J.W. (1984). Modern Financial Theory, Corporate Strategy, and Public Policy: Another Perspective. *The Academy of Management Review* 9: 152–157.

Penrose, E.T. (1959). The Theory of the Growth of the Firm. Wiley, New York.

Perold, A.F. (2004). The Capital Asset Pricing Model. *Journal of Economic Perspectives* 18: 3–24.

Peteraf, M.A. (1993). The Cornerstones of Competitive Advantage: A Resource-based View. *Strategic Management Journal* 14: 179–191.

Petersen, M.A. (2005). Estimating Standard Errors in Finance Panel Data Sets: Comparing Approaches. NBER Working Paper. Version as of April, 2005. Available on the internet on: http://www.nber.org/papers/w11280.

Phillips, R. (2003). Stakeholder Legitimacy. *Business Ethics Quarterly* 13: 25–41.

Picot, A. and Schuller, S. (2001). Vertragstheoretische Analyse des Risk-Managements. In Lange, K.W. and Wall, F. (eds.) *Risikomanagement nach dem KonTraG*. pp. 236–258. Verlag Franz Vahlen, München.

Pinkowitz, L. (2000). The Market for Corporate Control and Corporate Cash Holdings. SSRN Working Paper. Version as of January, 2000. Available on the internet on: http://ssrn.com/abstract=215191.

Pitelis, C.N. (2004). (Corporate) Governance, (Shareholder) Value and (Sustainable) Economic Performance. *Corporate Governance* 12: 210–223.

Plasmans, J. (2006). Modern Linear and Nonlinear Econometrics. Springer, Dordrecht.

Post, J.E., Preston, L.E. and Sachs, S. (2002). Managing the Extended Enterprise: The New Stakeholder View. *CALIFORNIA MANAGEMENT REVIEW* 45: 6–28.

Prahalad, C.K. (1997). Corporate Governance or Corporate Value Added? Rethinking the Primacy of Shareholer Value. In Chew, D. (ed.): *Studies in International Corporate Finance and Governance Systems*. pp. 46–56. Oxford University Press, New York.

Priem, R.L. and Butler, J.E. (2001). Is the Resource-Based "View" a Useful Perspective for Strategic Management Research? *Academy of Management Review* 26: 22–40.

Pritsch, G. and Hommel, U. (1997). Hedging im Sinne des Aktionärs. *DBW* 57: 672–693.

Pyndick, R.S. and Rubinfeld, D.L. (1998). Econometric models and Economic Forecasts. International Editions 1998. Irwin/McGraw-Hill. Boston etc.

Quinn, D.P. and Jones, T.M. (1995). An Agent Morality View of Business Policy. *Academy of Management Review* 20: 22–42.

Rajan, R.G. and Zingales, L. (1995). What Do We Know about Capital Structure? Some Evidence from International Data. *The Journal of Finance* 50: 1421–1460.

Rajan, R.G. and Zingales, L. (1998). Power in a Theory of the Firm. *The Quarterly Journal of Economics* 113: 387–432.

Rajan, R.G. and Zingales, L. (2000). The Governance of the New Enterprise. In Vives, X. (ed.). *Corporate Governance – Theoretical and Empirical Perspectives*. pp. 201–227. Cambridge University Press, Cambridge etc.

Rawls, S.W., III, and Smithson, C.W. (1990). Strategic Risk Management. *Continental Bank Journal of Applied Corporate Finance* 2: 6–18.

Reinganum, M.R. (1981) A New Empirical Perspective on the CAPM. *The Journal of Financial and Quantiative Analysis* 16: 439–462.

Richter, R. and Furubotn, E. (1999). Neue Institutionenökonomik. 2nd edition. J.C.B. Mohr, Tübingen.

Roberts, R.W. and Mahoney, L. (2004). Stakeholder Conceptions of the Corporations: Their Meaning and Influence in Accounting Research. *Business Ethics Quarterly* 14: 399–431.

Robins, J.A. (1992). Organizational Considerations in the Evaluation of Capital Assets: Toward a Resource-based View of Strategic Investment by Firms. *Organization Science* 3: 522–536.

Roll, R. and Ross, S.A. (1994). On the Cross-Sectional Relation between Expected Returns and Betas. *The Journal of Finance* 49: 101–121.

Ross, S.A. (1973). The Economic Theory of Agency: The Principal's Problem. *The American Economic Review* 63: 134–139.

Ross, S.A. (1977). The Determination of Financial Structure: The Incentive-Signalling Approach. *Bell Journal of Economics* 8: 23–40.

Rowley, T.J. (1997). Moving Beyond Dyadic Ties: A Network Theory of Stakeholder Influences. *The Academy of Management Review* 22: 887–910.

Rumelt, R.P. (1974). Strategy, Structure, and Economic Performance. *Harvard University Press*. Cambridge, MA.

Santomero, A.M. (1995). Financial Risk Management: The Whys and Hows. *Financial Markets, Institutions & Instruments* 4: 1–14.

Sarig, O.H. (1998). The effect of leverage on bargaining with a corporation. *The Financial Review* 33: 1–16.

Schmidt, R.H. and Terberger, E. (1999). Grundzüge der Investitions- und Finanzierungstheorie. 4. Auflage. Gabler, Wiesbaden.

Schwetzler, B. and Reimund, C. (2004). Valuation Effects of Corporate Cash Holdings: Evidence from Germany. HHL Working Paper. Version as of January, 2004. Available on the internet on: http://papers.ssrn.com/abstract=490262.

Seth, A. and Thomas, H. (1994). Theories of the Firm: Implications for Strategy Research. *Journal of Management Studies* 31: 165–191.

Shankman, N.A. (1999). Reframing the Debate Between Agency and Stakeholer Theories of the Firm. *Journal of Business Ethics* 19: 319–334.

Shapiro, A.C. (1990). Modern Corporate Finance. Macmillan, New York.

Shapiro, A.C. and Balbirer, S.D. (2000). Modern Corporate Finance. Prentice-Hall, New Jersey.

Shapiro, A.C. and Titman, S. (1986). An Integrated Approach to Corporate Risk Management. In Stern, J.M. and Chew, D.H. (eds): *The Revolution in Corporate Finance*. pp. 215–229, Basil Blackwell Ltd., Oxford.

Sharpe, W. (1964). Capital Asset Prices: A Theory of Market Equilibrium under Conditions of Risk. *The Journal of Finance* 19: 425–442.

Sharpe, W. (1991). Capital Asset Prices with and without Negative Holdings. *The Journal of Finance* 46: 489–509.

Shavell, S. (1998). Contracts. In Newman, P. (ed.): *The New Palgrave Dictionary of Economics and the Law,* Vol. 1, pp. 436–445. Macmillan Reference Limited, London.

Simon, H. (1985). Human Nature in Politics: The Dialogue of Psychology with Political Science. *American Political Science Review* 79: 293–204.

Skoulakis, G. (2005). Panel Data Inference in Finance: Least-Squares vs Fama-MacBeth. Northwestern Working Paper. Version as of October, 2005.

Smith, C.W. and Stulz, R.M. (1985). The Determinants of Firm's Hedging Policies. *Journal of Financial and Quantitative Analysis* 20: 391–405.

Smith, C.W. (1995). Corporate Risk Management: Theory and Practice. *The Journal of Derivatives* 2: 21–30.

Smith, C.W. (2005). Managing Corporate Risk. Working Paper. Forthcoming in Espen Eckbo, B. (ed.). *Handbook of Corporate Finance: Empirical Corporate Finance.* Elsevier/North-Holland.

Speckbacher, G. (1997). Shareholder Value und Stakeholder Ansatz. *DBW* 57: 630–639.

Speckbacher, G. (2003). The Economics of Performance Management in Nonprofit Organizations. *NONPROFIT MANAGEMENT & LEADERSHIP* 13: 267–281.

Speckbacher, G. and Wentges, P. (2005). A Note on Stakeholder Theory and Risk: Implications for Corporate Cash Holdings and Dividend Policy. Forthcoming in *Frontiers in Finance and Economics.*

Spence, M. (1974). Competitive and Optimal Responses to Signals: An Analysis of Efficiency and Distribution. *Journal of Economic Theory* 7: 296–332.

Spremann, K. (1996). Wirtschaft, Investition und Finanzierung. 5. Auflage. Oldenbourg, München.

Stiglitz, J.E. (1985). Information and Economic Analysis: A Perspective. *The Economic Journal* (Supplement) 95: 21–41.

Stimson, J.A. (1985). Regression in Space and Time: A Statistical Essay. *American Journal of Political Science* 29: 914–947.

Stock, J.H. and Watson, M.W. (2003). Introduction to Econometrics. Addison Wesley, Boston et al.

Stulz, R.M. (1984). Optimal Hedging Policies. *Journal of Financial and Quantitative Analysis* 19: 127–140.

Stulz, R.M. (1990). Managerial Discretion and Optimal Financing Policies. *Journal of Financial Economics* 14: 501–521.

Stulz, R.M. (1996). Rethinking Risk Management. *Bank of America Journal of Applied Corporate Finance* 9: 8–24.

Stulz, R.M. (2000). Merton Miller and Modern Finance. *Financial Management* 29: 119–131.

Stulz, R.M. (2003). Risk Management and Derivatives. Thomson South-Western, Mason.

Subramaniam, V. (1996). Underinvestment, Debt Financing, and Long-term Supplier Relations. *Journal of Law, Economics and Organization* 12: 459–477.

Sundaram, A.K. and Inkpen, A.C. (2004). The Corporate Objective Revisited. *Organization Science* 15: 350–363.

Taylor, P. and Lowe, J. (1995). A Note on Corporate Strategy and Capital Structure. *Strategic Management Journal* 16: 411–414.

Teece, D.J. (1998). Capturing Value from Knowledge Assets: The New Economy, Markets for Know-how, and Intangible Assets. *CALIFORNIA MANAGEMENT REVIEW* 40: 55–79.

Tirole, J. (1999). Incomplete Contracts: Where Do We Stand? *Econometrica* 67: 741–781.

Titman, S. (1984). The Effect of Capital Structure on a Firm's Liquidation Decision. *Journal of Financial Economics* 13: 137–151.

Titman, S. and Wessels, R. (1988). The Determinants of Capital Structure Choice. *The Journal of Finance* 43: 1–19.

Trevino, L.K. and Weaver, G.R. (1999). The Stakeholder Research Tradition: Converging Theorists–Not Convergent Theory. *Academy of Management Review* 24: 222–227.

Tufano, P. (1996). Who Manages Risk? An Empirical Examination of Risk Management Practices in the Gold Mining Industry. *The Journal of Finance* 51: 1097–1137.

Tufano, P. (1998). Agency Costs of Corporate Risk Management. *Financial Management* 27: 67–77.

Van Horne, J.C. (1995). Financial Management and Policy. 10th Edition. Prentice-Hall, London.

Vicente-Lorente, J.D. (2001). Specificity and Opacity as Resource-based Determinants of Capital Structure: Evidence for Spanish Manufacturing Firms. *Strategic Management Journal* 22: 157–177.

Vilasuso, J. and Minkler, A. (2001). Agency Costs, Asset Specificity, and the Capital Structure of the Firm. *Journal of Economic Behavior & Organization* 44: 55–69.

Wang, H.C., Barney, J.B. and Reuer, J.J. (2003). Stimulating Firm-specific Investment through Risk Management. *Long Range Planning* 36: 49–59.

Wang, H.C. and Barney, J.B. (2006). Employee Incentives to Make Firm Specific Investments: Implications for Resource-based Theories of Corporate Diversification. *Academy of Management Review* 31: 466–476.

Watson, R. and Wilson, N. (2002). Small and Medium Size Enterprise Financing: A Note on Some of the Empirical Implications of a Pecking Order. *Journal of Business Finance & Accounting* 29: 557–578.

Welch, I. (2000). Views of Financial Economists on the Equity Premium and on Professional Controversies. *Journal of Business* 73: 501–537.

Wentges, P. (2000). Eine Stakeholder-orientierte Analyse der Berücksichtigung des Risikos im Rahmen des Shareholder Value-Konzeptes. *DBW* 60: 199–209.

Wentges, P. (2002). Corporate Governance und Stakeholder-Ansatz. Implikationen für die betriebliche Finanzwirtschaft. DUV, Wiesbaden.

Wernerfelt, B. (1984). A Resource-Based View of the Firm. *Strategic Management Journal* 5: 171–180.

White, H. (1980). A Heteroskedasticity-consistent Covariance Matrix Estimator and a Direct Test for Heteroskedasticity. *Econometrica* 48: 817–838.

Wicks, A.C. and Berman, S.L. (2004). The Effects of Context on Trust in Firm-Stakeholder Relationships: The Institutional Environment, Trust Creation, and Firm Performance. *Business Ethics Quarterly* 14: 141–160.

Williamson, O.E. (1985). The Economic Institutions of Capitalism. The Free Press, New York.

Williamson, O.E. (1988). Corporate Finance and Corporate Governance. *The Journal of Finance* 43: 567–591.

Williamson, O.E. (1993). Opportunism and its Critics. *Managerial and Decision Economics* 14: 97–107.

Williamson, O.E. (1998). Transaction Cost Economics: How it Works; Where it is Headed. *De Economist* 146: 23–58.

Williamson, O.E. (2002). The Theory of the Firm as Governance Structure: From Choice to Contract. *Journal of Economic Perspectives* 16: 171–195.

Williamson, O.E. (2005a). Transaction Cost Economics. In Menard, C. and Shirley, M.M. (eds.). *Handbook of New Institutional Economics*. pp. 41–65. Springer, Dordrecht.

Williamson, O.E. (2005b). The Economics of Governance. *American Economic Review* 95: 1–18.

Wooldridge, J.M. (2002). Econometric Analysis of Cross Section and Panel Data. The MIT Press, Cambridge.

Wooldridge, J.M. (2006). Introductory Econometrics. A Modern Approach. 3rd Edition. Thomson South-Western, Mason.

Zingales, L. (1998). Corporate Governance. In Newman, P. (ed.): *The New Palgrave Dictionary of Economics and the Law*. pp. 497–503. Macmillan Reference Limited, London.

Zingales, L. (2000). In Search of New Foundations. *The Journal of Finance* 55: 1623–1653.

FSC
www.fsc.org
MIX
Papier | Fördert gute Waldnutzung
FSC® C083411

Kolibri 360 GmbH
Ferdinand-Jühlke-Straße 7
99095 Erfurt, Deutschland
produktsicherheit@kolibri360.de